# THE DANISH EU OPT-OUTS

This book offers the first comprehensive legal study dedicated to the understanding of the Danish EU opt-outs.

The impact of these is significant, falling as they do within Union citizenship, the euro, defence cooperation and the Area of Freedom, Security and Justice. Through a re-examination of the opt-outs individually, collectively and temporally, the book sheds light on their legal design and their interplay between international law, EU law and national law. This pioneering book takes a legal-doctrinal approach, which provides readers with a solid understanding of the opt-outs. Academics, judges and European Union civil servants will find this invaluable.

# The Danish EU Opt-Outs

## *Their Legal Significance, Past and Present*

Christian Thorning

•HART•
OXFORD • LONDON • NEW YORK • NEW DELHI • SYDNEY

HART PUBLISHING

Bloomsbury Publishing Plc

Kemp House, Chawley Park, Cumnor Hill, Oxford, OX2 9PH, UK

1385 Broadway, New York, NY 10018, USA

29 Earlsfort Terrace, Dublin 2, Ireland

HART PUBLISHING, the Hart/Stag logo, BLOOMSBURY and the Diana logo are trademarks of Bloomsbury Publishing Plc

First published in Great Britain 2024



A catalogue record for this book is available from the British Library.

A catalogue record for this book is available from the Library of Congress.

Library of Congress Control Number: 2024940200

ISBN: HB: 978-1-50998-094-9
ePDF: 978-1-50998-096-3
ePub: 978-1-50998-095-6

Typeset by Compuscript Ltd, Shannon

# *Preface*

IN 1992, AS I was in the midst of my law studies, the Edinburgh Decision was adopted, by which four EU opt-outs for Denmark were created. At the time, I never would have imagined that the opt-outs would one day be the subject of academic research conducted by me, which ultimately would result in a book by my hand.

I chose a career that covers different corners of diplomacy – many of which are unrelated to law. However, my law background continues to be a pillar of my professional life. Early on in my career, I was entrusted with chairing the so-called drafting group that, during the Danish presidency of the EU in 2002, prepared the accession treaty for the then 10 new Member States. I believe this was the occasion on which my passion for EU law was ignited.

The recent 30th anniversary of the opt-outs made me realise that the moment was ripe for me to return to this subject and, by conducting an in-depth legal analysis, make a humble contribution to academia. By this book, I wish to share my legal thoughts on the rather complex, and in my view fascinating, subject matter of the special Danish position within EU law.

Although the opt-outs are labelled as 'Danish', they are not exclusively relevant to Denmark. Their anchoring in Danish law, EU law and international law is testimony to their relevance beyond Denmark. It is my hope and belief that this book may prove useful for a wide spectrum of interlocutors.

Christian Thorning
*Baghdad*
*April 2024*

# *Acknowledgements*

I owe a vast amount of gratitude to several people without whom this book would not have been possible.

First of all, I am very thankful for the unwavering support that I have received from Professor Ramses A Wessel and Dr Justin Lindeboom at the University of Groningen. Their constructive comments offered in their respective roles as my supervisor and co-supervisor helped me immensely to focus and develop my academic thinking, which in turn greatly enhanced my ability to complete an earlier version of the manuscript that led to my award of a doctoral degree.

I should also like to give my thanks to the many colleagues and friends, also within the academic and judicial communities, with whom I have enjoyed countless enlightening and inspiring conversations over the years.

I am thankful to Global Editorial Director Sinéad Moloney at Hart Publishing for her trust and support, and for shepherding this book through the publishing process.

Last but certainly not least, I wish to thank my closest family for the encouragement, sparing and unfaltering spirit without which this project would not have come to fruition.

# *Contents*

# *List of Abbreviations*

| | |
|---|---|
| AG | Advocate General |
| Alm. del | *Almindelig del* (Ordinary Part) |
| AFSJ | Area of Freedom, Security and Justice |
| APF | African Peace Facility |
| Bull EC | Bulletin of the European Community |
| CAR | Central African Republic |
| CFSP | Common Foreign and Security Policy |
| CJEU | Court of Justice of the European Union |
| CMP | Coordinated Maritime Presence |
| COREPER | Committee of the Permanent Representatives of the Governments of the Member States to the European Union |
| CSDP | Common Security and Defence Policy |
| EASO | European Asylum Support Office |
| EBA | European Banking Authority |
| EDF | European Defence Fund |
| EC | European Community/Communities |
| ECB | European Central Bank |
| ECLI | European Case Law Identifier |
| Ecofin | Economic and Financial Affairs Council |
| EDIDP | European Defence Industrial Development Programme |
| EEAS | European External Action Service |
| EEC | European Economic Community |
| EIS | Europol Information System |
| EMS | European Monetary System |
| EMU | European Monetary Union |

| | |
|---|---|
| EPF | European Peace Facility |
| EPPO | European Public Prosecutor's Office |
| ERTA | European Road Transport Agreement (name of CJEU-instituted principle of implied external powers of the EC/EU) |
| ESCB | European System of Central Banks |
| ESDP | European Security and Defence Policy |
| ERM | European Exchange Rate Mechanism |
| EU | European Union |
| EUMC | European Union Military Committee |
| EUMT | European Union training mission |
| Eurodac | The European Asylum Dactyloscopy Database |
| EUROPOL | European Police Office/European Union Agency for Law Enforcement Cooperation |
| EUROJUST | European Union Agency for Criminal Justice Cooperation |
| EUU | *Europaudvalget* (European Committee) |
| E12 | European Intervention Initiative |
| FRONTEX | European Agency for the Management of Operational Cooperation at the External Borders of the Member States of the European Union |
| GAM | The Free Aceh Movement |
| ICJ | International Court of Justice |
| IGC | Intergovernmental Conference |
| JHA | Justice and Home Affairs |
| MEP | Member of European Parliament |
| MINUSMA | The United Nations Multidimensional Integrated Stabilization Mission in Mali |
| MPCC | Military Planning and Conduct Capability |
| NATO | North Atlantic Treaty Organization |
| OJ | Official Journal of the European Union |
| OCT | Overseas Countries and Territories |

| | |
|---|---|
| PESCO | Permanent Structured Cooperation. |
| PNR | Passenger Name Record |
| PPU | Urgent Preliminary ruling Procedure (at the CJEU) |
| QMV | Qualified Majority Voting |
| SAA | Stabilisation and Association Agreement |
| Saml | *Samling* (Parliamentary Session) |
| SATCEN | European Union Satellite Centre |
| SOFA | Status of Forces Agreement |
| SRM | Single Resolution Mechanism |
| SRF | Single Resolution Fund |
| SSM | Single Supervisory Mechanism |
| TCA | The EU's Trade and Cooperation Agreement with the UK |
| TEC | Treaty Establishing the European Community |
| TEU | Treaty on European Union |
| TFEU | Treaty on the Functioning of the European Union |
| TSCG | Treaty on Stability, Coordination and Governance in the EMU |
| UfR | *Ugeskrift for Retsvæsen* (weekly journal for the Judiciary) |
| UN | United Nations |
| UK | United Kingdom of Great Britain and Northern Ireland |
| WA | UK Withdrawal Agreement |
| WEU | Western European Union |
| VCLT | Vienna Convention of the Law of Treaties |

# *Table of Cases*

**Court of Justice of the European Union**

**Advocate General Views**



**Danish Jurisprudence**

# *Table of EU Secondary Law*

# *Table of Reports and Official Danish Memoranda*

**Danish Institute for International Studies**



**Danmarks Nationalbank**



**EU konsulenten (Folketinget)**



**Justitsministeriet**

### Tænketanken Europa



### Udenrigsministeriet



### Udenrigsministeriet & Forsvarsministeriet



### Økonomiministeriet & Finansministeriet

# 1

# *Introduction*

## I. PRELIMINARY REMARKS

IN A REFERENDUM in June 1992, the Danish electorate rejected the approval of the then new EU treaty known as the Maastricht Treaty. This meant that the anticipated European Union could not be established unless a special solution was found to accommodate the Danish concerns. Such a solution was agreed by the EU leaders already in December 1992, which in turn enabled the Maastricht Treaty to be ratified the following year. Denmark, however, was left in a 'special position', encompassing four legally defined opt-outs.

The year 2023 marked half a century for Denmark as a Member State of the European Union (EU).[1] It also marked 30 years since the above-mentioned solution in law, known principally as the Edinburgh Decision,[2] was created to overcome a major political constraint that otherwise would have put the entire European integration project in jeopardy.

While the opt-outs have to some extent been discussed, analysed and debated by judges, politicians, scholars and others over the years, there still exists a level of legal uncertainty and sometimes confusion around the scope, content and context of the opt-outs.

The opt-outs cannot be properly understood or appreciated without the benefit of knowing the full, and at times complex legal journey they have undertaken as a consequence of the European integration process. Through a re-examination of the opt-outs individually, collectively and temporally, this book sheds light on the legal issues pertinent to the opt-outs. As part of the discussion, new viewpoints and propositions are offered with a view to closing gaps in the legal understanding.

This book therefore forms the first comprehensive analysis of the Danish opt-outs and their effects in EU law.

[1] Together with the United Kingdom (UK) and Ireland, Denmark became a Member State of the then European Communities (EC) on 1 January 1973.

[2] Decision of the Heads of State or Government, meeting within the European Council, concerning certain problems raised by Denmark on the Treaty on European Union [1992] OJ C348/1.

## II. INTRODUCING THE DANISH OPT-OUTS

The opt-outs fall within four specific areas of EU cooperation: (i) Union citizenship; (ii) the third stage of Economic and Monetary Union (EMU) (the euro); (iii) defence cooperation; and (iv) the area that prior to the Lisbon Treaty was known as Justice and Home Affairs (JHA), now referred to as the Area of Freedom, Security and Justice (AFSJ).

In light of the European integration process, the opt-outs have – in different ways, as will be thoroughly explored in this book – been lifted from the Edinburgh Decision, an instrument under international law, and incorporated into EU treaty law. Furthermore, the continuous European integration process has necessitated that the opt-outs undergo certain adaptations.

Attempts to change the special position of Denmark have occurred three times; each time by way of addressing a particular opt-out separately. The first two attempts concerned, respectively, the opt-out from the third stage of the EMU (the euro) and the special position within the AFSJ. Both attempts failed as they were overruled by referenda in Denmark, with the result that the special Danish position on these policy matters has been left unchanged.[3]

The third attempt concerned the abolition of the defence opt-out. Following a successful referendum held on the matter in June 2022, the defence opt-out was subsequently abolished. Hence, Denmark no longer holds a special position within this particular field of cooperation; rather, Denmark participates in the cooperation just as any other Member State does.[4] Nonetheless, it is considered to be of value to include a full discussion of this opt-out in the present book with a view to ensuring and maintaining its comprehensive nature.

Although commonly referred to as 'Danish' opt-outs, the opt-outs are not exclusively relevant in a Danish legal context. They form part not only of Danish law but also of both international and EU law, which stretches their relevance beyond Denmark.

The study of the opt-outs is of relevance as seen from two perspectives: the 'operational' and the 'conceptual'.

First, with regard to the operational perspective, it is observed that the areas covered by the special position of Denmark are not insignificant areas of EU cooperation. On the contrary, they are arguably at the forefront of the EU agenda, as they include, amongst other things, topical issues such as migration, asylum, and combating terrorism and organised crime. Also, the financial crisis of 2008, leading to the sovereign debt crisis, highlighted the importance of but also the challenges to the euro cooperation, which in any case arguably stands as a backbone of the very construction of the EU.

The first 30 years of the evolving and vitally important European defence cooperation took place with Denmark as a side-lined Member State, unable to participate in actions with defence implications.

[3] See the following chapters on the respective opt-outs.

[4] See ch 5, section IV.

A thorough understanding of the special legal position of Denmark within these important and topical areas of EU cooperation is therefore necessary for stakeholders at large within the Union, including citizens and businesses, as well as the EU institutions and other Member States. That also applies to external stakeholders and counterparts, including third countries and international organisations, which may not be fully conscious of the limitations to the scope of their agreements with the EU that may occur as a consequence of the opt-outs.

Essentially, the aim here is to locate and assess the extent of the holes that the opt-outs leave in the fabric of EU cooperation, and how, if at all, such holes have been patched up.

Second, from the conceptual perspective, it is argued that the special Danish position constituted a novel legal tool to overcome political constraints on the European integration process that emerged at a particular point in time. Understanding the way in which this special Danish position was first introduced by the Edinburgh Decision as a very special addition to European treaty-lawmaking, and how it has developed since, offers an opportunity to reflect upon and appreciate it from a theoretical-legal viewpoint. As such, it offers a legal-doctrinal contribution to the wider study of differentiated integration within the EU as a concept, a process and a system.

This book also offers the opportunity to define the Danish 'opt-out' situation seen in relation to the defined British/Irish 'opt-in' regime within the AFSJ. More generally, a chance is provided to assess the limitations that the special Danish position contains, should it be considered to act as a potential template in other situations where European integration is constrained by the internal dynamics of a Member State.

## III. GAPS IN LEGAL UNDERSTANDING

The Danish opt-outs have been studied from different angles. Contributions taking a non-legal viewpoint offered by political scientists, international relations experts and economic experts are plentiful. They provide valuable insights into various aspects related to the Danish position. Many have taken a normative approach.[5]

[5] See, eg, the report by the Danish Institute for International Studies, *De danske forbehold over for den Europæiske Union – udviklingen siden 2000* (DIIS 2008); and recently the specific report by the same institute on the Defence opt-out, *Europæisk forsvarssamarbejde og det danske forsvarsforbehold* (DIIS 2019). See also P Svensson, 'The Danish Yes to Maastricht and Edinburgh. The EU Referendum of May 1993' (1994) 17(1) *Scandinavian Political Studies* 69; N Petersen, 'Denmark and the European Union 1985-96. A Two-level Analysis' (1996) 31(2) *Cooperation and Conflict* 185; D Naurin and R Lindahl, 'Out in the cold? Flexible integration and the political status of Euro opt-outs' (2010) 11(4) *European Union Politics* 485; GR Olsen, 'How Strong is Europeanisation, Really? The Danish Defence Administration and the Opt-Out from the European Security and Defence Policy' (2011) 12(1) *Perspectives on European Politics and Society* 13; L Miles and A Wivel (eds), *Denmark and the European Union* (Abingdon, Routledge, 2014); TB Olesen, 'Denmark in Europe 1973–2015: Processes of Europeanization and "Denmarkization"' (2015) 11(4) *Journal of Contemporary*

Of the political scientists, Adler-Nissen is a leading and widely published scholar in this field.[6]

Legal literature dealing in a comprehensive way with the various legal aspects of all four Danish opt-outs individually and horizontally is, on the other hand, less exhaustive.

Major volumes covering general and fundamental aspects of EU law written by well-respected legal scholars tend naturally to include mention of the Danish opt-outs, but without providing comprehensive coverage of their breadth and depth.[7]

The core Danish reference volume on EU law, *EU-Karnov*, covers aspects of the opt-outs with the overall aim of describing the law as it is applied in practice, rather than conducting academic legal reflection.[8] A separate volume, *EU-Retten i Danmark*,[9] aims to uncover how EU law is implemented and applied in Denmark. Except for the opt-out on Union citizenship, this volume discusses the remaining opt-outs in dedicated chapters. True to the aim of the volume, the focus is on Denmark and Danish law.

The Edinburgh Decision did attract some attention from legal scholars, and an academic debate unfolded after it, related both to its content and to its

*European Research* 312; A Wivel, 'As Awkward as They Need to Be: Denmark's Pragmatic Activist Approach to Europe' in MS McCallion and A Brianson (eds), *Nordic States and European Integration: Awkward Partners in the North* (Cham, Palgrave Macmillan, 2018) 13; MD Jensen and P Nedergaard, 'Danish European Union Policies: Sailing Between Economic Benefits and Political Sovereignty' in PM Christiansen, J Elklit and P Nedergaard (eds), *The Oxford Handbook of Danish Politics* (Oxford, Oxford University Press, 2020) 487.

[6] See, eg, R Adler-Nissen, 'The Diplomacy of Opting Out: A Bourdieudian Approach to National Integration Strategies' (2008) 46(3) *Journal of Common Market Studies* 663; 'Behind the scenes of differentiated integration: circumventing national opt-outs in Justice and Home Affairs' (2009) 16(1) *Journal of European Public Policy* 62; 'Opting Out of an Ever Closer Union: The Integration *Doxa* and the Management of Sovereignty' (2011) 34(5) *West European Politics* 1092; *Opting out of the European Union* (Cambridge, Cambridge University Press, 2014); 'The Vocal Euro-outsider: The UK in a Two-speed Europe' (2016) 87(2) *The Political Quarterly* 238. See also R Adler-Nissen and T Gammeltoft-Hansen, 'Straitjacket or Sovereignty Shield? The Danish Opt-Out on Justice and Home Affairs and Prospects after the Treaty of Lisbon' (2010) *Danish Foreign Policy Yearbook* 137.

[7] For relatively short references, see, eg, A Dashwood et al, *Wyatt and Dashwood's European Union Law*, 6th edn (Oxford, Hart Publishing, 2011); K Lenaerts and P van Nuffel, *Europees Recht*, 6th edn (Antwerp, Intersentia, 2017); RH Folsom, *European Union Law including BREXIT in a nutshell*, 9th edn (Saint Paul, MN, West Academic Publishing, 2017); PJ Kuijper et al (eds), *The Law of the European Union*, 5th edn (The Hague, Wolters Kluwer, 2018); R Schütze, *European Union Law*, 2nd edn (Cambridge, Cambridge University Press, 2018); P Craig et al, *European Union Law*, 4th edn (Cambridge, Cambridge University Press, 2019); P Craig and G de Búrca, *EU Law – text, cases, and materials*, 7th edn (Oxford, Oxford University Press, 2020). C Blumann and L Dubouis, *Droit institutionnel de l'Union européenne*, 2nd edn (LexisNexis Litec, 2005) mention that the Maastricht Treaty sparked constitutional problems in several Member States, including France and Germany, but fall short of explicitly mentioning the Danish case.

[8] See the introductory remarks of JH Danielsen et al (eds), *EU-Karnov*, vol 1 (Copenhagen, Karnov Group Denmark, 2015).

[9] BE Olsen and KE Sørensen (eds), *EU-retten i Danmark* (Copenhagen, Jurist- og Økonomforbundets Forlag, 2018).

construct.[10] The debate naturally was influenced by the stage of the European integration process as it appeared at the time.

Academics have since published contributions over the years in the form of book chapters, articles, op-eds, etc, on aspects of the Danish opt-outs.[11]

In relation to the referenda held respectively on the euro, AFSJ and defence opt-outs, the Danish authorities published memoranda with legal analyses so as to provide the public with general information on the topics.[12] The documents formed part of the parliamentary process as well. Legal scholars followed suit with targeted contributions.[13]

Whilst the existing literature provides good insights into many aspects of the individual opt-outs, there is not an abundance of literature available. Moreover, scholars tend to focus on an individual opt-out or examine the opt-outs from a particular moment in time.

It can be said that the existing literature dedicated to the Danish opt-outs remains limited in scope and that clarity on the legal impact of the opt-outs

[10] See, eg, D Howarth, 'The Compromise on Denmark and the Treaty on European Union: A legal and Political Analysis' (1994) 31(4) *Common Market Law Review* 765; D Curtin and R van Ooik, 'Denmark and the Edinburgh Summit: Maastricht without tears: A Legal Analysis' in D O'Keeffe and PM Twomey (eds), *Legal Issues of the Maastricht Treaty* (Chichester, Wiley Chancery, 1994) 349; J Shaw, 'The Treaty of Amsterdam: Challenges of Flexibility and Legitimacy' (1998) 4(1) *European Law Journal* 63.

[11] They include, eg, S Peers, 'In a World of Their Own – Justice and Home Affairs Opt-Outs and the Treaty of Lisbon' (2007) 10 *Cambridge Yearbook of European Legal Studies* 383; M Wind and S Adamo, 'Is Green Better than Blue? The Danish JHA opt-out and the Unilateral Attempt to Attract Highly Skilled Labour' (2015) 17 *European Journal of Migration and Law* 329; D Curtin, 'Brexit and the EU Area of Freedom, Security, and Justice: Bespoke Bits and Pieces' in F Fabbrini (ed), *The Law & Politics of Brexit* (Oxford, Oxford University Press, 2017) 183; E Herlin-Karnell, 'Between flexibility and disintegration in EU criminal law' in B de Witte, A Ott and E Vos (eds), *Between Flexibility and Disintegration: The State of EU law today* (Cheltenham, Edward Elgar Publishing, 2017) 384; S Peers, 'Differentiated integration and the Brexit process in EU Justice and Home Affairs' in AR Servent and F Trauner (eds), *The Routledge Handbook of Justice and Home Affairs Research* (Abingdon, Routledge, 2017) 253; D Thym, 'Supranational Differentiation and Enhanced Cooperation' in R Schütze and T Tridimas (eds), *Oxford Principles of European Union Law*, vol I (Oxford, Oxford University Press, 2018) 847; G Butler, 'The European Defense Union and Denmark's Defence opt-out: A Legal Appraisal' (2020) 25 *European Foreign Affairs Review* 117; A Engel, 'Opting in or opting out? The EU's variable geometry in the area of freedom, security and justice' in R Pereira, A Engel and S Miettinen (eds), *The Governance of Criminal Justice in the European Union* (Cheltenham, Edward Elgar Publishing, 2020) 39; C Thorning, 'De Danske Forbehold' in U Neergaard and KE Sørensen (eds), *Danmark og EU gennem 50 år – en milepæl* (Copenhagen, Djøf Forlag, 2023) 175. One or more of the Danish opt-outs have also figured as part of a wider discussion of differentiated integration among political scientist and others, see the references listed in ch 7 of this book.

[12] Økonomiministeriet and Finansministeriet, 'Danmark og euroen' (2000); Justitsministeriet, 'Samarbejdet om retlige og indre anliggender – En analyse af EU-lovgivning omfattet af retsforbeholdet' (Rosendahls Schultz Grafisk, 2015); Udenrigsministeriet and Forsvarsministeriet, 'EU's sikkerheds- og forsvarspolitiske samarbejde og det danske forsvarsforbehold – Redegørelse' (Europaudvalget 2021–22 EUU Alm.del – Bilag 416, 2022).

[13] See, eg, D Schraff and F Schimmelfennig, 'Does differentiated integration strengthen the democratic legitimacy of the EU? Evidence from the 2015 Danish opt-out referendum' (2020) 21(4) *European Union Politics* 590; U Neergaard and G Butler, 'Denmark's Defence opt-out, the Forthcoming Referendum, and the Changing Face of EU Defence and Security Arrangements' (2022) 95 *EU Law Live* 2.

has not yet been fully established. Testimony to that is the fact that questions regarding the Danish opt-out within the AFSJ in relation to the external competence of the EU continue to trouble the Court of Justice of the European Union (CJEU).[14]

Furthermore, notable confusion about the Danish and British special legal positions may have come about, with the Danish position mistakenly taken as being equal to that of the United Kingdom (UK).

More generally, the special legal position of the UK may have had a tendency to overshadow that of Denmark. The UK gained a reputation for being the 'champion' of opt-outs,[15] and the UK was joined by Ireland and Denmark 'in its drive to secure opt-outs'.[16] Cardwell even posed the question whether Brexit marked the end of exceptionalism within the EU.[17] Although the UK and Denmark may well have had different interpretations of what it means to be exceptional, it is a fact, as will be explored in this book, that notwithstanding the abolition of the Danish defence opt-out, Denmark remains the sole Member State with a comprehensive, special position under EU law, which otherwise is alien to all other EU Member States.

## IV. THE LEGAL QUESTIONS

The main question that this book aims to answer is to what extent and how the Danish opt-outs hold legal significance in EU law.

This question is too vast to be addressed head on. Therefore, answers to additional questions are sought first, on the basis of which the answer to the main question ultimately will be distilled.

As already indicated, a proper understanding of the opt-outs must start by examining the legal specificities of their birth. Consequently, it is only pertinent, first, to seek the answer to the following question: In what legal order, and how, were the opt-outs originally designed?

Second, the European integration process has gradually evolved since the opt-outs were first established. This journey would naturally have impacted on the opt-outs in relation both to their legal construction as well as the effects they have within the evolving EU law. To address this double challenge, one must ask a two-part question, the parts of which are interlinked, albeit distinct.

[14] eg Opinion 1/19 *Istanbul Convention* ECLI:EU:C:2021:198. See discussion in ch 6, sections III.C and III.D.

[15] M Kendrick, 'Brexit the Ultimate Opt-out: Learning the Lessons on Differentiated Integration' (2022) 7(3) *European Papers* 1211.

[16] A Łazowski, *Inside but out? The United Kingdom and the European Union* (Oxford, Oxford University Press, 2017) 501.

[17] PJ Cardwell, 'The End of Exceptionalism and a Strengthening of Coherence? Law and Legal Integration in the EU Post-Brexit' (2019) 57(6) *Journal of Common Market Studies* 1407.

The first part: How has the European integration process affected the opt-outs? The answer to this question will necessarily include a discussion of how the layouts of the opt-outs have changed, including by a transfer from one legal order to another.

Once that is established, the interlinked second part may be addressed essentially by replying to the following question: What are the effects in EU law of the individual opt-outs? This question could alternatively be phrased as a question on what kind of EU cooperation Denmark is *not* part of, bearing in mind that depending on the extent of the European integration process on the respective subject matter covered by each opt-out, the answer may vary during the course of the opt-outs' existence.[18] By finding this answer, eradication of possible misconceptions relating to the scope of the respective opt-outs is provided. Also, a closer look at the nature of the respective opt-outs will be taken in order to understand why it has proved possible, in certain cases, to introduce mitigating measures, and to assess to which legal order these measures belong.

Furthermore, a discussion of the comparative nature of the legal differences between the concept within EU law of an opt-out, on the one hand, and that of an opt-in, on the other hand, becomes relevant and will therefore form part of the analysis.

Third, it is pertinent to ask the following question – which essentially is in the category of an antonym – with a view to providing a complete picture: How could the special Danish position be changed?

The complete abolition of an opt-out naturally constitutes the ultimate change. That has indeed been executed in relation to the defence opt-out. On what legal basis that played out is in itself interesting to examine. Furthermore, a less fundamental change than abolition is, as will be explained later, an option in relation to the AFSJ opt-out.

Fourth and finally, as part of conceptualising the opt-outs with a view to providing a full and comprehensive legal picture, an analysis of a comparative character is called for, with the aim of establishing how the Danish opt-outs compare to other forms of differentiated integration within EU law and how the opt-outs fit with the concept of unity of EU law.

This book does not, however, aim to embark on a substantive discussion of the vast issue of differentiated integration as such, nor is that required to define the similarities and notably differences between the Danish opt-outs and other forms of differentiated integration within EU law, including the later-introduced concepts of enhanced and permanent structured cooperation. With a view to providing a picture as complete as possible on the issue of an opt-out seen in light of the broader concept of differentiated integration, a brief discussion of the judgment of the Danish Supreme Court in the so-called *Ajos* case is included in this respect.[19]

[18] In case of the defence opt-out, the question should necessarily be formulated in the past tense.

[19] Judgment of the Danish Supreme Court, Case no 15/2014, *DI, acting on behalf of Ajos A/S v Estate of A*, UfR 2017.824H.

## V. THE APPROACH

This book deliberately focuses strongly on the legal-doctrinal approach rather than on judicial policy. Consequently, the book does not offer qualitative assessments of the legal situation, nor does it formulate suggestions as to how the law should or should not evolve. The aim is to provide the reader with a solid legal understanding of the law and its application, on the basis of which one may draw one's own conclusions of a normative character.

Throughout the book, the opt-outs remain the subject. This implies that the author approaches the subject matter to the extent possible by zooming out from the opt-outs to the wider national, EU and international law perspectives and not the other way around. Furthermore, thorough analyses of the relevant areas of EU cooperation are not the objective and thus will not be conducted.[20] For the purpose at hand, a brief outline will suffice.

Moreover, it is also not the aim of this book to provide an assessment of the EU integration process, including offering an assessment of a possible role for the opt-outs in shaping (holding back) that process either retrospectively or when looking to the future of Europe. Rather, reference points to essential elements of the European integration process will be included in the analysis, as deemed appropriate to establishing how this in turn may have affected the opt-outs from a legal point of view. Notable reference points are the changes brought about by the Treaties of Amsterdam and Lisbon, respectively, and naturally by the Maastricht Treaty that caused the subject of this study to arise in the first place.

An analytical method is utilised to bring to light precisely what happened in the evolution of the EU integration process and how that affected the opt-outs. The approach is thus a deliberate methodological choice that is considered crucial for laying the foundation for understanding the legal effects of the opt-outs during the course of their existence, which subsequently will be explained and analysed as an integral part of this book.

The study contains elements of a comparative nature: in general, by addressing the opt-outs in light of the European integration process; and, more specifically, by reflecting on the differences in law between an opt-out *versus* flexible cooperation. Comparisons with arrangements held by other Member States will also appear, including by looking at and discussing the opt-out model *versus* the opt-in model.

Considerations on political reasoning and political implications, practical and diplomatic challenges and economic wisdom would be much better served by socio-political and economic studies and are therefore left to those disciplines. However, the legal-doctrinal findings of this book may serve as input for

[20] Over the years, scholars have published numerous and brilliant accounts on this aspect, to which this book refers and on which it builds.

non-legal studies. Clarity regarding the legal parameters that regulate, and at times limit, the political choices and tighten the room for manoeuvre in areas covered by the Danish opt-outs would be of importance in any context.

## VI. TERMINOLOGY

Before embarking on the subject of the Danish opt-outs in the remainder of this book, it seems appropriate to provide some preliminary remarks concerning the vocabulary used to label the special Danish position.

Confusion and possible misconceptions are potentially already born at the point when a label is applied to the special Danish position. The terminology varies. The terms used are not necessarily synonyms, although they may seem to be used interchangeably.

In relation to the Edinburgh Decision, a neutral terminology referring to laying out 'a set of arrangements' to overcome certain problems raised by Denmark on the Treaty on European Union (TEU) is used to describe the special position of Denmark, which that instrument then instituted.[21] As will be explored in this book, the original provisions from the Edinburgh Decision later found their way into the EU Treaty. In this connection, no particular labelling of the special position of Denmark was effected either, the exception being Protocol No 16 to the EU Treaties on the Danish position regarding the third stage of the EMU. In this Protocol, reference to Denmark is made as a country with 'an exemption'. However, the Protocol also states that the rules for Member States with a 'derogation' apply to Denmark.[22] As will be seen in chapter 4, the notion of 'a Member State with a derogation' has a special defined legal meaning within that particular part of EU cooperation, which does not translate to other parts of the treaty complex.

Among scholars and political actors, a variety of different terms are in use to describe the special Danish position. In the Danish language, actors often use the term '*forbehold*',[23] which in English translates to 'reservation'. While that term has a well-defined legal meaning under treaty law,[24] it may not necessarily correspond to the nature of the Danish position. In Denmark, the term '*undtagelse*' is occasionally used as well. This translates into English as 'an 'exemption', which traditionally means being free from an obligation.[25] To this definition it seems

[21] Decision of the Heads of State or Government (n 2). Discussed in ch 2.

[22] Protocol No 16 on Certain Provisions relating to Denmark [2016] OJ C 202/287. Discussed in ch 4.

[23] Recently used in the volume marking the 50th anniversary of Danish EU Membership, U Neergaard and K Engsig-Sørensen (eds), *Danmark og EU Gennem 50 år – En Milepæl* (Copenhagen, Djøf Forlag, 2023).

[24] Vienna Convention on the Law of Treaties, pt II, sec 2.

[25] *Concise Oxford English Dictionary Luxury Edition* (Oxford, Oxford University Press, 2009) 498.

only appropriate to add that it also implies being free from enjoying a right or a privilege, as the case may be. The Danish term *'undtagelse'* also translates into the English term 'derogation', which means to deviate from something.[26]

Finally, the term 'opt-out' is also widely used in a Danish context. The first part of the term originates from Latin *optare*, which means 'to choose' or 'to wish', and 'opt-out' is thus defined as meaning 'choosing not to participate'.[27]

The terms 'opt-out' and 'opt-in' should not be used interchangeably, as the latter represents a different legal situation. This particular issue will be analysed as part of the discussion of the AFSJ in chapter 6.

The title of the present book uses the term 'opt-outs' for the special Danish situation. That is because it arguably is the most commonly used term and as such provides the reader with a clear understanding as to what is addressed. The term 'opt-out' will thus also figure as the most commonly used term in the book. It is, however, without prejudice to the outcome of the legal discussion to follow.

Upon completion of the various analyses undertaken in the book, it will be possible, as part of the conclusions in chapter 8, to revert to the terminology issue with a view to determining the appropriate way of labelling the special Danish position.

## VII. STRUCTURE

The study of the four opt-outs commences in chapter 2, which is dedicated to their common origin. As such, it examines how in law and within which legal order the opt-outs originally were designed, and discusses the legality of the structure established at the time.

With a solid understanding of the historical context for the opt-outs and the legal nature of the original concept created to house them, chapters 3 to 6 take an in-depth look at each of the opt-outs with a view to 'mapping-out' how the opt-outs, individually, have adapted to the evolution of EU law in light of the European integration process since 1992. The two-part question, on the one hand regading what the effects of the European integration process on the opt-outs have been, and on the other hand as to what effects the opt-outs have in EU law, is answered in the form of four parts, each relating to one specific opt-out. The four parts will eventually be combined in the final concluding chapter.

The question on legal issues related to changing the special Danish position is addressed in dedicated sections within chapters 4 to 6, with the points of departure being the respective situations when the issues emerged.

The individual analyses of each opt-out conducted in dedicated chapters 3 to 6 may appear asymmetrical in length and depth. This is, however, merely

[26] ibid 386.
[27] ibid 1004.

a natural consequence of the differences in the legal complexities within the respective opt-outs, which the analyses will demonstrate and clarify.

The question of a general and horizontal nature on the interplay with the concept of differentiated integration is dealt with in chapter 7, which will draw upon the prior findings on the characteristics of the opt-outs.

Finally, the book is rounded off with a set of final and comprehensive conclusions in chapter 8.

# 2

# *Locating the Common Origin of the Opt-Outs*

## I. INTRODUCTION

AS MENTIONED IN chapter 1, the birth of the Danish opt-outs from four specific areas of EU cooperation took place at the meeting of the European Council in Edinburgh in December 1992. In this chapter, this common origin of the opt-outs is explored with a view to establishing within what legal order, and how, the opt-outs originally were designed.

To achieve this, it is necessary first to outline very briefly the events leading up to the meeting of the European Council in Edinburgh. This is done in section II.

The solution that emerged from the Edinburgh European Council to 'the problems raised by Denmark in light of the outcome of the Danish referendum on 2 June 1992 on the Maastricht Treaty',[1] discussed in section III, is complex in the sense that it comprises a number of documents. Most of this chapter is devoted to taking a closer look at these original documents to ascertain their legal nature and function within the overarching solution. This is achieved by first outlining the central elements in each document, followed by an analysis of their legal nature and, as part thereof, by assigning them to the legal order (international law, EU law or Danish law) to which they may belong. Discussion of the compatibility of the legal structure adopted for the opt-outs with the EU legal order forms a central part of the analysis.

The discussion of the legal nature of the instruments and texts examined is based on the view that both conclusions of the European Council and declarations attached to EU Treaties form part of EU law, but without that necessarily meaning that they can be legally enforced as such.[2] The instruments in question may provide guidance and may often be used to interpret other, legally enforceable instruments of EU law, that is, such as may be invoked before the CJEU. In this way, conclusion texts and declarations may very well have legal effects even though they are not legally enforceable as such. The same observation applies to instruments falling within international law.

[1] Presidency Conclusion Part A, point 2, Bull EC 12-1992, vol 25.

[2] See, for an early discussion on the issue of the legal nature of decisions from the European Council, J Werts, *The European Council* (The Hague, TMC Asser Instituut, 1992) 134.

Against this background, documents, which are not legally enforceable as such, will be discussed in order to ascertain the input (policy, interpretational or procedural) they provide to the legal construction to which they belong.

An in-depth analysis of the definition, scope and nature of the four opt-outs is not part of this chapter. Rather, that analysis follows in chapters 3 to 6, which all take the relevant texts from Edinburgh as their points of departure.

This chapter rounds off in section VIII by setting out the Edinburgh documents in a table that orders them according to their individual attribution and affiliation. Overall conclusions are drawn in section IX.

## II. SETTING THE SCENE FOR THE EDINBURGH SUMMIT

The agenda for the meeting of the European Council held in Edinburgh on 11–12 December 1992 was rather substantial. Among several other items, the Council was invited to address sensitive issues of an institutional nature. This included the need to reach a decision on the numbers of seats in the European Parliament for each Member State, considering the then recent German reunification, as well as to decide on the location of the geographical seats of a number of institutions. Also on the agenda was the so-called 'Delors II Package' on the future financing of the Community, as well as pertinent foreign policy issues like the emerging crisis in the Former Yugoslavia. The European Council thus had to agree 'on solutions to a very wide range of issues which are essential to progress in Europe'.[3] Among those was one additional agenda item, which related to the ratification process of the then newly drafted Maastricht Treaty establishing the European Union.

This last-mentioned agenda item was certainly not a routine one. The Danish electorate had rejected the Maastricht Treaty in a referendum on 2 June 1992. As the matter stood at the time of the European Council Meeting, the prospect of the Maastricht Treaty's ever entering into force looked grim given that one Member State, Denmark, had failed to ratify it.[4] However, Denmark had undertaken substantial work prior to the Edinburgh meeting with a view to breaking the deadlock.

Following the outcome of the Danish referendum, an internal political process was initiated in Denmark. It involved most of the Danish political parties, with the then left-wing opposition parties playing a leading role. The outcome was enshrined in a political Memorandum entitled 'Denmark in Europe'.[5] The short and to-the-point Memorandum outlined in its core part four derogations for Denmark from specific areas of cooperation within the Maastricht Treaty,

[3] Presidency Conclusion (n 1).
[4] Recalling that ratification by all Member States is required, see current Art 48 TEU.
[5] 'Denmark in Europe', Markedsudvalget 1992–93, MKU Alm. del bilag 70, part A.

approval of which would enable Denmark to vote for a second time on ratification of the Treaty.[6]

In the months leading up to the Edinburgh summit, intense diplomatic activities took place, notably on the side of Denmark. The Danish Foreign Minister presented the Memorandum during a tour that autumn to all the capitals of the Member States, and later the issue was discussed at a couple of meetings by the Foreign Ministers of the Member States. In parallel to and in concert with the activities of the Government, the leader of the Danish Social Democratic Party, and as such effectively the leader of the opposition in the Danish Parliament, himself reached out to his European counterparts. On this basis, the scene was set for the European leaders to resolve the matter in Edinburgh.[7]

## III. THE EDINBURGH SOLUTION

The terminology used to describe the outcome of the Edinburgh meeting on the Danish issue varies. At times it may be unclear which precise texts the terminology used includes. With the aim of providing some clarity, a set of terminology definitions should therefore be established from the outset.

First, it is noted that the European Council used terminology whereby it 'has agreed on' a 'set of arrangements' to meet the Danish concerns. The agreement in the form of these arrangements is set out in Part B of the Presidency Conclusions from the European Council meeting.[8] Its structure is as follows: a short conclusion serves as a sort of recital to the agreed arrangements, which are subsequently included in three annexes; Annex I reproduces what would become known as 'the Edinburgh Decision', and Annexes II and III, respectively, reproduce a set of declarations. Part B is entitled 'Denmark and the Treaty on European Union'. As will be explored and discussed in what follows, Part B in its entirety was treated as a combined body of text and is published as such in the *Official Journal*.[9]

Second, the Danish Government also talked about 'the agreement' reached in Edinburgh and referred to it as 'the so-called Edinburgh Agreement'.[10] For Denmark, this term included the Edinburgh Decision with related declarations (ie the texts annexed to Part B of the conclusions), as well as the conclusions reached by the European Council regarding the issues of greater transparency

[6] An outline and analysis of the memorandum follows in section IV.

[7] For an account of events, see, eg, N Petersen, 'Denmark and the European Union 1985–96. A Two-level Analysis' (1996) 31(2) *Cooperation and Conflict* 185; TB Olesen, *Den svære dans. Danmark og det europæiske samarbejde* (Copenhagen, Gads Forlag, 2022).

[8] Presidency Conclusion Part B, Bull EC 12-1992, vol 25.

[9] Denmark and the Treaty on European Union [1992] OJ C348/1.

[10] The explanatory notes to the Danish ratification Bill L177, Folketingstidende saml 1992–93, col 6703.

and subsidiarity.[11] The last two aspects had also been mentioned as areas of concern in the Danish Memorandum, 'Denmark in Europe'. They were, however, treated as part of the ordinary Part A of the Presidency Conclusions and not as part of Part B on the specific arrangements on Denmark.

The Edinburgh Agreement thus has a broader scope than the *specific* agreement on the set of arrangements entitled 'Denmark and the Treaty on European Union'. To complicate matters, the analyses that follow in this book will reveal that even some elements of the proclaimed 'specific' arrangements on Denmark are in fact of a general nature.

In any case, the Edinburgh *Agreement* should not be taken as synonymous with the Edinburgh *Decision*. The latter forms the core part of the former as the prominent element of the *arrangements* within Part B of the conclusions. The Edinburgh Decision was clearly also perceived by the Danish Government as the core document, and is as such explicitly mentioned and addressed in the operative part of the ratification Bill that followed.[12]

Third, it is worth recalling that the European Council was guided in its work by the Memorandum drafted by the Danish political parties. The document in its entirety forms part of the explanatory notes to the Danish ratification Bill, which underlines the importance attached to it by the Danish legislators.[13]

All texts are, as we shall see, of importance, albeit in different ways. Consequently, they are all included in the analysis that follows in this chapter. Seen together, this combined set of texts forms what it is proposed to refer to as the comprehensive Edinburgh *solution*.

The individual documents forming the Edinburgh solution are presented and subsequently analysed in the following sections, with the Danish Memorandum as the natural starting point.

## IV. THE DANISH MEMORANDUM

### A. Outline of the Danish Memorandum

All parties in the Danish Parliament except for *Fremskridtspartiet* (the Progress Party) adopted the Memorandum 'Denmark in Europe' on 30 October 1992.[14]

The Memorandum initially notes that the narrow result of the Danish 1992 referendum on the Maastricht Treaty, with 50.7 per cent voting 'no' compared to 49.3 per cent voting 'yes', required that 'the political parties must formulate

[11] ibid.

[12] Both the Edinburgh Decision and the ratification Bill are discussed in detail in section VII.A and B.

[13] On the status of *travaux préparatoires* in Danish legislation, see the Danish Ministry of Justice's guidance note on the quality of legislation, Justitsministeriet, 'Lovkvalitesvejledningen' (2007).

[14] 'Denmark in Europe' (n 5).

*a national compromise* which can unite the population on Denmark's participation in further EC cooperation'.[15] In a Danish context, the Memorandum is thus often referred to as 'The National Compromise'.[16]

The Memorandum is divided into three parts: (A) introductory remarks; (B) a Danish proposal to the other Member States; and (C) the Danish position on enlargement of the EU.

The introductory remarks within Part A contain a statement of a fundamental character. It reads:

> The Danish 'no' to European Union on 2 June 1992 reflected the fact that the majority of Danes do not wish a United States of Europe. It was not, however, a 'no' to EC membership or European cooperation.[17]

Further on, the text reads:

> Europe needs binding cooperation. This is a pre-condition for progress in Europe, with peace, employment and the environment being given pride of place. The EC is the natural framework for such cooperation …[18]

Part C of the Memorandum offers full backing for the European integration process in the geographical sense, by making the following call regarding the prospect of future enlargement:

> Under the Danish Presidency, a wide-ranging conference must be called to look at the development prospect for European cooperation.[19]

Between these two sets of political pledges, the Memorandum's middle Part B contains a proposal on how to move forward with the stalled Maastricht Treaty in light of the result of the Danish referendum. The Danish politicians rightly observed:

> As a result of the referendum of 2 June, the Bill on Denmark's ratification of the Maastricht Treaty lapsed. Denmark and the eleven other countries which signed this treaty are therefore faced with a real problem which can be solved only by all twelve countries together.[20]

Part B of the Memorandum is divided into two sections. Under the subheading 'Issues of common interest', the first section presents Danish views on the issues of enhanced transparency and respect for the principle of subsidiarity within the then area of European Communities (EC) cooperation. In addition, viewpoints are highlighted on the extent of the cooperation within the fields of social and economic policies, consumer protection and the environment.

[15] ibid (emphasis added).
[16] Petersen (n 7).
[17] 'Denmark in Europe' (n 5).
[18] ibid.
[19] ibid, Part C. Denmark was at the time the incoming EU presidency after the UK.
[20] ibid, Part B, section 2.

The subsequent second section outlines issues of particular interest for Denmark. In this regard, the Danish politicians insisted on a solution (the term 'agreement' is used) whereby Denmark effectively would become 'shielded' from four specific elements of cooperation under the new Treaty regime. The Memorandum formulated it as follows:

1) Denmark does not participate in the so-called defence policy dimension, which involves membership of the Western European Union and a common defence policy or a common defence.
2) Denmark does not participate in the single currency and the economic policy obligations linked to the third stage of Economic Monetary Union. However, Denmark attaches great importance to participating in exchange-rate cooperation as formulated within the EMS and in the form which is to be carried forward in the second stage. Denmark must remain involved in close exchange-rate cooperation within the EC, even if and when other EC countries move into the third stage. Denmark will thus retain its national powers over financial and monetary policy, including legislation on the National Bank of Demark.
3) Denmark will have no obligations in connection with citizenship of the Union. However, for EC citizens living in Denmark it will retain the right to vote and to stand as a candidate at municipal elections and introduce both aspects for elections to the European Parliament.
4) Denmark cannot agree to transfer sovereignty in the areas of justice and police affairs, but can participate in the intergovernmental cooperation which has existed to-date. This means that Denmark cannot agree to parts of the third pillar being transferred to the area of supranational cooperation in the first pillar.[21]

The Memorandum further states that any solution addressing the aspects listed above should respect the Danish referendum; it should be legally binding; and it should be without any time limit. The detailed legal form of the arrangement was explicitly left to the forthcoming negotiations to determine.

A pledge that Denmark, on the other hand, would not prevent the other Member States from pursuing further cooperation within the said areas immediately follows these requirements. Equally, it was made clear that Denmark otherwise fully participated in the then EC cooperation.

Last but not least, the Memorandum stated that a new referendum (on Danish approval of the Maastricht Treaty) was to be held once an agreement had been successfully drawn up and in so far as the Danish Parliament could recommend it to the electorate.[22]

## B. Legal Analysis of the Danish Memorandum

The Danish Memorandum was drafted and agreed upon by the political parties acting in an informal political setting. It is testimony to a long parliamentary

[21] ibid.
[22] ibid.

tradition in Denmark of finding solutions to major political questions through multi-party cooperation that even crosses otherwise political dividing lines. According to Svensson, 'the decision-making process of this compromise was an extreme manifestation of the peculiar arrangement of Danish minority parliamentarism'.[23] The Memorandum is by nature and by its intent a political document giving political directions for a legal solution to be agreed accordingly.

There are two notable takeaways from the Memorandum. The first is that the document clearly identified four areas of cooperation designated as requiring special rules vis-à-vis the participation of Denmark. The policy areas identified corresponded largely to concerns raised from the left-wing spectrum of the political arena in Denmark prior to the intergovernmental conference (IGC) on the Maastricht Treaty.[24] The concrete and relatively concise way in which they were described arguably proved helpful in finding a lasting solution at the meeting in Edinburgh. As we shall see, this solution in its legal form was indeed closely based on the directions given by the Memorandum.[25]

While keeping this in mind, the second takeaway is that the Memorandum also communicated a clear political message from the broad majority of the Danish political parties, including those in government and those that incidentally soon were to come into government.[26] The message is one of a general commitment to continuous and active Danish participation in the European project. Given the context, it is thus clear that the envisaged legally binding opt-outs were also seen from a political point of view as exceptions to an otherwise positive Danish commitment to EU cooperation. This is not without relevance for the legal interpretation of the opt-outs that subsequently was established. That issue is addressed in detail in chapters 3 to 6, reaching its conclusion in chapter 8 of this book.

The Danish Memorandum ('The National Compromise') is classified as a political document that is not legally enforceable as such, although it provided valuable policy input to the construction of the opt-outs at the time, as well as continuous interpretational input to the understanding of the legal scope of the opt-outs. The latter is accentuated by the fact that the Memorandum is reproduced in the explanatory notes to the Danish ratification Bill.[27]

[23] P Svensson, 'The Danish Yes to Maastricht and Edinburgh. The EC Referendum of May 1993' (1994) 17(1) *Scandinavian Political Studies* 69, 71.

[24] Petersen (n 7).

[25] There is one notable modification, though, given the form of the final Danish position on Union citizenship, see ch 3.

[26] There was a change of Danish Government in 1993.

[27] See further section VII.B.

## V. PRESIDENCY CONCLUSION, PART A (IN PART)

### A. Outline of the Presidency Conclusion, Part A (in Part)

The Danish Memorandum advocated the promotion of transparency in the EU decision-making process and respect for the principle of subsidiarity. These were not Denmark-specific issues as such but were of a more general nature, and the Danish viewpoints were already shared by several other Member States. In fact, concrete deliberations on addressing these issues had already commenced at an extraordinary meeting of the European Council in Birmingham on 16 October 1992. At that point, a so-called Birmingham Declaration had been adopted.[28]

In the general Part A of the Presidency Conclusion from Edinburgh, these issues were further advanced, including by adopting an overall approach to the application of the subsidiarity principle attached as Annex no 2. Furthermore, the European Council expressed itself in detail in the subsequent Annex no 3, regarding the implementation of the Birmingham Declaration on transparency.

Part A of the Conclusion also deals with the challenge of unemployment in Europe as part of an outline for promoting economic recovery by way of a declaration produced in Annex 4. In the Danish Memorandum there is a call for a strengthened, coordinated effort to increase employment in Europe. Arguably, it appears to be a shortcoming of the text of the explanatory notes to the later Danish ratification Bill, that the matter was not explicitly included in the Danish Government's definition of what constituted 'The Edinburgh Agreement'.[29]

### B. Legal Analysis of Presidency Conclusion, Part A (in Part)

Following the definition adopted at the time by the Danish Government, relevant elements within Part A of the Council Conclusion were considered to be part of the Edinburgh Agreement since they addressed issues raised in the Danish Memorandum.[30] However, the texts are all detached from the specific arrangements concerning Denmark within Part B. They should be assessed as what they are, namely, ordinary texts originating from the European Council. The ordinary legal status attributed to conclusions from the European Council thus applies. In this respect, a couple of observations may prove pertinent.

It is recalled that the European Council was established by agreement among the heads of government as well as the President of France during a meeting

[28] Conclusion of the Birmingham European Council, Bull EC 10-1992, para 1.8.

[29] The explanatory notes to the Danish ratification Bill L177 (n 10). See further on the ratification Bill, section VII.B.

[30] Part A of the Conclusion also addressed other issues from the extensive agenda of the European Council meeting, which had no reference to the Danish Memorandum.

in 1974, and was later brought into the Treaty system by way of the Single European Act (SEA) 1986. The Lisbon Treaty further developed the scope of the European Council and elevated it to a European Institution.[31] Throughout, its main role has remained to 'provide the Union with the necessary impetus for its development and shall define the general political directions thereof. It shall not exercise legislative functions.'[32]

The principal tool of the European Council is one of adopting conclusions. Originally, these conclusions were drawn by the Presidency, as was the case from the meeting in Edinburgh in 1992. Today, they are adopted as collective conclusions by the European Council. This change has not altered their functions as regards policy setting and policy steering; they may have huge political and practical influence, including on subsequent legislation.[33]

Against that background, this study classifies the conclusions of the European Council in Part A as a part of EU law, although they cannot be legally enforced as such, but they provide guidance and may be used to interpret other, legally enforceable, instruments of EU law. In the concrete case, the European Council remarked at its subsequent meeting in Copenhagen in June 1993 that the principles it had spelled out in Edinburgh regarding democracy, subsidiarity and openness would indeed 'guide' the implementation of the new treaty (the Maastricht Treaty).[34]

## VI. OUTLINE OF THE PRESIDENCY CONCLUSION, PART B

The combined set of texts in Part B, that is the Conclusion text itself together with the documents set out in the Annexes, form a united body of texts addressing the Danish issue. The Edinburgh Decision is its centrepiece.

In this section, each element is presented individually. In section VII, a legal analysis of these elements is also undertaken by addressing them individually, whilst at the same time keeping a necessary eye on the unity they form.

### A. Outline of the Text of Part B of the Conclusion

The Conclusion text itself within Part B is rather brief. It forms a prelude to the arrangements agreed to meet the Danish concerns, first by recalling the background and then by following with some general considerations.

[31] C Thorning, 'EU's institutioner' in JH Danielsen et al (eds), *EU-Karnov 2015*, vol 1 (Copenhagen, Karnov Groupe Denmark, 2015) 110.

[32] Art 15 TEU.

[33] Thorning (n 31).

[34] Conclusions of the Copenhagen European Council, 21–22 June 1993, Bull EC 6-1993, Introduction.

More specifically, the European Council first recalls the fundamental legal requirement for ratification of the envisaged Maastricht Treaty by all Member States for it to enter into force. In this context, the European Council notes the various elements listed in the Memorandum 'Denmark in Europe'. Against that background, the European Council declares that it has agreed on a set of 'arrangements ..., which are fully compatible with the Treaty, are designed to meet Danish concerns, and therefore apply exclusively to Denmark and not to other existing or acceding Member States'.[35]

These arrangements are subsequently outlined. First, a decision that is included in Annex I to the Presidency Conclusions; second, two Declarations from the European Council included in Annex II to the Presidency Conclusions; and, third, three unilateral Declarations from Denmark in Annex III, including a so-called 'Final Declaration', the European Council having taken cognisance of them all.

## B. Outline of the Edinburgh Decision

The Edinburgh Decision bears the formal title 'Decision of the Heads of State and Government, meeting within the European Council, concerning certain problems raised by Denmark on the Treaty of European Union'.[36]

The Decision is divided into five sections. The first four sections, A to D, institute four Danish 'opt-outs' from four areas of Union law. Section E contains certain final provisions.

In the short Preamble, a couple of points are made. First, the leaders declare their desire to settle particular problems that specifically concern Denmark, as raised in the Memorandum 'Denmark in Europe', while at the same time observing that this is done 'in conformity with the Treaty on European Union'.[37] Second, the Heads of State and Government note that Denmark does not intend to make use of the outlined provisions in such a way so as to prevent closer cooperation and action among Member States within the framework of the Union and its objectives.[38]

The Decision then lists the particular special provisions for Denmark within four specified areas of EU cooperation. A thorough examination of each of these four provisions will be conducted in chapters 3 to 6. At this stage, it will suffice to summarise them as follows:

A Union citizenship: Union citizenship does not in any way take the place of national citizenship, which in turn is settled solely by reference to the national law of the Member State concerned.

[35] Denmark and the Treaty on European Union (n 9).
[36] ibid Annex I.
[37] ibid Preamble, first recital.
[38] ibid fifth (final) recital.

B EMU (the euro): with reference to the Danish EMU Protocol,[39] Denmark has notified that it will not participate in the third stage. The notification takes effect on the entry into force of the present Decision. Denmark continues to participate fully in the second stage of EMU.

C Defence policy: Denmark does not participate in the elaboration and implementation of decisions and actions of the Union that have defence implications but will not prevent the development of closer cooperation between Member States in this area.

D Justice and Home Affairs (JHA): Denmark participates fully in cooperation on JHA on the basis of the provisions of Title VI of the TEU.[40]

The final provisions in Section E serve two purposes: first, to determine that the date of the entry into force of the Decision is linked to that of the Maastricht Treaty. It is further stated that the duration of the Decision shall be governed by the then Article Q ('The Treaty is concluded for an unlimited period.') and Article N(2) of TEU. The latter Article provided for the calling of an IGC in 1996 to review certain provisions of the Treaty.[41]

The second purpose of the final provisions relates to the termination of all or part of the Decision. That call is exclusively placed in the hands of Denmark. At any time, Denmark is entitled, in accordance with Danish constitutional requirements, to inform the other Member States that it no longer wishes to avail itself of all or part of the Decision. In that event, Denmark will henceforth be obliged to apply in full all relevant measures then in force and which Denmark until that time would not have been part of as a consequence of the relevant provisions of the Decision.

## C. Outline of the Declarations

The *First Declaration* of the European Council set out in Annex II to Part B of the Presidency Conclusions addresses issues highlighted in the Memorandum 'Denmark in Europe' that are not covered by the Edinburgh Decision nor as part of the general deliberations reflected in Part A of the Presidency Conclusions.

In this respect, the European Council declared that the TEU does not prevent Member States from maintaining – or introducing – more stringent measures on

[39] Current version: Protocol No 16 on certain provisions relating to Denmark [2016] OJ C202/287. The Protocol already formed part of the Maastricht Treaty (then as Protocol No 12) and provided Denmark with a right not to participate in the third stage of EMU, if Denmark so decided. See further the discussion in ch 3.

[40] The then Title VI, also known as the third pillar, was cooperation of an intergovernmental nature in contrast to the supranational character of cooperation within the first pillar.

[41] The result of that IGC would be the Amsterdam Treaty. The significance of the refence to Art N(2) is discussed in section VII.A.ii in relation to a discussion of why references to the Danish constitutional procedures are made in a couple of the Danish declarations.

working conditions/social policies; attaining a high level of consumer protection; and regarding the protection of the environment. At the same time, it is underlined that any such measures by the Member States should be compatible with the then Treaty Establishing the European Community (TEC). Furthermore, it is declared that each Member State may pursue its own policy with regard to distribution of income, and may maintain or improve social welfare benefits.

The *Second Declaration* of the European Council relates to Section C (Defence Policy) of the Edinburgh Decision. The European Council notes that Denmark would renounce its right to exercise the Presidency of the Union in any case involving the elaboration and implementation of decisions and actions of the Union that have defence implications.

In Annex III to Part B of the Presidency Conclusion, the *first unilateral Danish Declaration* relates to Section A of the Edinburgh Decision concerning Union citizenship. Denmark presents its view on the differences between the Union citizenship and a national citizenship, as well as its views on which rights are to be derived from which kind of citizenship.[42]

The *second Danish Declaration* concerns JHA cooperation and thus relates to Section D of the Edinburgh Decision. Denmark recalls its constitutional requirements in relation to potential changes to the nature of the cooperation.[43]

The third and last Declaration in Annex III, entitled 'Final Declaration', remarks *in fine* that the Edinburgh Decision and the Declarations all are compatible with the Treaty, without calling its objectives into question.

## VII. LEGAL ANALYSIS OF THE PRESIDENCY CONCLUSION, PART B

A comprehensive legal analysis of the specific arrangements agreed on Denmark, that is the Edinburgh Decision with the accompanying Declarations plus the conclusion text of Part B, requires a two-level approach. First on the macro level, looking at the instruments from the point of view of international law and EU law. Second, from the micro perspective, whereby the arrangements are viewed from a national Danish legal angle.

The two levels are distinct but interact. If one were to look at the situation purely on a single level, one might run the risk of missing essential points on the other level that are necessary to complete the picture. Consequently, both levels are explored and taken into consideration in the legal analysis that unfolds in the remaining part of this chapter.

Section VII.A is dedicated to the macro level. Section VII.B then looks at the Danish level, which is centred on the legislation providing for a second referendum and subsequent Danish ratification of the Maastricht Treaty. Even with this

[42] See the discussion of Union citizenship in ch 3.

[43] The requirements alluded to in the Declaration are those laid down in the Danish Constitution, Art 20. On that issue, see section VII.B.

attempt to structure the analysis, overlap cannot be avoided, so cross-references will appear.

## A. Legal Analysis of the Presidency Conclusion, Part B – Macro Level

In principle, the Member States could have chosen to make use of an instrument of primary EU law to settle the issue of 'certain problems', as raised by Denmark vis-à-vis the Maastricht Treaty following the negative outcome of its referendum. Even though no changes to the Maastricht Treaty as such were foreseen, a special Danish position could, in principle, have been enshrined directly in the EU Treaties.

However, one has to be very idealistic to imagine that a treaty-change process with such a 'surgical' purpose can be performed without seriously running the risk of opening the infamous Pandora's Box. In any case, it would have triggered the opening of the treaty-change procedure, including a call for an IGC, and it would ultimately have required subsequent ratification of the outcome by all Member States according to their respective national constitutional requirements. That was not an option at the Edinburgh Summit.

Already two days after the Danish June referendum, the Portuguese Presidency convened a meeting on 4 June 1992 of the EU Foreign Ministers in the Norwegian capital, Oslo. At that meeting, the so-called Oslo Declaration was adopted, whereby the Foreign Ministers declared that the ratification process of the Maastricht Treaty should continue in the other 11 Member States and that renegotiation of the Maastricht Treaty was excluded.[44] Effectively, that meant that convening an IGC, even if 'only' with a view to adding to the treaty by inserting provisions to cater for the Danish situation, was excluded in advance.[45] However, the Oslo Declaration stated that all (other) possibilities for continuous Danish participation in EU cooperation should be kept open. These 'possibilities' thus translated into the adoption of the specific set of arrangements on Denmark, with the Edinburgh Decision at its core.

### *i. Legal Analysis of the Edinburgh Decision*

The Edinburgh Decision stands out, as it is here that the four opt-outs are instituted and defined. Therefore, the legal analysis holds the Edinburgh Decision as its point of departure.

[44] The Oslo Declaration was subsequently endorsed by the European Council at its meeting in Lisbon on 26–27 June 1992, see Presidency Conclusion, section I.1, Bull EC 1992. By the autumn of 1992, all Member States except for the UK, Germany and Denmark had ratified the Treaty.

[45] The situation was thus very different from the one emerging years later, when the electorates in the Netherlands and France, respectively, rejected the Constitutional Treaty, which did lead to a new IGC and eventually to a new treaty, the Lisbon Treaty.

When examining the Edinburgh Decision, what is immediately remarkable is that the Decision is adopted by the Heads of State and Government *meeting within* the European Council. It is thus clearly not a decision *of* the European Council. It is not a piece of secondary EU legislation either. Although the latter may appear obvious, the Danish Government nevertheless found it necessary to underline this point during the process of parliamentary scrutiny of the subsequent Danish ratification Bill.[46]

In the eyes of the Danish Government, there was no doubt that the Edinburgh Decision was an instrument under international law. This was explicitly stated several times in the explanatory notes to the Danish ratification Bill,[47] and repeated in the Government's reply to subsequent questions from the Parliamentary Scrutiny Committee,[48] as well as repeated during the deliberation in Parliament.[49] It follows implicitly that the Edinburgh Decision was viewed as not forming part of EU law.

To emphasise the legally binding nature of the Edinburgh Decision under international law, the Decision was, at Denmark's request, registered by the UK in the registry for treaties at the United Nations (UN) headquarters in New York. The combined texts of the Presidency Conclusions Part B led to registration as follows: 'Decision constituting an agreement concerning certain problems raised by Denmark on the Treaty on European Union (with conclusions and declarations). Concluded at Edinburgh on 12 December 1992.'[50] This step ensured conformity with the provisions in Article 102(1) of the Charter of the United Nations in accordance with Article 80 of the Vienna Convention on Law of Treaties (VCLT). The UK's action may be regarded as a function of a depositary under Article 77(g) VCLT. Compliance with the registration requirement in Article 102(1) of the UN Charter is a prerequisite for invoking an international agreement before any UN body, including the International Court of Justice (ICJ) in accordance with Article 102(2) of the Charter. The issue of jurisdiction did become a discussion point, as will be explored further below.

At the level of the EU, the entire content of Part B of the Presidency Conclusions was equally treated as a separate, combined body of text and published as such in the *Official Journal*. It thus corresponds to the set of texts registered with the UN in New York, albeit with a shorter title in the EU version.[51] It is listed in the C-series, that is the information section, which generally includes recommendations and resolutions, etc. Given that the texts all originate from conclusions of the European Council, the C-series and not the L-series, which contains legislation, appears to be the correct listing. Even so, listing in the C-series does not

[46] Reply to parliamentary questions: Markedsudvalget 1992–93 – L177, svar på spørgsmål 21–23.
[47] Folketingstidende, saml 1992–93 – L177.
[48] Reply to parliamentary questions (n 46).
[49] Folketingstidende, saml 1992–93, cols 6705 and 6706.
[50] 1765 UNTS no I-30685.
[51] Denmark and the Treaty on European Union [1992] OJ C348/1.

indicate that the text – and notably the Edinburgh Decision – should not be attributed any legal status.[52]

Hjalte Rasmussen described the Edinburgh Decision as 'an international agreement'.[53] Hartley argued that the Member States wanted the decision to be legally binding, and he described the result as 'an international agreement in a simplified form'.[54] The form, the context and the procedure followed for the adoption of the Edinburgh Decision all testify to the fact that the Edinburgh Decision does indeed constitute a multilateral legal instrument binding the contracting parties under international law. Thus it is 'a treaty' under Article 2(a) VCLT. The contracting parties are the 12 Member States of the EU, including Denmark. The signatory parties are thus exactly the same as for the EU Treaties, including the Maastricht Treaty, all of which are concluded exclusively by the Member States.

Moreover, the Edinburgh Decision clearly relates to the TEU as instituted by the Maastricht Treaty, since its entire purpose is to settle the problems identified by Denmark in relation to the ratification of the Maastricht Treaty. The essential question thus becomes how the relationship between the Edinburgh Decision and the EU Treaties should be classified in law. To answer that question, the general treaty law is consulted first.

The nature of the opt-outs instituted in the Edinburgh Decision appears to be as reservations by Denmark vis-à-vis certain specific elements of the Maastricht Treaty. In general treaty law, the notion of a 'reservation' of a signatory as regards certain treaty obligations is regulated in Article 19 VCLT. However, the way in which such a reservation is instituted in accordance with that provision differs from what happened by way of the Edinburgh Decision. The Decision was not deposited together with the Maastricht Treaty but drafted and concluded at a later date. Despite some similarities in their nature, this author considers that the opt-outs do not constitute reservations as understood by the VCLT.[55]

Article 31 VCLT lays out general rules on interpretation of a treaty; it states that a subsequent agreement between the parties regarding the interpretation of the treaty or the application of its provisions may be taken into consideration. With the possible exception of the element on the Union citizenship,[56] the Edinburgh Decision does not provide any general interpretational input into the Maastricht Treaty. Instead, it determines the legal position of one treaty party,

[52] At one point in time treaties were generally published in the C-series, see *OSCOLA*, 4th edn (Faculty of Law, Oxford University) para 2.6. The recent Lisbon Treaty is published in Series C [2007] OJ C306/1.

[53] H Rasmussen, *EU-ret i kontekst* (Copenhagen, Gad Jura, 1995) 109.

[54] TC Hartley, 'Constitutional and international aspects of the Maastricht Treaty Agreement' (1993) 42(2) *International and Comparative Law Quarterly* 234.

[55] See Rasmussen (n 53) 11. Against, Münch, referred to in RA Wessel, *The European Union's Foreign and Security Policy. A legal Institutional Perspective* (The Hague, Kluwer Law International, 1999) 138.

[56] See the discussion in ch 3.

Denmark, on certain policy matters. Consequently, the Edinburgh Decision does not seem to correspond fully to an add-on *interpretational* agreement (treaty) in the sense of Article 31 VCLT.[57]

This leaves the Edinburgh Decision as a separate 'stand-alone' treaty entered into among the EU Member States and binding them as contracting parties under international law, without the Edinburgh Decision at the same time forming part of EU law.

This was indeed a novelty, and not surprisingly sparked some confusion and debate among scholars at the time. Krunke found that the Edinburgh Agreement, including the Edinburgh Decision, had a 'strange' character from a legal point of view.[58] Other scholars wondered whether the construction of the Edinburgh Decision as a separate instrument under international law nevertheless had a legal impact directly under EU law, notably vis-à-vis the issue of jurisdiction of the CJEU.

Curtin and Van Ooik argued in 1994 that Sections A, B and E of the Edinburgh Decision would come under the jurisdiction of the CJEU, because these sections concerned interpretation of the Rome Treaty. On the other hand, the remaining Sections C and D would not fall under the competence of the CJEU since they concerned the then intergovernmental pillars of the Maastricht Treaty. According to these scholars, the latter sections fell within the competence of the ICJ.[59] Howarth pointed to a potential issue in this regard due to the fact that, at the time, only seven of the then 12 EU Member States had accepted the compulsory jurisdiction of the ICJ.[60]

In the explanatory notes to its ratification Bill, the Danish Government made reference to the ICJ as the body having jurisdiction over the Edinburgh Decision. However, the explanatory notes also stated:

> If, on the other hand, a specific case arises which makes it relevant, the Edinburgh Decision must, where appropriate, be included in the assessment when interpreting and applying the Maastricht Treaty. This applies to the Community institutions, including the European Court of Justice.[61]

Hartley somewhat similarly argued that the CJEU would probably take the Edinburgh Decision into consideration when interpreting the Maastricht Treaty,

[57] Against, see the British Government, which viewed the Edinburgh Decision as an agreement in the sense of Art 31 VCLT; see the replies of Prime Minister John Major, cited in D Howarth, 'The Compromise on Denmark and the Treaty on European Union: A legal and Political Analysis' (1994) 31(4) *Common Market Law Review* 772. See also Wessel (n 55).

[58] H Krunke, 'Peoples' Vengeances. From Maastricht to Edinburgh: The Danish Solution' (2005) 1 *European Constitutional Law Review* 339.

[59] D Curtin and R van Ooik, 'Denmark and the Edinburgh Summit: Maastricht without tears: A Legal Analysis' in D O'Keeffe and PM Twomey (eds), *Legal Issues of the Maastricht Treaty* (Chichester, Wiley Chancery, 1994) 358.

[60] Howarth (n 57) 797.

[61] The explanatory notes to the Danish ratification Bill L177, Folketingstidende saml 1992–93, col 6705 (author's own translation).

as the case might be. He added, however, that the CJEU would not thereby necessarily have regarded itself to be bound by the Decision.[62] On the other hand, Hartley opposed the notion that the ICJ would be competent.[63]

The Edinburgh Decision was not judicially challenged at the time, nor has it been since. Consequently, neither the CJEU nor the ICJ has ruled on the matter of jurisdiction. Recent case law of the CJEU interpreting Article 263 of the Treaty on the Functioning of the European Union (TFEU) suggests that the CJEU may possibly consider itself to lack jurisdiction to rule on the legality of the Edinburgh Decision.[64] On the other hand, given the particularities of the instrument examined in the cases in question, its conclusion may not necessarily apply to the Edinburgh Decision as well.

Furthermore, as will be explored in chapters 3 to 6, the elements of the Edinburgh Decision have subsequently been incorporated into EU law as a legal offshoot of the European integration process. Although the Edinburgh Decision remains in force, the evolution of EU law has limited the relevance of the Decision as a potential interpretational instrument for the CJEU. Its relevance is not, however, eliminated. Concrete examples to that effect have emerged in relation to Section A on Union citizenship, which are examined in chapter 3.

This leaves us with the fundamental issue of the relation between the Edinburgh Decision and EU law, and the fact that the European leaders went to lengths to ensure that what had been agreed in Edinburgh was in conformity with the TEU.[65]

Naturally, this is a crucial issue, as the opposite would constitute a fundamental breach of EU law. Any changes to the EU treaty system may only be made by adhering to the decision-making procedure the Member States themselves have laid down in the EU Treaties.[66] This procedure was not followed in the case of the adoption of the Edinburgh Decision.

With a view to assessing the validity of the multiple statements originating not only from the Member States but also from the Commission as part of the European Council, a closer look at the substance of the four 'opt-outs' as instituted by the Edinburgh Decision is required.

When taking such a closer look, it is clear that all four of them share one, important characteristic, which is that they all regulate Denmark's position in relation to *potential* development of European integration that might occur sometime in *the future*. At the same time, the Edinburgh Decision and associated texts make it clear that the position of Denmark as laid out in no way prevents

[62] Hartley (n 54) 234.
[63] ibid 235.
[64] See Joined Cases C-684/20 P and C-685/20 P *Eleanor Sharpston v Council of the European Union and Representatives of the Governments of the Member States* ECLI:EU:C:2021:485/486.
[65] Declared in the conclusion text of Part B, in the Final Declaration as well as in the recital to the Edinburgh Decision.
[66] Currently Art 48 TEU.

foreseen or potential integration from taking place.[67] Moreover, no changes to the Maastricht Treaty, to the EU Treaties in general or to the *acquis* were necessitated or called for by the opt-outs instituted in the Edinburgh Decision.

Given that background, the only outstanding question is whether the Edinburgh Decision compromised treaty obligations undertaken by Denmark at the time. To that end, clarification of the characteristics of the respective opt-outs becomes essential.

First, the opt-out by which Denmark will not join in the then foreseen but at that time still unrealised third stage of the EMU relates directly to a concession already given to Denmark by way of the Maastricht Treaty.[68] The provision in Section A of the Edinburgh Decision activating this concession does not challenge any treaty rights and obligations pursuant to the Maastricht Treaty.

Second, the opt-out on Union citizenship, as well as the one on cooperation within the AFSJ, essentially regulates potential development of European integration within these areas by stating the position of Denmark in this respect, which essentially means: (i) that Union citizenship does not replace national citizenship (which, incidentally, no one disputed nor thought to change); and (ii) that Denmark will cooperate fully on AFSJ matters as long as they remain part of the (then) third-pillar cooperation. Changes to these legal situations, as far as Denmark is concerned, requires in both cases the observation of the rules laid out in Article 20 of the Danish Constitution.[69] Again, the position of Denmark did not breach any commitments or obligations undertaken by Denmark by way of signing the Maastricht Treaty.

Third, the defence opt-out also relates to the future by excluding Danish participation in concrete Council initiatives and actions that may emerge within the area of the common security and defence policy. The important thing to note is that Denmark would not have been legally required to take part in such actions under EU law given the special rules of the Treaty governing this field of cooperation. Moreover, and as explicitly recalled in the definition of this opt-out, Denmark does not, by its non-participation, prevent the other Member States from proceeding with concrete initiatives within the field. Once again, the special Danish position established does not run counter to Denmark's obligations under the Treaty; on the contrary, Denmark limits its own rights.[70]

When these specificities are taken into consideration, the conclusion is that the construction of the Edinburgh Decision as an instrument of international law not forming part of the EU Treaties, although complementing it by outlining the position of Denmark on the identified concrete areas, was legally sound.[71]

[67] Recitals to the Edinburgh Decision and repeated in Section C on defence.

[68] At the time it was Protocol No 12; in its current version it is Protocol No 16 on certain provisions relating to Denmark [2016] OJ C 202/287.

[69] See on the issue of Art 20 the discussion in section VII.B.

[70] See further the discussion of Denmark's giving up its 'veto' in section VII.A.iii.

[71] Certain scholars were less convinced. As an example, Thym has described the outcome from Edinburgh as 'legally dubious', see D Thym, '"United in Diversity" – The Integration of Enhanced Cooperation into the European Constitutional Order' (2010) 6/11 *German Law Journal* 1743.

The choice of terminology, '*Decision* of the Heads of State and Government …', does not have an impact on its legal status. As concluded above, the instrument is a 'treaty' binding under international law, and that remains so 'whatever its particular designation', as set out in Article 2(a) VCLT.

One could reflect on the fact that, in general terms, the terminology 'Decision' is used for an instrument adopted by an empowered body with a view to regulating particular issues vis-à-vis a specific subject to which the Decision is addressed. Although that is clearly not the case here, the European Council underlined in Part B of the Conclusion text that the set of arrangements agreed would apply exclusively to Denmark and not to other existing or acceding Member States. In light thereof, and by avoiding the term 'treaty' or 'protocol' but instead using 'Decision', the special character of the Edinburgh Decision, as distinguished from the EU Treaties, becomes clear.

The Edinburgh Decision contains no provisions on ratification, nor on signatures. The Decision enters into force without further formalities on the stipulated date, which is the date of entry into force of the Maastricht Treaty.

That sparked some criticism by scholars.[72] Criticism, in particular of the issue of no ratification, would certainly be pertinent if the Edinburgh Decision were to be viewed as corresponding to a protocol under EU law, in which case the decision-making procedure stipulates a general ratification process in all Member States. However, the Edinburgh Decision is not EU law and the ratification requirement under EU law does not apply. International treaty law does not prescribe ratification as a general rule, as seen in Articles 11 and 24 VCLT. Consequently, the lack of a ratification requirement did not compromise the sound legal character of its construction.

In the case of Denmark, the Edinburgh Decision formed part of its ratification procedure and became woven into the legal fabric of Danish legislation. That will be explained and discussed when addressing the microlevel in section VII.B. First, the elements associated with the Edinburgh Decision need to be analysed at the macro level.

### *ii. Legal Analysis of the Declarations*

Declarations are instruments frequently used by parties entering into treaty obligations and are associated with an agreed treaty. Unlike the treaty instrument itself, declarations are not legally enforceable as such. That said, they do form part of the combined legal structure of which the legally enforceable instrument under international law, the treaty, forms the centre. Declarations may have interpretative guidance and, in this sense, have legal effects.

The Declarations associated with the Edinburgh Decision formally fall into two categories. The first category in Annex II comprises two Declarations of the European Council; the other category, in Annex III, contains three unilateral

[72] See Curtin and Van Ooik (n 59).

Danish Declarations. Irrespective of the category, the Declarations do not all serve the same purpose. Nor does their relevance necessarily depend on the category to which they belong.

What is clear is that all five Declarations are instruments formally forming part of international law, as they all belong to the same set of texts registered as such with the UN in New York and treated as such by the EU side when published as a separate entity in the *Official Journal* under the heading 'Denmark and the Treaty on European Union'. Their more precise legal value, function and potential effects depend largely on their respective content.

As regards the content of the *first Declaration of the European Council*, it consists of views offered by the European Council on the limitations to the competences of the Union within a number of Union policy issues (working conditions, social policy, consumer protection and protection of the environment). Its purposes may well be regarded as forming a calming response to an internal Danish *political* concern at the time, relating to whether Denmark, after the entry into force of the Maastricht Treaty, would be able to maintain its welfare state and a green profile, which Denmark perceived to be further advanced than the EU average, possibly even as the most progressive of all EU Member States.

These policy issues are all left over from the list of concerns within the Danish Memorandum, as they had not been addressed elsewhere by the European Council and as such reflected in the Part A of the Conclusion; nor were they destined to become opt-outs. To ensure that the comprehensive Danish concerns as raised in the Memorandum were all addressed, the Declaration was necessary.

Even though the Declaration forms part of the body of texts that address Danish concerns and, according to the initial statement in the text of Part B of the Conclusion, 'apply exclusively to Denmark and not to other existing or acceding Member States',[73] it simply is not true in the case of this particular Declaration. The Declaration explicitly aims at general applicability.[74] The nature of the Declaration thus corresponds to the text in Part A of the Conclusion; neither is Denmark-specific and neither relates to the substance addressed in the Edinburgh Decision.

The character of the substance of the Declaration is, however, somewhat different from the text in Part A of the Conclusion on the other policy items from the Danish Memorandum. The latter items are addressed in a more advanced sense, as the European Council in Part A of the conclusions sets out concrete guidelines,[75] whereas the content in the Declaration is more declaratory as to how the European Council reads (the limits to) the relevant treaty provisions.

[73] Denmark and the Treaty on European Union (n 51) Part B, the Conclusion text.

[74] Reference is made to 'any Member State' as not being prevented from maintaining or introducing more stringent protection measures compatible with the EC Treaty within the then listed policy areas.

[75] See section V.

In this regard, Howarth speculated whether it might have proved helpful in the Danish context that the Declaration was indeed one from the European Council, that is that the Commission was also a party thereto.[76] However, nothing in the explanatory notes to the Danish ratification Bill suggests that this was an issue to which particular attention was paid by the Danish Government. Nonetheless, and given the fact that the Commission holds a central position by way of its right of initiative in the rule-making procedure of the EU, the value of a Declaration originating in the European Council is arguably higher than it would have been if it had originated in the Member States alone. That is so even though the Declaration of the European Council arguably only largely repeated what already followed from the Treaty to a large extent.[77]

Whereas the first Declaration formally belongs to the body of international law, by its content it is solely related to the scope of the TEU and not to the Edinburgh Decision at all. As such, it may potentially be given interpretational effects within EU law, even though it does not form part thereof.

The *second Declaration of the European Council* serves a different purpose and, unlike the first Declaration, does relate to the special position of Denmark as instituted by the Edinburgh Decision. More specifically, it addresses the way in which the Council should function in the event that Denmark, as a consequence of the defence opt-out, were to abstain from performing a role as chair of the particular Council formation. This Declaration thus provides procedural guidance in this respect.

The *first Declaration* of Denmark also relates to the Edinburgh Decision, as it offers extensive interpretational views on the legal boundaries of Union citizenship and as such elaborates on the provisions in Section A of the Edinburgh Decision.[78] In its last part, reference is made to the then Article 8e TEC.[79] The treaty provision makes it possible to strengthen or add to the rights of Union citizenship, provided it was adopted in accordance with the respective constitutional requirements of the Member States. In light thereof, Denmark recalled the procedure in Article 20 of the Danish Constitution, which potentially could become relevant in such a scenario. Interestingly, Denmark did not declare itself to be shielded from such changes due to its opt-out.

The *second Danish Declaration* largely serves the same purpose as the last part of the first Declaration on Union citizenship. The second Declaration relates to Section D of the Edinburgh Decision, in which Denmark's full participation in the then intergovernmental third-pillar cooperation on JHA (now AFSJ) is confirmed. However, a potential 'pillar-jump' was provided for in the then Article K.9 TEU, whereby actions under the intergovernmental third-pillar cooperation on JHA by way of a unanimous decision of the Council, could be

[76] Howarth (n 57).
[77] ibid 786. Howarth refers as an example to Art 2.5 of the Protocol on Social Policy.
[78] On the substance, see ch 3.
[79] Currently Art 25 TFEU.

transferred to the first pillar. In the Declaration, Denmark recalled its constitutional requirements in the event that this was to happen.[80] The Declaration did not give any indication as to whether Denmark potentially would support such a unanimous decision at all. In the explanatory notes to the Bill on Danish ratification, the Government mentioned that Denmark would not be take part in any further deepening or expansion of the cooperation within any of the four areas addressed in the Edinburgh Decision.[81] In a written reply to a parliamentary question as to how this statement should be understood, the Government did not elaborate and refused to take a position on Article K.9 due to the fact that there were no concrete plans to actually make use of that provision.[82] In the Memorandum 'Denmark in Europe', the political parties had been more straightforward. They stated that Denmark, for its part, could not support the transfer of parts of the third pillar to the supranational cooperation in the first pillar.

Article K.9 was never invoked. However, the matter later formed part of the IGC leading to the Amsterdam Treaty, which did transfer part of the then third pillar cooperation to the then first pillar. As it turned out, Denmark maintained its opt-outs, with the consequence that the new treaty provisions on supranational AFSJ cooperation did not become applicable to Denmark.[83]

At this point, it may be useful to revert to the reference to the then Article N(2) found in the final Section E of the Edinburgh Decision, which de facto pointed to the IGC leading to the Amsterdam Treaty.[84] Section E states that the Edinburgh Decision is governed by Article N(2) and equally by Article Q (now Article 53 TEU). The latter provision states that the Treaty is concluded for an unlimited period, which was of particular importance, since it was made clear in the Danish Memorandum that the sought-after agreement on the Danish opt-outs should not only be legally binding but also concluded for an unlimited period. That condition was thus met. However, the parallel reference to Article N(2) nonetheless indicates a potential time limit, in so far as the special Danish position that was instituted potentially could change and possibly even be abolished as part of changes to the Treaties foreseen as emerging at the upcoming IGC. One could read this as a form of political reassurance from Denmark to the other Member States that the Danish opt-outs potentially were foreseen as being short-lived.[85] If that was indeed the case, it turned out to be a grave miscalculation.

[80] The requirements are those laid down in the Danish Constitution, Art 20. See section VII.B.

[81] The explanatory notes to the Danish ratification Bill L177, Folketingstidende saml 1992–93, col 6711.

[82] Reply to parliamentary questions, Markedsudvalget Alm del 1992–93, L177. – svar på spørgsmål 38 + 39.

[83] For details see ch 6.

[84] Section E, para 1 reads 'This decision will take effect on the date of entry into force of the Treaty on European Union; its duration shall be governed by Articles Q and N(2) of that Treaty.'

[85] In an interview in January 2023, retired Ambassador and former Permanent Representative of Denmark to the EU, Poul Skytte Christoffersen, stated that the opt-outs of the Edinburgh Decision

The third Declaration, *the 'Final Declaration*', provides interpretational views, notably by declaring that the Edinburgh Decision and the associated Declarations are compatible with the Treaty and do not call its objectives into question.[86]

Howarth, as well as Ware and Millar, immediately after the 1992 Edinburgh European Council, discussed whether the unilateral Danish Declarations should be considered legally binding.[87] Howarth observes that '[a]ny legal difference between the sections of the decision [the Edinburgh Decision, Sections A and D respectively] and the unilateral declarations is … irrelevant and need worry only the legal theorists'.[88] Howarth concludes that the purpose of the Declarations can only be seen as political.

Curtin and Van Ooik did not regard the Final Declaration as a unilateral Danish Declaration.[89] The Declaration is, however, listed in Annex III under the heading 'Unilateral Declarations of Denmark …'. The Danish Government itself considered it to be one of three Danish Declarations,[90] and it is hard to see why this should not be the correct understanding. In any case, the formal difference between the Declarations of the European Council and the unilateral Danish Declaration fades in view of the fact that the European Council took 'cognisance' of all unilateral Danish Declarations.[91] The Member States, for their part, repeated this 'cognisance' in the Preamble to the Edinburgh Decision. Arguably, the European Council and the Member States would not have done this had they not shared the views expressed in the three Danish Declarations, or at least they would not have done this if the Danish views were perceived to be incorrect.

As previously mentioned, this study regards all of the Declarations within Part B of the Presidency Conclusion, which form part of the combined body of texts 'Denmark and the Treaty on European Union', as falling within international law, with the Edinburgh Decision at its core; albeit that the Declarations themselves are not individually enforceable as such.

It is furthermore held that, even though the Declarations do not form part of EU law, the views set out in the First Declaration of the European Council on the boundaries of Union citizenship may be given interpretational effects within EU law, just as is the case with the provisions of Part A of the Edinburgh Decision, when the corresponding treaty provisions are examined by the CJEU.[92]

at the time 'by us all' were believed to be short-lived, see 'Danmarks grå EU-eminence: "Vi var på mange måder et besværligt medlemsland fra starten"' *Altinget* (12 January 2023) at www.altinget.dk.

[86] On the validity of this statement, see the discussion in section VII.A.i.

[87] Howarth (n 57) 789–90; R Ware and V Millar, 'The Maastricht Debate: Clarifications, "Opt-Outs" and Amendments' (1993) House of Commons Research Paper 93/3.

[88] Howarth (n 57) 789–90.

[89] Curtin and Van Ooik (n 59) 354.

[90] Explanatory notes to the Danish ratification Bill L177, Folketingstidende saml 1992–93, col 6711.

[91] Stated in the text of the Conclusion, Part B.

[92] As far as Section A of the Edinburgh Decision is concerned, the CJEU has indeed done so in Case C-135/08 *Janko Rottman v Freistaat Bayern* ECLI:EU:C:2010:104, as well as in Case C-689/21

The two statements of a procedural nature regarding the Danish constitutional requirements, made by the Danish Government, are of such a nature that they hardly offer any legal value. The one on AFSJ sends a political message that the Danish position regarding cooperation only on an intergovernmental level – potentially – could be changed subject to the outcome of the said procedures. Likewise, the Final Declaration serves a political objective by reiterating that the outcome of the 1992 Danish referendum has been accommodated. The validity of the statement that it has been done in a legally sound way naturally depends on an independent examination thereof.[93]

### *iii. Legal Analysis of the Text of Part B of the Conclusion*

The Conclusion text serves a purpose that is somewhat similar to preambular remarks to operational provisions in a legally binding instrument. This may explain why the text of the Conclusion was included in the combined body of texts 'Denmark and the Treaty on European Union', which has the Edinburgh Decision at its core and which is binding under international law. The Edinburgh Decision itself contains an ordinary set of preambular remarks. Not surprisingly, some repetition occurs from the Conclusion text. The conclusions themselves are, however, not legally enforceable in their own right. The text provides interpretational input to the Edinburgh Decision.

Given that the text also forms part of the complete set of conclusions originating from the meeting of the European Council, arguably the text also forms part of EU law in the same way as the other conclusions from the European Council. It provides interpretational input as to the compatibility of the subsequent, outlined arrangements on Denmark with EU law.

As in the case of the Final Declaration, the statement made on the conformity of the agreed arrangements with EU law does not in itself create a legal fact. Its validity depends on a legal examination of the said arrangements, notably the Edinburgh Decision.

### *iv. Legal Analysis of the Presidency Conclusion, Part B – Combined Impact*

A remaining issue is the question of whether Denmark, by the Edinburgh Decision and associated texts, gained anything of substance in addition to what was already encompassed in the Maastricht Treaty.

The question certainly formed part of the political debate in Denmark leading up to the referendum in May 1993.[94] At the time, certain scholars and

*X v Udlændinge- og Integrationsministeriet* ECLI:EU:C:2023:626 (see discussion in ch 3, section III). However, as far as can be detected, the CJEU has never referred to the said Declaration in its jurisprudence.

[93] The conclusion drawn above following such an examination is affirmative.

[94] See, as an example the substantial and critical minority statement by the 'Progress Party' in the report of the Scrutiny Committee on the ratification Bill, *Betænkning afgivet af Markedsudvalget den 19. marts 1993*, Markedsudvalget 1992–93, L176/177/178, bilag 25.

journalists found that this was not the case but rather that it was 'an intelligent illusion'.[95]

Curtin and Van Ooik argued that the four 'exceptions' were not exceptions per se, as they did not give Denmark anything that was not already in the Treaty.[96]

Howarth seemed to agree with this statement as far as the issues of Union citizenship and of cooperation within the area of JHA were concerned; however, he did not agree as regards the two other Danish opt-outs on the third stage of the EMU and on defence cooperation.[97]

Even though Howarth thus recognised an impact on defence, actually describing it as the one derogation possibly having the biggest impact,[98] he was both confused and somewhat puzzled that Denmark pursued a policy of giving up its 'veto' over this part of EU cooperation. He put it like this: 'It is odd, however, to consider this a Danish negotiation victory in that it limits the role of a Danish European Council Presidency and the use of the Danish veto on defence related policy-making.'[99] Howarth reiterated his argument by saying that, within the defence cooperation, Denmark could simply have kept the option to 'veto' a possible development of European integration that Denmark did not want instead of depriving itself of all influence over the formation of defence-related cooperation.[100]

That argument is questionable. A situation whereby Denmark was left able to block all unwelcome developments by virtue of the unanimity provision would effectively have hindered the adoption of all concrete second-pillar initiatives with defence implications. That did not constitute a sustainable way forward.

Second and decisively, the majority of the Danish political parties *did* want to impose a legally binding element of self-constraint on the room for manoeuvre of any Danish government, making sure that the issue of possible Danish participation in any action with defence implications could not arise at all.[101] What the Edinburgh Decision did was effectively to bar Denmark from participation in all future actions with defence implications. As already argued in this chapter, this did not conflict with the Treaty obligations, as the rules laid out in the Treaty did not oblige Denmark to take part in such actions. On the other hand, the Treaty did not exclude it. The Edinburgh Decision did, and thus delivered, as something new, the required legal outcome.

[95] See Krunke (n 58) 343.
[96] Curtin and Van Ooik (n 59).
[97] Howarth (n 57) 800–02.
[98] ibid.
[99] ibid 801.
[100] ibid 776–78. The term 'veto' is used by Howarth in relation to an ordinary unanimity procedure, which is different from 'a veto' as a special competence to reject an adopted initiative, eg the right of veto of a Head of State vis-à-vis the legislator. Arguably, the latter situation would constitute the proper use of the term, although it should be recognised that 'veto' has widely spread to describe a 'no vote' within an unanimity procedure.
[101] 'Denmark in Europe' (n 5).

Furthermore, as Krunke rightly pointed out on a more general note not specific to the defence opt-out:

> [T]he power of clarification and interpretation should not be underestimated. Clarifying how specific articles must (and must not) be interpreted can prove to be of great importance later on, and it must be seen as a way of controlling the extent of the cooperation.[102]

With the benefit of hindsight, what seems to have been generally overlooked at the time was the impact the Edinburgh Decision would gain by way of locking the Danish position to the status quo, regardless of future evolutions within the defined areas of cooperation. Arguably, the impact of the Edinburgh Decision on Denmark's position on (notably) defence cooperation and the AFSJ for 30 years to come was not apparent in 1992–93.

The Danish self-constraint was further strengthened by the way in which the opt-outs were incorporated into Danish law and, as such, the legal effect arising from the micro level. Section VII.B will explore this further.

## B. Legal Analysis of the Presidency Conclusion, Part B – Micro Level

The Danish political parties that drafted the Memorandum 'Denmark in Europe' endorsed the outcome of the Edinburgh European Council meeting. The outcome was found to have ticked, to a large extent, all of the required boxes.[103] On that basis, the way was paved for a new Danish referendum on ratification of the Maastricht Treaty.

However, it was not possible to proceed directly to a new referendum. The previous referendum was based on the Bill on Danish ratification of the Maastricht Treaty, which had been adopted by the Danish Parliament in late spring of 1992. However, as a consequence of the negative result of the 1992 referendum, that Bill was rejected.[104]

The Danish Government, which had changed in the meantime from centre-right to centre-left, therefore proceeded by tabling a new set of Bills on the ratification of the Maastricht Treaty and on holding a new referendum on the issue.

In order to understand the way in which the legislation was composed, some basic observations on the Danish constitutional system may prove helpful.

First and fundamentally, Denmark generally adheres to a dualist system, which is reflected in the relevant Articles 19 and 20 of the Constitution. The former regulates treaty-making and includes a requirement for the Government

[102] Krunke (n 58) 349.

[103] Formally recognised by a large majority of the parties in the Danish Parliament in a statement made in the scrutiny report on the ratification Bill, *Betænkning afgivet af Markedsudvalget den 19. marts 1993* 1, Markedsudvalget 1992–93, L176/177/178, bilag 25.

[104] See Art 20 of the Danish Constitution.

to obtain parliamentary ratification consent prior to ratification by the Government of a treaty, see Article 19(1).

Second, Article 20 was inserted into the Constitution at its last revision in 1953. It was drafted to prepare for Denmark's joining international agreements of a character that would reach beyond traditional treaties. As such, it constituted the legal basis for Danish membership of the EC in 1973.[105]

Article 20 reads:

> (1) Powers vested in the authorities of the Realm under this Constitutional Act may, by statute to a certain specified extent, be delegated to international authorities set up by mutual agreement with other states for the promotion of international rules of law and cooperation.
>
> (2) For the enactment of a Bill dealing with the above, a majority of five-sixths of the Members of the Folketing shall be required. If this majority is not obtained, whereas the majority required for the passing of ordinary Bills is obtained, and if the Government maintains it, the Bill shall be submitted to the electorate for approval or rejection in accordance with the rules for referenda laid down in Section 42.[106]

The essential matter is thus whether Denmark's accession to a new treaty implies that powers vested in the authorities of the realm are being delegated. This is commonly referred to as an issue of 'transfer of sovereignty'.[107] It is a legal definition, which may well differ from a politically or publicly perceived understanding of what constitutes sovereignty. It is purely a national legal definition. What may be considered transfer of sovereignty in one Member State, and treated accordingly, may not be considered as a matter of sovereignty in another.[108]

In Denmark, the issue of the applicability of Article 20 of the Danish Constitution has been clarified by the Danish Supreme Court, which has ruled has follows:

> Application of the qualified procedure according to Article 20 of the constitution is necessary to the extent that it is left to an international organisation to exercise legislative, administrative or judicial authority with direct effect in this country [Denmark] or to exercise other powers, which according to the constitution belong to the authorities of the Kingdom, including the power to enter into treaties with other states.[109]

[105] See, for a general account, JH Danielsen, 'Delegation of Sovereignty – Article 20 of the Danish Constitution: The story of a successful operation but a dead patient?' in H Koch et al (eds), *Europe, The New Legal Realism* (Copenhagen, DJØF's Forlag, 2010) 135.

[106] The English translation originates from refworld.org.

[107] See the legal comments on Art 20 in JP Christensen, JA Jensen and MH Jensen, *Grundloven med kommentarer* (Copenhagen, Jurist- og Økonomforbundets Forlag, 2015).

[108] As a prominent example, there are differences on the definition of the matter between Denmark and the UK. On the UK position, see eg B Laffan, 'Sovereignty: Driving British Divergence' in F Fabbrini (ed), *The Law & Politics of Brexit* (Oxford, Oxford University Press, 2021) 240. For a general, academic discussion of sovereignty and the EU, see N Walker, 'Sovereignty and Differentiated Integration in the European Union' (1998) 4 *European Law Journal* 355.

[109] Judgment of the Supreme Court in the so-called '*Maastricht Case*', UfR U.1998.800 (author's own translation). The case emerged after the Danish ratification of the Maastricht Treaty. The

The Danish Supreme Court has thus essentially defined what constitutes 'transfer of sovereignty' in a Danish legal context.

In the event that Article 20 is applicable, the qualified procedure laid out regarding the enactment of such an adopted Bill, including ultimately by way of a referendum, must be followed. On the other hand, if no power is being delegated by the ratification Bill, in the sense defined by the Supreme Court, the Article 20 procedure does not apply. The holding of referendum is not prescribed.[110]

It is the legal tradition in Denmark that the Danish Ministry of Justice makes the assessment in concrete cases on the question of delegation of power. The Ministry does so by producing a thorough legal analysis of the matter in the form of a specific Memorandum.[111] The Ministry of Justice had produced such a legal assessment prior to the 1992 Bill on accession to the Maastricht Treaty. The Ministry pointed to a number of elements in the Maastricht Treaty that indeed led to delegation of new powers from Denmark to the Union in the legal sense of Article 20 of the Constitution. The procedure laid down in that Article was consequently applicable.

Given that the Maastricht Treaty had not been amended, the same conclusion applied in 1993. However, the political scene in the Danish Parliament had changed. In 1992, there was no five-sixths majority in Parliament for the adoption of the 1992 ratification Bill, and the June 1992 referendum had been a direct consequence thereof as the final step in the Article 20 procedure. In 1993, the political situation had changed as a result of the preceding broad political engagement on providing for the Edinburgh Solution. So, even though the procedure in Article 20 continued to be applicable, it would not provide for a referendum on the 1993 ratification Bill, as an overwhelming majority of the MPs in the Danish Parliament would approve this Bill. Since holding a new referendum was a firm political requirement, a different legal-technical solution had to be found.

The solution to accommodating a legally binding *second* referendum on the ratification of the Maastricht Treaty was a package of three Bills: L176, L177 and L178. The issue of Danish ratification of the Maastricht Treaty was regulated by L177.[112] This Bill is referred to as the Main Bill or the Ratification Bill.

As previously mentioned, non-ratification is the default procedure of the Edinburgh Decision itself, as the requirement for its entering into force is solely linked to that of the entry into force of the Maastricht Treaty.

Nonetheless, for Denmark it was essential that the Edinburgh Decision formed part of the renewed Danish legislation on ratification of the Maastricht

Supreme Court dismissed claims that the Danish ratification had infringed the provisions of the Constitution, including Art 20.

[110] M Sørensen, 'Udtalelse til Folketingets Markedsudvalg af januar 1971' (1971) *Juristen* 431.

[111] This procedure has been followed in Denmark in relation to all EU treaty changes throughout the years, as well as in relation to Denmark's accession in the first place.

[112] *Forslag til Lov om Danmarks tiltrædelse af Edinburgh-Afgørelsen og Maastricht-Traktaten*, Lovtidende, saml 1992–93, L177.

Treaty and, not least, the subsequent referendum. The explanatory notes to the Ratification Bill read as follows:

> The rights and obligations that follow from the Maastricht Treaty are specified in the Edinburgh Decision, and the significance of the Maastricht Treaty for Denmark follows from this Treaty with accompanying protocols and declarations as well as from the Edinburgh Decision with associated declarations, see § 2 of the Bill. It is for this purpose that it is proposed that the Edinburgh Decision with accompanying declarations be approved.[113]

Under the title 'Act on Denmark's accession to the Edinburgh Decision and the Maastricht Treaty' (author's own translation), the legal construction of the Ratification Bill was as follows: by Article 1(1) the Edinburgh Decision was 'approved'. The subsequent provision in Article 1(2) reads 'Denmark can *then* ratify the Maastricht Treaty …'.[114] In other words, Denmark did not *ratify* the Edinburgh Decision but the *approval* thereof was made a prerequisite, under Danish law, for the Danish ratification of the Maastricht Treaty.

To underline the importance of the political Memorandum 'Denmark in Europe', which was presented prior to Edinburgh, that Memorandum was included in its entirety as a part of the explanatory notes to the Bill.

Second, in the adjoining Bill L176,[115] the Edinburgh Decision, along with the associated Declarations, were added to the list of 'treaties, etc' contained in Article 4 of the Danish Act of Accession to the EU.[116] This list is essential in a Danish constitutional context, as it forms the basis for Denmark's membership of the EU.[117] The Edinburgh Decision is listed in the Accession Act immediately after the Maastricht Treaty. The recitals to the Edinburgh Decision state that the unilateral Declarations of Denmark will be associated with its act of ratification. It is unclear why this was highlighted; in any case, the Decision, as well as both sets of associated Declarations, formed part of the Danish ratification package. However, unlike in the case of the registration with the UN and the publication of the arrangements made in the *Official Journal*, the Danish Bill does not include the text of Part B of the Conclusion. This may be perceived as a shortcoming on the Danish side, but given the short preambular character of the Conclusion text, it would hardly have contributed much anyway.

[113] Explanatory notes specifically to Art 1, Folketingstidende, saml 1992–93, L177, col 6737 (author's own translation).

[114] Ratification Bill L177 (n 112) (author's own translation, emphasis added).

[115] *Forslag til lov om ændring af lov om Danmarks tiltrædelse af De Europæiske Fælleskaber*, Folketingstidende, saml 1992–93, L176.

[116] *Lov om Danmarks tiltrædelse af de europæiske fællesskaber*, Act no 447 of 11 October 1972 with later amendments (*Retsinformation*). For a general discussion of the Act, see NS Lauridsen and J Nymann-Lindegren, 'Tiltrædelsesloven dengang og nu' in U Neergaard and KE Sørensen (eds), *Danmark og EU Gennem 50 år – en milepæl* (Copenhagen, Djøf Forlag, 2023) 155.

[117] In the 2017 ruling of the Danish Supreme Court in the so-called *Ajos Case*, Case no 15/2014, *DI, acting on behalf of Ajos A/S v Estate of A*, UfR U.2017.824H, the Supreme Court reasoned largely by referring to the said list of 'treaties, etc'. The case is discussed in ch 7, section V.

As a direct consequence of the Edinburgh Decision, the provisions of the Maastricht Treaty relating to the third stage of the EMU, as well as Article K.9 (AFSJ), were explicitly excluded from the listing in the Act of Accession. In this way, these parts of the Maastricht Treaty were not made applicable to Denmark.

Third and finally, the set of Bills was completed by a separate Bill on holding a referendum on 18 May 1993.[118] Legally, the Bill meant that the parliamentary ratification consent to the Danish ratification of the Maastricht Treaty pursuant to Article 19(1) of the Constitution, and which would be given by the Parliament's adoption of the ratification Bill, was 'carved out' and put up for a referendum. This was done in accordance with the provisions laid out in Article 42 of the Danish Constitution. It followed a back-up model that already had been conceived by Professor Max Sørensen in relation to the Danish accession to the EC.[119] From a legal point of view, this implied that the new referendum in May 1993 was just as legally binding as the previous one in June 1992. The legal bases were different, but both referenda were held on the basis of provisions of the Constitution. They were thus both legally binding upon the Danish Government and the Parliament. For the sake of good order, this was explicitly made clear in the explanatory notes to the referendum Bill L178.[120]

A remaining issue relates to how to, from a Danish point of view, go about potential future changes to the special Danish position as instituted by the Edinburgh Decision. The matter was explicitly addressed in the explanatory notes to the Ratification Bill.

Initially, it was pointed out that neither the Maastricht Treaty nor the Edinburgh Agreement could undergo changes without Danish approval, in which respect the Government added that the procedure to be followed in Denmark, including on parliamentary participation and on the issue of a renewed referendum, would be determined by Denmark itself in accordance with the provisions of the Constitution.[121] This statement seemingly referred to a situation involving a new IGC, which the Maastricht Treaty already envisaged under the then Article N(2) TEU.[122]

The issue was not left at this, however. When making reference to the legal right for Denmark unilaterally to terminate the Edinburgh Agreement in whole or in part, it was noted that seven of the parties in the Danish Parliament

[118] *Forslag til lov om afholdelse af folkeafstemning om forslag til lov om Danmarks tiltrædelse af Edinburgh-Afgørelsen og Maastricht-Traktaten*, Folketingstidende, saml 1992–93, L178.

[119] Lauridsen and Nymann-Lindegren (n 116) 158. The situation did not materialise in 1972 since a referendum at that time followed directly from the Art 20 procedure.

[120] At one point there was a debate among legal scholars as to whether it would constitute an infringement of the Danish Constitution if a referendum was held despite the fact that Art 20 does not provide for it. See H Koch, 'Grundlovsstridige EU-folkeafstemninger' in H Koch et al, *Politik og jura. Festskrift til Ole Espersen* (Copenhagen, Forlaget Thomson, 2004). It would suffice to note that this argument has not gained momentum.

[121] See Folketingstidende, saml 1992–93, col 7612.

[122] See also the discussion in section VII.A.ii.

had agreed that this could only happen following a renewed referendum.[123] Moreover, during the deliberations of the Bill in the plenary session of the Danish Parliament, the Foreign Minister repeated that the Danish position, as set out in the Edinburgh Decision, only could be changed by way of holding a new referendum.[124]

Against this background, Krunke concluded that the Danish population was promised a referendum before any of the four exceptions (the opt-outs) could be abolished.[125] Krunke recognised that the Ratification Bill could not alter the provisions of Article 19 and 20 of the Constitution; nevertheless, she considered that the promise made to seek popular confirmation in a referendum of any changes to the Edinburgh Decision constituted a precondition, just as did the Edinburgh Decision itself, for the Danish ratification of the Maastricht Treaty. Given that the promise was made as part of the ratification legislation, in Krunke's eyes, it had 'considerable legal force'.[126]

This author has sympathy for Krunke's reasoning. It is worth underlining that in Danish legal tradition, which may vary from the legal traditions in other European countries, the explanatory notes to a Bill form an integral part of that Bill. Their status as *travaux préparatoires* is given great interpretive attention in determining the legal impact of the Bill when it has later been enacted. This is the case as regards both the Executive and the Judiciary.[127]

The first time the issue of a new referendum became relevant after the entering into force of the Edinburgh Decision was in 2000, at which point the Government proposed to abolish the euro opt-out.[128] The Government explicitly addressed the referendum question as follows:

> In connection with the set of bills on Denmark's accession to the Edinburgh Agreement and the Maastricht Treaty, the 7 parties entered into a political agreement which implies that Denmark's position on four main elements of the Maastricht Treaty, including the third phase of the Economic and Monetary Union, can only be changed through a referendum. … It is absolutely crucial for the government that both the letter and the spirit of this agreement are observed. Regardless of whether a majority of 5/6 is achieved, the government will, in accordance with the agreement between the 7 parties, ensure that the question of Denmark's accession to the common currency is submitted to the electorate for approval or rejection according to the rules in § 42 of the constitution.[129]

[123] Folketingstidende, saml 1992–93, col 6736. Among the political parties to the agreement were those that formed the government coalition.

[124] ibid col 5374.

[125] Krunke (n 58) 355.

[126] ibid.

[127] See the Danish Ministry of Justice's guidance note on the quality in legislation, Justitsministeriet, 'Lovkvalitesvejledninge' (2007) point 2.8. As a prominent example from the Judiciary, see the judgment of the Danish Supreme Court in the *Ajos Case* (n 117).

[128] See further ch 4, section III.A.

[129] Explanatory notes to Bill 288; *Forslag til lov om Danmarks deltagelse i den fælles valuta*, Folketingstidende, saml 1999–2000, L288 (author's own translation).

It is not crystal clear from the wording whether the Government acted due to a perception that it was legally bound to do so pursuant to the legislation on the Danish ratification of the Maastricht Treaty, to which it refers. However, over the years a widely-held opinion seems to have formed among Danish scholars, that adherence to an absolute referendum requirement on any changes to the opt-outs is rooted in a political – and not a legal – obligation.[130] In any case, the result is the same.

In 2000, the Government most certainly found itself to be bound by at least a *political* requirement to hold a referendum in accordance with a well-established Danish parliamentarian practice, to honour political agreements such as the one entered into on the referendum question from 1993.

Successive Danish Prime Ministers have since, on various occasions, confirmed that any changes to the opt-outs require approval in a Danish referendum. Notably, this viewpoint was reflected by the Government some 15 years later in relation to a proposed change to the Danish position within the AFSJ.[131] Most recently that was the case in connection with the abolition of the defence opt-out.[132]

What it implies is that the political room for manoeuvre of any Danish government on the matter of EU cooperation falling within the scope of the opt-outs was constrained from the outset. Any changes would require confirmation by a referendum. This requirement is perceived as a mandatory one and respected as such, regardless of what follows pursuant to the procedure in Article 20 of the Danish Constitution.

In other words, the way in which the Edinburgh Decision was approved politically in Denmark and legislated for in national law meant that, on the matter of the Danish opt-outs, direct democracy took precedence over parliamentary democracy, which otherwise dominates Danish rule-making, from this point on. This was certainly an innovation.[133]

## VIII. OVERVIEW OF THE DOCUMENTS FORMING THE EDINBURGH SOLUTION

Building on the findings in this chapter, Table 2.1 provides a structured and condensed overview of the combined set of documents by which the 'Danish

[130] See, as an recent example, TB Olesen, 'Danmark i Europa – de lange linjer 1945–2022' in Neergaard and Sørensen (eds) (n 116) 58.

[131] See reply to parliamentary questions: EUU (2015–16) L29, *svar på spørgsmål* 110. On the general issue of the proposed changes to the AFSJ position, see ch 6.

[132] See further ch 5.

[133] It adds to the discussion above in section VII.A.iii on the combined impact of the Edinburgh Decision. Furthermore, it is noted that the Edinburgh Decision also had the effect that a referendum on Denmark's not becoming part of the third stage of the EMU was held as an integral part of the

concerns' were resolved in Edinburgh. The Edinburgh Decision appears in bold font as it constitutes the core document.

The design of Table 2.1 follows the methodological approach of this book, and as such lists the relevant documents in the first column, indicating to which terminological framework they belong, that is, the Edinburgh Agreement and/or the set of arrangements on Denmark as defined in the Part B of the Presidency Conclusion.[134] In the second column, reference is made to the parties to which the documents are attributed. That is followed in column 3 by the affiliation of each document according to the findings of the analysis; and finally an outline in column 4 of what role the document plays as part of the entire construction erected to resolve the Danish issue.

The table may serve as a useful reference point for the original opt-outs when, in the following chapters, in-depth analysis of each of them is undertaken.

**Table 2.1** Documents Forming the Edinburgh Solution

| DOCUMENT | PARTIES | AFFILIATION | ROLE |
|---|---|---|---|
| Danish Memorandum 'Denmark in Europe'<br>(The National Compromise) | Denmark | Danish law (formal *travaux préparatoires)* | <u>Policy/interpretational input</u><br>Outlining the opt-outs as well as other elements handled outside the scope of opt-outs |
| Presidency Conclusion A<br>Conclusion text + annexes (in part)<br>Part of:<br>*The Edinburgh Agreement* | EU Presidency quoting European Council | EU law | <u>Policy input/guidance</u><br>Advancing certain non-Danish specific issues raised in the Danish Memorandum |
| Presidency Conclusion B<br>Conclusion text<br>Part of:<br>*The Edinburgh Agreement + Arrangements on Denmark* | EU Presidency quoting European Council | International law<br>EU law | <u>Interpretational input</u><br>Outlining the framework for the arrangements to meet the Danish concerns |

*(continued)*

vote on the Edinburgh Decision and the Maastricht Treaty and not, as originally envisaged, potentially at a later stage and in principle only if the procedure in Art 20 of the Constitution would have prescribed it, see Krunke (n 58) 348.

[134] The latter published in the *Official Journal* under the title 'Denmark and the Treaty on European Union' [1992] OJ C348/1.

Table 2.1 *(Continued)*

| DOCUMENT | PARTIES | AFFILIATION | ROLE |
|---|---|---|---|
| Presidency Conclusion B<br>Annex I: **Edinburgh Decision**<br><br>Part of:<br>*The Edinburgh Agreement + Arrangements on Denmark* | The Member States of the EU | International law<br>Danish law | Legislation<br>Instituting four Danish opt-outs:<br>A) Union citizenship<br>B) 3rd stage of the EMU (euro)<br>C) Defence<br>D) AFSJ cooperation |
| Presidency Conclusion B<br>Annex II: European Council Declaration 1<br><br>Part of:<br>*The Edinburgh Agreement + Arrangements on Denmark* | European Council | International law<br>Danish law | Policy input<br>Addressing certain non-Danish specific issues raised in the Danish Memorandum |
| Presidency Conclusion B<br>Annex II: European Council Declaration 2<br><br>Part of:<br>*The Edinburgh Agreement + Arrangements on Denmark* | European Council | International law<br>Danish law | Procedural input<br>Relates to opt-out C.<br>Prescribes the procedure in the Council following Denmark's renouncing of the Council Presidency on defence matters |
| Presidency Conclusion B<br>Annex III: Unilateral Declaration 1<br><br>Part of:<br>*The Edinburgh Agreement + Arrangements on Denmark* | Denmark | International law<br>Danish law | Interpretational input/ policy input<br>Relates to opt-out A.<br>Relates to Union citizenship versus national citizenship.<br>Danish constitutional procedure in case of changes to the above |
| Presidency Conclusion B<br>Annex III: Unilateral Declaration 2<br><br>Part of:<br>*The Edinburgh Agreement + Arrangements on Denmark* | Denmark | International law<br>Danish law | Policy input<br>Relates to opt-out D.<br>Danish constitutional procedure in case of 'pillar- jump' within the AFSJ |

*(continued)*

Table 2.1 *(Continued)*

| DOCUMENT | PARTIES | AFFILIATION | ROLE |
|---|---|---|---|
| Presidency Conclusion B<br>Annex III: Unilateral Declaration 3 (Final Declaration)<br><br>Part of:<br>*The Edinburgh Agreement + Arrangements on Denmark* | Denmark | International law<br>Danish law | Policy/interpretational input<br>Statement regarding the outcome of the Danish 1992 referendum.<br>Views on the legal compatibility between the Edinburgh Solution and the EU Treaty |

## IX. CONCLUDING REMARKS

The analysis conducted in this chapter provides the answer to the question of how the opt-outs originally were designed. In brief, the answer is that it was done in a legally novel way, rooted in two legal orders.

The terminology used for the combined solution found at the December 1992 European Council meeting in Edinburgh, to accommodate a Danish ratification of the Maastricht Treaty, is manifold: 'a set of arrangements', 'the Edinburgh Agreement' and 'the Edinburgh Decision' are widely used. These terms are not interchangeable as they do not cover the same number of texts. Also, regardless of statements to the contrary, not all of the issues addressed in the documents are in fact Denmark-specific; some elements have universal applicability. The immense time pressure under which steps into uncharted territory were taken in Edinburgh may well explain why such ambiguities occurred. Nonetheless, and importantly, the solution found proved solid, sustainable and adequate.

The political Memorandum from the Danish political parties, 'Denmark in Europe', served as strong guidance for the solution produced in Edinburgh. It has kept some relevance in relation to the interpretation of the intended scope of the opt-outs.

What was clear from the outset was that Denmark essentially made two requests. On the one hand, Denmark sought some general clarifications on how certain policy areas were to be governed pursuant to the new Treaty; and on the other hand, Denmark requested specific opt-outs within four defined policy areas. Both aspects were accommodated in Edinburgh.

The general Part A of the Presidency Conclusion addressed some of the general aspects. The rest are addressed in the First Declaration by the European Council, which forms part of the specific set of arrangements targeting Denmark and embedded in Part B of the Conclusion. Confusing as this may appear, it does not alter the fact that the substance of the Declaration has a general character and is not Denmark-specific. Although the Declaration forms part of Part B, it does not, by its substance, relate to the opt-outs. Together with the elements of Part A of the Conclusion, it is thus of less relevance to the remaining chapters of this book dedicated to the opt-outs.

Turning to the other aspect of the requests by Denmark, which undisputedly was the core one, namely the institution of four opt-outs, it is noted that this was accomplished in a legally binding way on two levels. First on the macro level, the Edinburgh Decision binds the contracting parties, which are the EU Member States, under international law. The instrument does not form part of EU law; however, it complements the Maastricht Treaty without changing it and without breaching any of the obligations that arise from it.

The creation of such an instrument among the EU Member States was a novelty. The reason why this legally was possible has everything to do with the characteristics of the substance of the opt-outs created by the Edinburgh Decision. They are directed towards potential, future development of European integration, which Denmark will not prevent from happening; on the other hand, Denmark itself will not be take part in such further integration. The non-participation of Denmark does not breach obligations undertaken by Denmark as a contracting party to the Maastricht Treaty. Moreover, no changes to the Maastricht Treaty nor to the *acquis* were necessitated or called for by the institution of the Danish opt-outs.

Second, the Edinburgh Decision is part of Danish law as it forms part of the 'treaties, etc' listed in the Danish Act of Accession. Furthermore, it follows from the Edinburgh Decision itself that the issue of its termination is a matter for Denmark alone. The way in which the Edinburgh Decision was legislated for under Danish law has ramifications for how this competence should be exercised by Denmark. The *travaux préparatoires* explicitly prescribe the holding of a referendum in Denmark on the matter. Even if this may not be a legally binding requirement, which on the other hand should not be fully ruled out, it is certainly a strong political requirement that has been observed ever since. On the issue of the opt-outs, Denmark thus chose to enhance direct democracy at the expense of the otherwise predominant parliamentary democracy.

The Edinburgh Decision is the core of the set of arrangements that also includes five associated Declarations. Together with the initial conclusion text of Part B, they all form part of a combined entity, registered as such at the UN in New York and published in the same format in the *Official Journal* in Brussels. The individual status of the Declarations and Conclusion text is, however, of a different nature than the Edinburgh Decision itself.

The analyses have documented that some of the Declarations provide interpretational input to the content and scope of the opt-outs. That is the case regarding the Danish Declaration on Union citizenship and, in more general terms, the Final Declaration. Although the Declarations are unilateral in character, the European Council took 'cognisance' of them. The views expressed on their legal interpretation are thus to be understood as having broader backing. The text of Part B of the Presidency Conclusion also provides views on the general legal character of the Edinburgh Decision.

The Second Declaration of the European Council, which relates to the Danish defence opt-out, provides procedural advice of a housekeeping nature on how to deal with the fact that Denmark, as a consequence of the opt-out, would not be mandated to chair meetings of the Council on the subject.[135]

The Declarations by Denmark on the AFSJ, as well as the last part of the Declaration on Union citizenship, serve a political purpose. It is argued that they may be read as sending a message of reassurance to Denmark's EU partners that the opt-outs may not have been intended to last for long. The reality was to turn out differently.

Reverting to the intended scope of the opt-outs, it is held that no spill-over was intended into Denmark's general engagement and cooperation as an EU Member State. The Danish Memorandum underlined that Denmark did not dissociate itself from its EU membership and that Denmark should not be isolated; on the contrary, Denmark should play an active role in Europe's continued development. Concretely, it called for active Danish engagement in the enlargement dossier, which did indeed happen immediately after Edinburgh.

At the same time as Denmark engaged in the ratification of the Maastricht Treaty, and by that the approval of the four opt-outs pursuant to the Edinburgh Decision, Denmark held the EU Presidency. At the concluding meeting of the European Council in Copenhagen in June 1993, the Council recognised, for the first time, the right of the countries of Central and Eastern Europe to join the EU, subject to the fulfilment of certain specified criteria for accession.[136] These criteria subsequently became known as the 'Copenhagen Criteria'. The active role played by the Danish Presidency was testimony to an unbroken Danish commitment to the European integration process.

Whereas it is not the aim of this book to explore, nor to contribute to analyses of, the political fallout from the Danish rejection of the Maastricht Treaty in 1992, it is pertinent to observe, as Howarth so aptly did, that '[t]he voting result threw the Community into a political and legal quagmire'.[137] In light thereof, it is quite remarkable that the European leaders were able, so quickly, to pull the Community out of the situation in which it found itself during the summer of 1992.[138]

[135] The normal rules for replacing the President, in the event of the President's being indisposed, apply in that situation.

[136] Conclusions of the Copenhagen European Council 21–22 June 1993, Bull EC 6-1993. A decision on opening accession negotiations with Sweden, Finland and Austria had already been reached in Edinburgh with full backing from the Danish side. Norway followed shortly thereafter.

[137] Howarth (n 57).

[138] For an account of the political dimensions, see former Danish Foreign Minister Per Stig Møller, 'Dansk Udenrigspolitik og EU-medlemskabet' in Neergaard and Sørensen (eds) (n 116) 77.

The then State Secretary in the Danish Ministry of Foreign Affairs, Ørstrøm-Møller, has drawn the following lesson from why it was possible for the Edinburgh Decision to be fostered, approved and enacted within a short period of time:

> [M]ake up your mind at an early stage defining what exactly you go for … Think before moving is wise; keep thinking without moving is not. In the Danish case the government had a clear perception of how to square the circle about a month after the rejection of the Maastricht Treaty, but manoeuvered gently and cautiously gradually getting a grip on the tiller.[139]

Determination and legal imagination, combined with a general and focused effort, paid off. Within one year, all Member States, including Denmark, did ratify the Maastricht Treaty, which entered into force on 1 November 1993. The solution that emerged from the European Council in Edinburgh meant, however, that Denmark was left with a special legally binding position within four defined areas of Union cooperation.

During the subsequent 30 years, the opt-outs matured in law in different ways. The remainder of this book will analyse how the continuous process of EU integration has impacted their legal shape and effects, and how they fit in with the evolved European legal order. In this respect, the importance and impact of the Edinburgh Decision will be assessed as part thereof.

[139] JØ Møller, 'Brexit: Lessons from Denmark' *OMFIF* (11 October 2016) at www.omfif.org/2016/brexit-lessons-from-denmark/.

# 3

# *Union Citizenship*

## I. INTRODUCTION

Following the general methodology adopted in this book, the relevant section of the Edinburgh Decision forms the point of departure for the analysis in section II. In the case of this opt-out, the analysis of the departure point by and large provides a complete answer to the question of the opt-out's legal effects. This in turn leads to an account of the subsequent European integration process that materialised in this field of cooperation, notably by way of the Amsterdam Treaty, which effectively attributed a rather peculiar role to this particular opt-out.

Misunderstandings as to the width of the scope of this opt-out may easily flourish; this is therefore addressed in section III as a continuation of the analysis of the opt-out's legal effects and the impact of the evolution of the EU law in question. In this regard, an account of the special Danish position on the acquisition of secondary residences in Denmark, viewed in light of the position on Union citizenship, is given in section IV. To accomplish this, the essential Danish legislation within this field is discussed. The descriptive nature of this account comes with a point that becomes clear when ultimately it is held up against the essence of the Union citizenship as defined in EU law. General concluding remarks are offered in section V.[1]

## II. IMPACT ON AND EFFECT OF THE UNION CITIZENSHIP OPT-OUT

Section A of the Edinburgh Decision on 'Citizenship' provides as follows:

> The provisions of Part Two of the Treaty establishing the European Community relating to citizenship of the Union give nationals of the Member States additional rights and protection as specified in that part. They do not in any way take the place

[1] On Union citizenship in general, see among many contributions, eg, T Kostakopoulou, 'European Union Citizenship: The Journey Goes On' in A Ott and E Vos, *Fifty Years of European Integration: Foundations and Perspectives* (The Hague, TMC Asser Press, 2009); D Kochenov (ed), *EU Citizenship and Federalism* (Cambridge, Cambridge University Press, 2017); D Thym (ed), *Questioning EU Citizenship* (Oxford, Hart Publishing, 2017).

of national citizenship. The question whether an individual possesses the nationality of a Member State will be settled solely by reference to the national law of the Member State concerned.[2]

The provision essentially comprises two parts. The first is a finding that Union citizenship, as regulated in the Treaty, gives the holder additional rights as well as additional protections. Given the context, this element is understood as an add-on to the rights enjoyed through the national citizenship held by the same individual or, put differently, as a derived condition of nationality.[3] However, it is worth observing that the rights deriving from Union citizenship as specified in the Treaty are for the most part directed towards Member States other than the one of which the individual is a national. This is because the rights are mainly associated with the right to free movement.[4] In this connection, Closa described the construction as one whereby Union citizenship adds a second circle of new rights, which may be enjoyed in any Member State. That is in addition to the nationality rights enjoyed within an individual's own particular Member State.[5]

The second part of Section A of the Edinburgh Decision elaborates on the additional character of Union citizenship. It is thus further emphasised, first, that Union citizenship does not replace national citizenship and, second, the matter of whether an individual holds national citizenship is to be resolved entirely through national legislation.

In the first unilateral Danish Declaration to the Edinburgh Decision, Denmark expanded on the understanding of what Union citizenship was and what it was not. The first two paragraphs of the Danish Declaration state as follows:

1. Citizenship of the Union is a political and legal concept which is entirely different from the concept of citizenship within the meaning of the Constitution of the Kingdom of Denmark and of the Danish legal system. Nothing in the Treaty of European Union implies or foresees an undertaking to create a citizenship of the Union in the sense of citizenship of a nation-state. The question of Denmark participating in any such developments does, therefore, not arise.
2. Citizenship of the Union in no way in itself gives a national of another Member State the right to obtain Danish citizenship or any of the rights, duties, privileges or advantages that are inherent in Danish Citizenship by virtue of Denmark's constitutional, legal and administrative rules. Denmark will fully respect all specific rights expressly provided for in the Treaty and applying to nationals of the Member States.[6]

[2] Denmark and the Treaty on European Union [1992] OJ C348/1.

[3] C Closa, 'Citizenship of the Union and Nationality of Member State' (1995) 32 *Common Market Law Review* 510.

[4] See Arts 20–22 TFEU.

[5] Closa (n 3) 493.

[6] Denmark and the Treaty on European Union (n 2).

In Denmark, acquisition of Danish citizenship is governed by the Constitution, Article 44 of which prescribes that a foreigner can obtain Danish citizenship only by an Act of Parliament. The process, known as naturalisation, is in practice handled twice a year, when the Minister of Justice tables a Bill containing the names of individuals to be naturalised, by the adoption (by simple majority) in Parliament of the said Bill. Furthermore, the issue of becoming a Danish citizen by birth, as well as other aspects of citizenship, is regulated in the Act on Citizenship.[7]

Against this background, it is held that it was of paramount importance to Denmark to underline that although Denmark, in the Declaration forming part of the Edinburgh Agreement, recognised Union citizenship as a political *and a legal* concept, it was found to be 'entirely different' (see the wording of the Danish Declaration, above) from Danish citizenship, which is acquired in accordance with the above-mentioned Danish rules.

In the subsequent paragraph 3 of the Danish Declaration, Denmark recalled that, already at the time, nationals of other Member States enjoyed the right under Danish law to vote and to stand as a candidate in municipal elections in Denmark. Paragraph 3 reads:

> 3. Nationals of the other Member States of the European Community enjoy in Denmark the right to vote and to stand as a candidate at municipal elections, foreseen in Article 8b of the European Community Treaty. Denmark intends to introduce legislation granting nationals of the other Member States the right to vote and to stand as a candidate for elections to the European Parliament in good time before the next elections in 1994. Denmark has no intention of accepting that the detailed arrangements foreseen in paragraphs 1 and 2 of this Article could lead to rules detracting from the rights already given in Denmark in that matter.[8]

This legal situation was otherwise foreseen as granting new rights under EU law as derived from Union citizenship, see Article 8b(1) of the then Treaty Establishing the European Community (TEC), introduced by the Maastricht Treaty. At the previous IGC in 1985 that led to the SEA, Denmark had unsuccessfully suggested the introduction into EU law of these rights of citizens of other Member States in relation to participation in elections at the municipal level.[9] At the IGC leading to the Maastricht Treaty, Denmark once again championed this view.[10] These particular rights deriving from Union citizenship were, however, viewed as controversial by a number of Member States, which pointed to difficulties of a constitutional nature. In light thereof, Article 8b(1) TEC explicitly allowed for derogations on this specific issue, if warranted by

[7] *Lovbekendtgørelse nr 1029 af 10 July 2018 om dansk indfødsret.*
[8] Denmark and the Treaty on European Union (n 2).
[9] C Closa, 'The Concept of Citizenship in the Treaty on European Union' (1992) 29 *Common Market Law Review* 1148.
[10] ibid 1155.

problems specific to a Member State. At the time, this was the case for, amongst others, Luxembourg.[11]

In the second part of paragraph 3 of its Declaration, Denmark made a commitment to ensuring that the same rights as already granted in Denmark in relation to municipal elections would also be applicable in relation to European Parliamentary elections. This was in conformity with the requirements provided for in Article 8b(2) of the then TEC introduced by the Maastricht Treaty.[12] Denmark even declared itself to be unwilling to accept that rules introduced by Article 8b TEC would have an effect detracting from the rights ensured by Danish rules. In other words, Denmark made it crystal clear that the legal position on the additional character of Union citizenship as laid out in Section A of the Edinburgh Decision had no bearing on this particular aspect of rights derived from Union citizenship.

Finally, Denmark referred in the fourth and final paragraph of the Declaration to its constitutional requirements, as laid out in Article 20 of the Danish Constitution.[13] This procedure would potentially become relevant in the event that the Council were to take steps to adopt provisions with a view to strengthening and expanding the rights falling within the concept of Union citizenship.[14] According to the Treaty provisions, such a decision would be subject to national ratification in each Member State.[15] Denmark's reference in the Declaration to its constitutional requirements was, therefore, of a reminding character; it did not allude to a special privilege for Denmark in this regard.[16]

Whereas the Declaration explicitly refers to Denmark and Danish legislation, and draw conclusions as to the legal effect of Union citizenship on that background, what stands out is that Section A of the Edinburgh Decision is formulated in a non-Denmark-specific way. It takes the form of a clarification of general legal facts.

There is no evidence to suggest that these facts were contested. In this regard, it is worth noting that already at the time of agreeing to the Maastricht Treaty, the Member States had made a joint declaration concerning the possession of national citizenship, which Section A of the Edinburgh Decision largely repeats. Declaration No 2, annexed to the final act of the TEU as established by the Maastricht Treaty, is worded as follows:

> The Conference declares that, wherever in the Treaty establishing the European Community reference is made to nationals of the Member States, the question whether an individual possesses the nationality of a Member State shall be settled solely by reference to the national law of the Member State concerned ...[17]

[11] ibid 1163.

[12] Art 8b(2) TEC contained the same in-built provision for a potential derogation from the rule as found in Art 8b(1). In current EU law, this provision is set out in Art 22 TFEU.

[13] On Art 20, see ch 2, section VII.B.

[14] Art 25 TFEU (former Art 8e TEC).

[15] Art 8e TEC.

[16] Closa (n 3) 512.

[17] Declaration on nationality of a Member State [1992] OJ C191/98.

Bearing these findings in mind, the evolution that subsequently took place seem rather logical. At least, it would be fair to assume that the point stressing the additional character of Union citizenship as formulated in the Edinburgh Decision was an issue of political importance not only to Denmark but also to most, if not all, of the other Member States.

In any case, already at the IGC that led to the Amsterdam Treaty in 1999, the distinction entailed in Section A of the Edinburgh Decision between national citizenship on the one hand and Union citizenship on the other was inserted into the Treaty provision establishing Union citizenship. The additional clause reads 'Citizenship of the Union shall be additional to and not replace national citizenship.' This has been retained until the present day, now Article 20(1) TFEU, and it is repeated, in a slightly different wording, in Article 9 TEU.[18]

That the Amsterdam Treaty incorporated the essence of Section A of the Edinburgh Decision into a general treaty provision in this way came as a natural development. It was logical given that Section A was formulated as it was, namely, as a statement of a general legal fact about Union citizenship. Even though it took the form of a Denmark-only provision, bearing in mind the initial statement of the European Council in the Conclusion text from Edinburgh that the arrangements agreed were designed to meet Danish concerns and as such were applicable exclusively to Denmark and not to other existing or acceding Member States,[19] that was legally not the case, and in this particular instance arguably not the intention either. Therefore, had the Amsterdam Treaty not elevated these provisions into a Treaty provision of a general character, it could have been suggested that this was indeed, at least henceforth, a special position applicable to Denmark only, whereas the concept of Union citizenship potentially had a different legal meaning in relation to the other Member States. The Amsterdam Treaty eradicated any prospect of making this wrongful assumption.[20]

The derogation in Article 8b TEC, which is applicable if warranted by problems specific to any Member State, has remained part of the Treaty provisions ever since the Maastricht Treaty. Today it is replicated in Article 22 TFEU. As made clear by the Danish Declaration forming part of the Edinburgh Agreement, this derogation has never been relevant for, and thus has never been invoked by, Denmark.

## III. POTENTIAL MISCONCEPTION AS TO THE SCOPE OF THE OPT-OUT

As discussed in section II, Section A of the Edinburgh Decision made some clarifications that, albeit undoubtedly regarded as very important, were nothing

[18] The Lisbon Treaty introduced the additional reference to the Union citizenship in Art 9 TEU that concerns the principle of equality.

[19] Denmark and the Treaty on European Union (n 2).

[20] See a discussion of how the CJEU has viewed Section A in section III.

more than the exposition of a legal reality already established by the Maastricht Treaty.

In the Danish political Memorandum presented prior to the Edinburgh European Council, the Danish politicians had requested a solution whereby 'Denmark will have no obligations in connection with citizenship of the Union'.[21] As already clear from the preceding discussion, the literal sense of that requirement was not fulfilled by the solution that emerged in the Edinburgh Decision.

It would therefore constitute a misconception to associate Section A of the Edinburgh Decision with an exemption for Denmark from the effects of Union citizenship. Such an exemption has never existed. On the contrary, by its Declaration forming part of the Edinburgh Agreement, Denmark did explicitly acknowledge Union citizenship as a concept of EU law.

Moreover, Denmark explicitly denounced the need to make use of the general possibility given by the Treaty to derogate from the specific obligation derived from Union citizenship, which ensures that citizens from other Member States are given access to participate in local electoral processes in other Member States.

The rights under the Treaties granted to nationals of Member States who at the same time automatically hold Union citizenship have been applicable to Denmark all along. At no point in time has Section A exempted Denmark therefrom. Put in a different way, the legal evolution of these rights, whether that has followed from new secondary legislation or from the jurisprudence of the CJEU, has raised no legal questions particular to Denmark's position.

Neergaard rightly observes that the development of the legal rights and obligations deriving from the concept of the Union citizenship, which have evolved over the years with the CJEU as the main driver, was in all likelihood not foreseen at the time of the drafting of Part A of the Edinburgh Decision.[22] That is undoubtedly true, but it cannot change the legal fact that they also have effect for Denmark.

This also holds true in relation to the very issue of acquisition and loss of nationality. Already in the so-called *Micheletti* case from the beginning of the 1990s, the CJEU had ruled that Member States must, when exercising their powers in this respect, have regard to EU law.[23] It is not surprising that the Court in this way clarified that Member States cannot exercise their competence with the effect that obligations of EU law are infringed. The Court has since had the opportunity to elaborate on what this entails in relation to Member States' granting and evoking national citizenship in light of the inherent relation to Union citizenship.

[21] 'Denmark in Europe', Markedsudvalget 1992–93, MKU Alm. del bilag 70, p 3.

[22] U Neergaard, '"A More United Union" and the Danish Conundrum' in AB Engelbrekt and X Groussot (eds), *The Future of Europe: Political and Legal Interaction Beyond Brexit* (Oxford, Hart Publishing, 2019) 256.

[23] Case C-369/90 *Mario Vicente Micheletti and others v Delegación del Gobierno en Cantabria* ECLI:EU:C:1992:295, para 10.

In the *Rottman* case, the Court referred to the above-mentioned Declaration No 2 from the ICG on the Maastricht Treaty, as well as to Section A of the Edinburgh Decision.[24] The Court remarked that both are elements that have to be taken into consideration as being instruments for the interpretation of the Treaty, especially for the purpose of determining the ambit of *ratione personae* under the Treaty.[25] The Court further stated that this was a matter for the CJEU to determine as part of its judicial review.[26] What is of significance when discussing the scope and impact of the Danish position pursuant to the Edinburgh Decision is the fact that the Court treats Section A in the way it is drafted, namely, as a general provision on the relation between national and Union citizenships and not as a Denmark-specific provision. Neither is it viewed as a derogation from treaty obligations. The Court applies the provisions of Section A on a par with Declaration No 2.

Subsequent questions on the subject matter of acquisition and loss of nationality have been brought before the CJEU.[27] The Court has clarified that although the question of acquisition and loss of nationality is a competence that lies 'solely' with the Member States, obligations of EU law and notably the principle of proportionality should be taken into account.[28] This is all the more so seen in the light of the Union citizenship, which, according to settled case law of the Court, is intended to constitute the fundamental status of nationals of the Member States.[29] Interestingly, a Danish court has also made a referral.[30] The Danish court did not anticipate any special status for Denmark pursuant to the Edinburgh Decision in this regard; on the contrary, it asked for clarification on the compatibility of Danish legislation with the matter in light of Denmark's undisputed obligations under EU law. With explicit reference to Section A of the Edinburgh Decision on Union citizenship, the Danish Government, however, argued that Denmark enjoyed a special position.[31] The Court reaffirmed its ruling in the *Rottman* case, namely, that Section A of the Edinburgh Decision serves a general

[24] Case C-135/08 *Janko Rottman v Freistaat Bayern* ECLI:EU:C:2010:104, para 4. An extract from Section A of the Edinburgh Decision is reproduced alongside text from Declaration No 2 under the heading referring to relevant EU law. Arguably, that does not necessarily mean that the Court implicitly hereby has ruled that the Edinburgh Decision is indeed an instrument of EU law per se.

[25] ibid para 40.

[26] ibid paras 46 and 48.

[27] Case C-221/17 *MG Tjebbes and Others v Minister van Buitenlandse Zaken* ECLI:EU:C:2019:189; and Case C-118/20 *JY v Wiener Landesregierung* ECLI:EU:C:2022:34. In these cases, no refence to the Edinburgh Decision is made. Instead, the Court relies on the treaty provisions on Union citizenship along with relevant international conventions.

[28] *Wiener Landesregierung* (n 27) para 58. The CJEU also points to obligations under international law, notably the Convention on the Reduction of Statelessness, see *Rottman* (n 24) paras 39 and 41.

[29] See, eg, *Tjebbes* (n 27) para 31.

[30] Case C-689/21 *X v Udlændinge- og Integrationsministeriet* ECLI:EU:C:2023:626.

[31] View of AG Szpunar in Case C-689/21 *X v Udlændinge- og Integrationsministeriet* ECLI:EU:C:2023:53, fn 45.

clarifying purpose.[32] The argument of the Danish Government was not accommodated.

The issue of other Member States' granting foreigners national citizenship, whereby the individuals concerned become Union citizens, also does not raise any questions in relation to the provisions of Section A of the Edinburgh Decision. Once an individual holds citizenship of a Member State, the treaty rights of a Union citizen are applicable.[33] Section A of the Edinburgh Decision underlines that issues relating to the settlement of national citizenship lie with the respective Member State.[34] That Union citizenship then becomes an additional part thereof is emphasised in both Section A and the corresponding treaty provisions. Differences in naturalisation policies under the legal regimes of the individual Member States are not addressed by Part A of the Edinburgh Decision.

## IV. THE DANISH PROTOCOL ON THE ACQUISITION OF 'SUMMERHOUSES'

At this point, it may be worthwhile to discuss the special Danish position in relation to the acquisition of real estate in Denmark, notably in the form of a secondary residence. The fact is that Denmark does enjoy a special position in this field under EU law; however, it would constitute a misconception to relate this position to the Danish position on Union citizenship.

The issue of a foreigner's acquisition of real estate in Denmark is regulated at constitutional level. Article 44 of the Constitution stipulates that this question should be regulated by an Act of Parliament. In other words, the Constitution ensures that there is not necessarily free access for non-Danish citizens to acquire real estate (land, houses and buildings) in Denmark.

The Danish Act on Acquisition from 1959 fulfilled this constitutional requirement.[35] The Act essentially stipulates that the right to acquire real estate in Denmark for persons not resident in the country, as well as for commercial entities, associations, etc that are not domiciled in Denmark, is made dependent on obtaining a special permission from the Danish Ministry of Justice. As the legislation shows, the legislators opted for a model whereby the decisive factor is not the question of citizenship but that of residence.[36] This is the first element to note in light of the later-introduced Union citizenship.

Immediately prior to Denmark's accession to the then European Economic Community (EEC), specific regulation was introduced in Denmark on secondary

[32] *X v Udlændinge- og Integrationsministeriet* (n 30) paras 26–28.

[33] See Art 20(1) TFEU together with Art 20(2) TFEU.

[34] Bearing in mind the obligations of EU law as clarified by the CJEU.

[35] Act no 344 of 23 December 1959. Latest consolidated version: *Lovbekendtgørelse* no 265 of 21 March 2014 on *erhvervelse af fast ejendom*.

[36] The explanatory note to the legislation indicates that by doing so, priority was given to the country's citizens, see *Forslag til lov om erhvervelse af fast ejendom*, Folketingstidende 1959–60, Tillæg A.

residences, which in Danish are referred to as 'summerhouses'. The 'Act on Summerhouses' essentially regulates the issue of commercial rental of secondary residences. As is the case concerning the acquisition of such a property from a non-domiciled buyer, the issue of renting it out on a commercial basis also requires prior special permission from the Danish Ministry of Justice.[37]

At the time of Denmark's accession to the then EEC in 1973, these two pieces of national legislation were in force in Denmark. As a consequence of EU membership, certain modifications to the Danish legislation on the acquisition of properties were made, although not in relation to the specific issue of acquisition of 'summerhouses'; and none was made to the 'Act on Summerhouses'. The Ministry of Justice maintained a relatively strict practice in relation to issuing the prescribed special permissions under both pieces of legislation. At the time, this was perceived not to infringe Denmark's obligations under EU law, while at the same time, from a Danish political point of view, it was considered important to ensure that Danish summerhouses effectively and mainly remained in the hands of the Danes.[38]

The issue was not a problem for many years, until the introduction in 1988 of Council Directive 88/361/EEC on the implementation of Article 67 TEC. At this stage of the EU integration process, it was deemed necessary to include a specific provision that made it possible for Denmark, at least temporarily, to maintain the legal status quo on the issue of access to buy summerhouses in Denmark. Article 6(4) of the Directive reads:

> Existing national legislation regulating purchases of secondary residences may be upheld until the Council adopts further provisions in this area in accordance with Article 69 of the Treaty. This provision does not affect the applicability of other provisions of Community law.[39]

From an EU law point of view, what is essentially at stake here is the principle of non-discrimination on grounds of nationality,[40] as well as the principle of free movement, notably of capital.[41]

During the IGC that led to the Maastricht Treaty, it was a Danish priority to ensure that the issue of acquisition of secondary residences in Denmark formally and permanently became regulated within primary EU law.[42] That was

[37] Originally enacted as *Lov* no 267 of 7 June 1972; now see *Lovbekendtgørelse* no 949 of 3 July 2013 on *sommerhuse, campering m.v.*

[38] See memos produceded for the parliamentary EU Committee: EU-konsulenten, 'EU-note om Sommerhusprotokollen', Europaudvalget 2015–16, EUU Alm.del EU-note E 46; KE Sørensen, 'Notat om sommerhusprotokollen og mulighederne for at skærpe kontrollen og sagsbehandlingen', Europaudvalget 2022–23 (2. samling) EUU Alm.del – Bilag 434.

[39] Council Directive 88/361/EEC for the implementation of Article 67 of the Treaty [1988] OJ L178/7.

[40] See Art 18 TFEU.

[41] Part Three, Title IV of the TFEU.

[42] N Petersen, 'Denmark and the European Union 1985–96. A Two-level Analysis' (1996) 31(2) *Cooperation and Conflict* 197 and fn 14.

accomplished by way of introducing a new specific protocol to the Treaty. This protocol has been continued to this day and has been subject only to technical adaptions. Protocol (No 32) on the Acquisition of Property in Denmark reads in its current form as follows:

> THE HIGH CONTRACTING PARTIES, DESIRING to settle certain particular problems relating to Denmark,
>
> HAVE AGREED UPON the following provisions, which shall be annexed to the Treaty on European Union and to the Treaty on the Functioning of the European Union:
>
>> Notwithstanding the provisions of the Treaties, Denmark may maintain the existing legislation on the acquisition of second homes.[43]

Ever since the Maastricht Treaty, Denmark has in this way explicitly enjoyed a special position under EU *treaty* law in this field.[44] From a legal point of view, particular attention should be put on the formulation as seen in the Protocol, that Denmark may 'maintain the existing legislation'. It suggests limits, and possibly even excludes changes, to the Danish legislation without that having an impact on the Danish position under EU law. Former Danish Foreign Minister Per Stig Møller has recalled that during the IGC that led to the Lisbon Treaty, certain Member States questioned the Protocol, and Møller argues that it only survived at Danish insistence. Møller warns Denmark not to tamper with the scope of the Protocol, as this, according to Møller, likely would change the *political* faith of the Protocol at the next IGC.[45] In any case, the issue of 'stand still' is closely monitored by the authorities in Denmark.[46]

Among the other Member States, only Malta has come to enjoy a somewhat similar position,[47] which is laid out in a protocol negotiated as part of Malta's accession to the EU.[48] Unlike the Protocol regulating the Danish situation, the Maltese version is more elaborate, including by explicitly requiring Malta to ensure the application of the derogation in a non-discriminatory way as well as ensuring equal treatment of citizens from all Member States. The restrictive formulation is likely a reflection of a more particular approach that has

[43] Protocol No 32 on the Acquisition of Property in Denmark [2016] OJ C202/317.

[44] At times, scholars erroneously attribute the fact that Denmark, ever since joining the EC, has enjoyed a special position on the issue to provisions forming part of the Danish accession treaty of 1972: see TB Olesen, 'Danmark i Europa – de lange linjer 1945–2022' in U Neergaard and KE Sørensen (eds), *Danmark og EU gennem 50 år – en milepæl* (Copenhagen, Djøf Forlag, 2023) 44.

[45] PS Møller, 'Dansk Udenrigspolitik og EU-medlemskabet' in Neergaard and Sørensen (eds) (n 44) 84.

[46] Reply from the Minister of Justice to parliamentary question: EUU Alm. del., Europaudvalget 2016–17 – svar på spørgsmål 309. For a comprehensive discussion, including of Case C-302/97 *Konle* ECLI:EU:C:1999:271, see Sørensen (n 38).

[47] Certain acceding Member States have gained temporary derogations on the matter. These arrangements have all since expired; see note produced by EU-konsulenten, 'EU-note om Sommerhusprotokollen' (n 38).

[48] Protocol No 6 on the acquisition of secondary residences in Malta [2003] OJ L236/947.

evolved on the part of the EU when accommodating permanent derogations from fundamentals of treaty law.[49]

In any case and as demonstrated above, the legal construction of the limits for EU citizens to acquire a secondary home in Denmark is *not* related to the Danish position on Union citizenship. It is a separate issue that involves a derogation from the principle of free movement, notably of capital, and as such regulated separately under EU law. With reference to Protocol No 32, Piris describes it as a derogation whereby non-nationals (ie non-Danes) are prohibited from buying second homes in Denmark.[50] Although this, to a large extent, is the de facto effect, the criterion governing the scope of the opt-out relates nonetheless not to nationality but to residence.

It is known to constitute a 'fifth Danish opt-out'.[51]

## V. CONCLUDING REMARKS ON THE UNION CITIZENSHIP OPT-OUT

From a dogmatic legal point of view, Section A of the Edinburgh Decision can hardly be described as either an 'opt-out' or any other form of a derogation from obligations under EU law. Unlike the general derogation that may be invoked pursuant to Article 22 TFEU, concerning the right of Union citizens to participate in election processes, Section A of the Edinburgh Decision does not derogate from treaty provisions that would otherwise lead to another result. It does not provide any exemptions for Denmark from the effects of Union citizenship. Rather, Denmark has explicitly recognised Union citizenship not only as a political but also as a legal concept under EU law. Although having made reference to Section A, the CJEU has not referred to Denmark as a Member State holding a special position within this field.[52] This non-derogative position of Denmark is not always fully reflected in the literature. For example, Schimmelfennig and Winzen state that 'The Danish opt-outs from the Maastricht Treaty in the areas of *Union citizenship* and Justice and Home Affairs impinge directly on individuals' civil rights.'[53] Moreover, it is misleading to claim that Denmark originally gained a position whereby 'EU citizenship' was not to be applied to Danish citizens.[54]

[49] The finding draws on the author's own experience, having served as chairman of the Council Working Group that drafted the accession treaty of Malta and others. See also Møller (n 45). On the issue of differentiation in relation to enlargements in general, see F Schimmelfennig and T Winzen, *Ever Looser Union. Differentiated European integration* (Oxford, Oxford University Press, 2020).

[50] J-C Piris, *The Future of Europe. Towards a Two-Speed EU?* (Cambridge, Cambridge University Press, 2011) 76, fn 40.

[51] See EU-Konsulenten as well as Sørensen (n 38).

[52] *Rottmann* (n 24) and *X v Udlændingestyrelsen* (n 30).

[53] Schimmelfennig and Winzen (n 49) section 11.2.2 (emphasis added).

[54] D Leuffen, B Rittberger and F Schimmelfennig, *Integration and Differentiation in the European Union. Theory and Policies*, 2nd edn (Cham, Palgrave Macmillan, 2022) 348.

Denmark does enjoy a special legal position under EU law regarding the acquisition of 'summerhouses'. It is, however, a separate matter regulated pursuant to EU primary law, and not related to the provision on Union citizenship pursuant to the Edinburgh Decision.

The effect of Section A of the Edinburgh Decision and the accompanying Declaration by Denmark served the purpose, at the time, of removing potential doubt or perceived ambiguity – notably in Denmark – that Union citizenship was indeed not equal to national citizenship and that the latter, in turn, remained an exclusive competence of the Member States. Despite the legal nature of the Edinburgh Decision, Section A on Union citizenship mainly served a political purpose for Denmark.[55]

The non-Danish wording of Section A, combined with its character as legal clarification, made its evolution into general treaty provisions appear rather straightforward. The text of the treaty provisions is not the same as that of Section A in the Edinburgh Decision. Notably, the element in Section A regarding national citizenship's being an exclusive Member State competence is not repeated. This may possibly be due to the fact that it had already been stated by all Member States in the Declaration attached to the Final Act of the Maastricht Treaty.[56] Therefore, the conclusion is that the essence of the Danish 'derogation' on Union citizenship, which notably is the point on the additional nature of Union citizenship, since the time of the Amsterdam Treaty, has formed part of primary EU law in the form of general applicable provisions.

It raises a question as to the status of Section A of the Edinburgh Decision. The Decision as such remains in force. In relation to the Danish ratification Bill on the Amsterdam Treaty, the Danish Government underlined in the accompanying explanatory notes to the Bill that the Amsterdam Treaty explicitly maintained the Danish opt-outs, including that on Union citizenship, and that this was done by referring to Denmark's position pursuant to the Edinburgh decision.[57] Naturally this was of importance to the Danish Government, since none of the four provisions from the Edinburgh Decision can be terminated unless this is confirmed in a referendum in Denmark.[58] This applies to the section on Union citizenship as well, which the Danish Minister of Foreign Affairs explicitly had confirmed back in 1993 in a reply to a question from the Scrutiny Committee of the Danish Parliament.[59] Such a referendum has never taken place and does not seem to be on the cards. Neergaard recently observed that in any case, the

[55] Closa (n 3) 512; and D Curtin and R Van Ooik, 'Denmark and the Edinburgh Summit: Maastricht without tears: A Legal Analysis' in D O'Keeffe and PM Twomey (eds), *Legal Issues of the Maastricht Treaty* (Chichester, Wiley Chancery, 1994) 359.

[56] Declaration on nationality of a Member State [1992] OJ C191/98.

[57] Explanatory Notes to Bill L1 of 26 March 1998 on Danish ratification of the Amsterdam Treaty, Folketingstidende, 1997–98, 2. Saml, L1, column 238.

[58] See ch 2.

[59] Reply to question 38 re Bill L177, Markedsudvalget Alm del.

likelihood would be an outcome whereby a majority of the electorate would vote 'no' if invited to give up this section of the Edinburgh Decision.[60]

Nevertheless, it seems pertinent to reflect on whether Section A, from the time it effectively was incorporated into the Amsterdam Treaty, has ceased to have legal effect. It seems to be a widely held view among scholars that Section A of the Edinburgh Decision, on Union citizenship, is indeed obsolete.[61]

It may be tempting to draw the same conclusion. However, doing so may prove to be a little too hasty. The reason for this is twofold. First, the CJEU has found it beneficial to make reference to Section A as being relevant for the interpretation of the Treaties.[62] This underlines the fact that the Edinburgh Decision is still in force and, seemingly, that Section A has been, and potentially still is, considered to have legal relevance in its own right. However, as previously discussed, the Court has not referred to Section A as a derogation, nor to its being Denmark-specific. Its value as an interpretational element arguably is a minor one since only the issue of Member State competence to grant national citizenship has not explicitly been transposed from Section A of the Edinburgh Decision into the treaty provisions on Union citizenship. Even so, as no competence on the matter is conferred on the Union, it follows from Article 4(1) TEU that it remains with the Member States.[63]

Second, the situation that Denmark rightly declared not to be relevant in 1992 should be kept in mind, namely, that '[n]othing in the Treaty of European Union implies or foresees an undertaking to create a citizenship of the Union in the sense of citizenship of a nation-state'.[64] Although currently still not relevant, potentially a future IGC could lead to changes in the legal character of Union citizenship vis-à-vis national citizenship in a manner contrary to the legal situation today as defined in Article 9 TEU and Article 20(1) TFEU.[65] Should such a situation occur, Section A of the Edinburgh Decision, underpinned by the accompanying Danish declaration forming part of the Edinburgh Agreement, would define the default Danish position at the IGC, which consequently would be that Denmark would not be inclined to be involved in such treaty changes. This default Danish position could only be changed following confirmation in a referendum in Denmark.[66]

[60] Neergaard (n 22) 256.

[61] ibid. See also H Krunke, '"Peoples" Vengeances. From Maastricht to Edinburgh: The Danish Solution' (2005) 1 *European Constitutional Law Review* 351.

[62] *Rottmann* (n 24) and *X v Udlændingestyrelsen* (n 30).

[63] To be exercised with respect to obligations pursuant to EU law as compared with the jurisprudence of the CJEU.

[64] Paragraph 1 of the unilateral Danish Declaration on the Union citizenship that forms part of the Edinburgh Solution, see Denmark and the Treaty on European Union [1992] OJ C348/1.

[65] Ideas to this effect were aired as part of the 2021–22 Conference on the Future of Europe (CoFE).

[66] If politically so wished, the holding of a referendum on the question could be done either separately and prior to the conclusion of an IGC or, alternatively and more likely, afterwards as part of the Danish ratification of the negotiated treaty changes.

Should the default position persist, a likely outcome could be the insertion into the EU Treaties of a proper opt-out for Denmark. In return, Denmark would not block the said treaty changes, true to the commitment undertaken in the Edinburgh Agreement. The situation would be comparable to the one Denmark found itself in at the time of the Amsterdam Treaty regarding the then-introduced treaty changes on cooperation within the AFSJ. Denmark did not oppose those changes to EU treaty law but ensured that, in parallel, a proper opt-out for Denmark within the area of EU cooperation was instituted under EU law.[67]

In sum, the legally defined Danish position on Union citizenship has never had the legal effect of a derogation but rather that of a general, legal clarification. Furthermore, besides playing a minor role as a general instrument for the interpretation of the treaties, and besides a binding effect on the Danish position at a potential IGC that would seek to 'create a citizenship of the Union in the sense of citizenship of a nation-state',[68] Section A of the Edinburgh Decision plays no active role in law today.

[67] See ch 6 on the impact of the European integration process on the Danish AFSJ opt-out.

[68] See the Danish Declaration, paragraph 1 (n 64). The position may only be changed following a positive outcome in a referendum.

# 4

# *Economic and Monetary Policy – The Euro*

## I. INTRODUCTION

THE INTRODUCTION OF the single currency, the euro, is the cornerstone of the third stage of EMU.[1] The special Danish position on this stage is therefore popularly referred to as the Danish euro opt-out.[2] This terminology is used where appropriate throughout the analysis undertaken in this book.

Answers to the question regarding the impact on the euro opt-out of the European integration process, as well as to the question on its legal effects, will be presented in section II, following a combined analysis of the relevant section of the Edinburgh Decision in light of relevant special provisions of EU Treaty law. This analysis is elaborated upon by comparing the special position of Denmark with the legal situation of a few other Member States.[3]

[1] See Art 3(4) TEU.

[2] See, eg, the website of the Danish Parliament at www.eu.dk/da/danmark-i-eu/de-danske-forbehold.

[3] See in general on the euro, including aspects of differentiation, F Allemand, 'The Impact of the EU Enlargement on Economic and Monetary Union: What Lessons Can Be Learnt From the Differentiated Integration Mechanisms in an Enlarged Europe?' (2005) 11(5) *Pean Law Journal* 586; F Amtenbrink, LA Geelhoed and S Kingston, 'Economic, Monetary and Social Policy' in PJG Kapteyn et al (eds), *Kapteyn & VerLoren van Themaat – The Law of the European Union and the European Communities* (The Hague, Kluwer Law International, 2008) 881; J Usher, 'The Evolution of Economic and Monetary Union – Some Legal Issues' in A Arnull, P Eeckhout and T Tridimas (eds), *Continuity and Change in EU Law: Essays in Honour of Sir Francis Jacobs* (Oxford, Oxford University Press, 2008) 297; E Ferran, 'European Banking Union and the EU single financial market: more differentiated integration, or disintegration?' *University of Cambridge Faculty of Law Research Paper 29/2014*; S Fabbrini, 'Emerging from the Euro Crisis: The Institutional Dilemmas of a Political Union' in M Dawson et al (eds), *Beyond the Crisis: The Governance of Europe's Economic, Political and Legal Transformation* (Oxford, Oxford University Press, 2015) 94; B de Witte, 'Euro Crisis Responses and the EU Legal Order: Increased Institutional Variation or Constitutional Mutation?' (2015) 11 *European Constitutional Law Review* 434; A Dashwood, 'Guest Editorial. Living with the Eurozone' (2016) 53(1) *Common Market Law Review* 3; T Beukers and M van der Sluis, 'Differentiated Integration from the Perspective of Non-Euro Area Member States' in T Beukers, B de Witte and C Kilpatrick (eds), *Constitutional Change Through Euro-Crisis Law* (Cambridge, Cambridge University Press, 2017) 143; S van den Bogaert and V Borger, 'Differentiated integration in EMU' in B de Witte, A Ott and E Vos, *Between Flexibility and Disintegration* (Cheltenham, Edward Elgar Publishing, 2017) 209; F Amtenbrink and C Herrmann (eds), *EU Law*

The first-ever attempt to alter the special Danish position as instituted by the Edinburgh Decision took place in 2000, with a view to abolishing the euro opt-out. Discussion of the legal framework governing the abolition of this opt-out, as well as the outcome of the 2000 endeavours, provide a first contribution in section III to the issue of how to change the special Danish opt-out position.

Section IV of this chapter is dedicated to discussion of the legal position of Denmark in relation to some of the major initiatives and measures that form part of the EU's monetary policies in light of the opt-out. Finally, concluding remarks on the euro opt-out are offered in section V.

## II. IMPACT ON AND EFFECT OF THE EURO OPT-OUT

### A. General Analysis of the Legal Status of Denmark on the Euro

The rather lengthy Section B of the Edinburgh Decision, on 'Economic and Monetary Union', reads as follows:

> 1. The Protocol on certain provisions relating to Denmark attached to the Treaty establishing the European Community gives Denmark the right to notify the Council of the European Communities of its position concerning participation in the third stage of Economic and Monetary Union. Denmark has given notification that it will not participate in the third stage. This notification will take effect upon the coming into effect of this decision.
> 2. As a consequence, Denmark will not participate in the single currency, will not be bound by the rules concerning economic policy which apply only to Member States participating in the third stage of Economic and Monetary Union, and will retain its existing powers in the field of monetary policy according to its national laws and regulations, including powers of the National Bank in the field of monetary policy.
> 3. Denmark will participate fully in the second stage of Economic and Monetary Union and will continue to participate in exchange-rate cooperation within the European Monetary System (EMS).[4]

None of the Declarations forming part of the Edinburgh Agreement from either the European Council or Denmark elaborate further on Section B of the Decision.

Section B refers to the Protocol on certain provisions relating to Denmark. This Protocol formed part of the Maastricht Treaty from the outset (as (then) Protocol No 12), and as such already catered for a potential Danish opt-out concerning the third stage of EMU.

*of Economic & Monetary Union* (Oxford, Oxford University Press, 2020); S Baroncelli, 'Differentiated Governance in European Economic and Monetary Union: From Maastricht to Next Generation EU' (2022) 7(2) *European Papers* 867.

[4] Denmark and the Treaty on European Union [1992] OJ C348/1.

The Protocol in its current form provides as follows:

PROTOCOL (No 16)
ON CERTAIN PROVISIONS RELATING TO DENMARK

THE HIGH CONTRACTING PARTIES,

TAKING INTO ACCOUNT that the Danish Constitution contains provisions which may imply a referendum in Denmark prior to Denmark renouncing its exemption,

GIVEN THAT, on 3 November 1993, the Danish Government notified the Council of its intention not to participate in the third stage of economic and monetary union,

HAVE AGREED UPON the following provisions, which shall be annexed to the Treaty on European Union and to the Treaty on the Functioning of the European Union:

1. In view of the notice given to the Council by the Danish Government on 3 November 1993, Denmark shall have an exemption. The effect of the exemption shall be that all Articles and provisions of the Treaties and the Statute of the ESCB referring to a derogation shall be applicable to Denmark.
2. As for the abrogation of the exemption, the procedure referred to in Article 140 shall only be initiated at the request of Denmark.
3. In the event of abrogation of the exemption status, the provisions of this Protocol shall cease to apply.[5]

The original version of paragraph 1 and the initial part of paragraph 2 of the Protocol read as follows:

1. The Danish Government shall notify the Council of its position concerning participation in the third stage before the Council makes its assessment under Article 109J(2) of this Treaty.
2. In the event of notification that Denmark will not participate in the third stage, Denmark shall have an exemption. The effect of …[6]

Thus, in its original form, the Protocol related to the future by regulating for a *possible* Danish position, taking the form of an opt-out in relation to a *foreseen*, although not yet materialised, third stage of EMU. Heber qualifies this original Danish position on the euro as a 'quasi opt-out', seemingly due to the fact that Denmark in this way was given an option to opt-out, which stood in contrast to the British legal position of opting out of the euro from the very outset and without hesitation.[7] Nonetheless, Section B of the Edinburgh Decision effectively activated the special position of Denmark, as already provided for in the corresponding Protocol to the Treaties.

[5] Protocol No 16 to the Treaty on European Union and the Treaty on the Functioning of the European Union [2016] OJ C 202/287.

[6] Protocol on certain provisions relating to Denmark, annexed to the Treaty establishing the European Community [1992] EUR-Lex, Document 11992M/PRO/DK.

[7] C Heber, *Enhanced Cooperation and European Tax Law* (Oxford, Oxford University Press, 2021) 20.

The Maastricht Treaty entered into force on 1 November 1993. On 3 November, the Danish Government formally notified the Council that Denmark did not intend to participate in the third stage of EMU. The notification was a formality given the explicit wording of the Edinburgh Decision; it served the purpose, however, of being a formal notification under EU law.[8]

The Amsterdam Treaty, as well as the Nice Treaty, carried over the original formulation of paragraph 1 of (now) Protocol No 16 on certain provisions relating to Denmark unchanged. The Lisbon Treaty, however, rectified the original generic wording regarding a possibility for Denmark to notify the Council of its intention in this field, by inserting a reference to the specific date, 3 November 1993, when this indeed had happened. The change made by the Lisbon Treaty did not alter the legal fact that Denmark had enjoyed a special position on the third stage of EMU ever since 1993, and that Denmark continues to do so. The Lisbon Treaty simply clarified that this had been the case.

It follows from the Edinburgh Decision that Denmark will not prevent the other Member States from cooperating within the fields of EU cooperation from which Denmark holds a derogation.[9] Naturally, that applies to the third stage of EMU as well. However, in this connection the unilateral Danish pledge was of less relevance. The Maastricht Treaty regulated the question in a general manner by way of a specific protocol attached to the then TEC. The Protocol declared the irreversible character of the Community's movement towards the third stage of EMU by signing the then new treaty provisions on EMU. In light thereof, the Protocol stipulated that all Member States, whether they fulfilled the conditions for the adoption of the single currency or not, should respect the will of the Community to enter the third stage and that no Member States should prevent that.[10]

On 1 January 1999, the third stage of EMU materialised.[11] This was in accordance with the deadline laid down by the Maastricht Treaty.[12] Although the Danish position on this third stage of EMU had already been activated in 1993, due to its very nature the opt-out only became effective in concrete terms from 1 January 1999.

The whole construction of the third stage of EMU implies that not all Member States necessarily formed part of it from the outset. An in-built process on the fulfilment of a set of convergence criteria has led to a situation of successive entries by Member States according to their own merits.[13] Once a Member State adopts the euro as its currency, the state is referred to as a Member State

[8] Document not available on EUR-Lex.

[9] See discussion in ch 2.

[10] Protocol on the Transition to the third stage of Economic and Monetary Union [1992] OJ C191/87.

[11] The euro as a physical currency was only introduced in 2002.

[12] Art 109J(3) TEC.

[13] See notably Art 140 TFEU. In 1999, Greece did not enter the third stage of EMU. See also the discussion of the EMU as an element of differentiated integration in ch 7.

whose currency is the euro.[14] These Member States all belong to the so-called 'Eurozone' and they meet within the informal body created in 1997 called the 'Euro Group'.[15]

Member States that have not been part of the third stage are formally referred to as 'Member States with a derogation'.[16] It is a derogation with different effects within the economic part of EMU, on the one hand, and the monetary side, on the other hand. Whereas most provisions on economic union are applicable to the Member States with a derogation, the important provisions on monetary union are not.

Protocol No 16 defines the legal position of Denmark as one of 'an exemption'. Nonetheless, Denmark falls into the group of Member States with a derogation, given the stipulation in the Protocol that all articles and provisions of the Treaties and the Statute of the European System of Central Banks (ESCB) referring to a derogation shall be applicable to Denmark.[17]

### B. The Danish Position on the Euro Compared to Certain Other Member States

The special Danish position within EMU differs from the one formerly in place for the UK.[18] The British situation was regulated in much more detail than the Danish one. Moreover, the provisions relating to the UK had greater effects. As an example, the UK was only obliged to 'endeavour to avoid' an excessive deficit, whereas the general rule in Article 126(1) TFEU provides that Member States 'shall avoid' excessive government deficits.[19] In contrast to the UK, the general rule in that Article applies to Denmark, as the Treaty does not make exceptions for non-euro Member States, that is 'Member States with a derogation', to which group Denmark belongs.

Member States with a derogation are, however, exempted from a number of provisions of the Treaties. Article 139(2) TFEU lists those treaty provisions that are not applicable to Member States with a derogation. As an example, the coercive means of remedying an excessive deficit in a Member State do not apply.[20] Article 139(2) TFEU also clarifies that the reference in the listed treaty provisions

[14] Title VIII, ch 4 TFEU.

[15] The Euro Group was formally recognised by Protocol No 14 on the Euro Group [2016] OJ C202/283, adopted as part of the Lisbon Treaty. The informality of the Group is explicitly stated in Art 1.

[16] Art 139 TFEU.

[17] Protocol No 16 (n 5) para 1.

[18] Protocol No 15 on certain provisions relating to the United Kingdom of Great Britain and Northern Ireland [2016] OJ C202/284.

[19] A Rosas and L Armati, *EU Constitutional Law. An Introduction*, 3rd edn (Oxford, Hart Publishing, 2018) 115.

[20] Art 126(9) and (11) TFEU.

to 'Member States' is to be understood as referring to Member States that have adopted the euro as their currency.

Beyond the lists in Article 139 TFEU, Articles 136 and 137 TFEU contain provisions that explicitly apply to Member States whose currency is the euro. Although not mentioned in Protocol No 16, those treaty provisions do not apply to Denmark either. This follows from the very nature of the provisions in question, and is equally the case in relation to other Member States who have not – yet – adopted the euro. In the case of Denmark, this legal fact is underpinned by the provision in paragraph 2 of Section B of the Edinburgh Decision.

Legal scholars Rosas and Armati observe that 'the position of a political unwilling state is not necessarily different from that of an economic unable one'.[21] On the other hand, scholar in political science Adler-Nissen argues that there are huge differences between voluntary and involuntary euro-outsiders.[22] Notwithstanding how one approaches that question, the ultimate difference between the Danish situation and that of all other Member States is that, unlike all other Member States, Denmark is not obliged to join the third stage of EMU if and when the necessary economic criteria are fulfilled.[23] After Brexit, no other Member State enjoys the same legal position under the Treaties.[24]

Following a Swedish referendum in 2003, Sweden has pursued a policy of not adopting the euro. However, Sweden does not have an exemption under the Treaties from participation in the third stage of EMU. Sweden is by legal definition a Member State with a derogation, in accordance with Article 139 TFEU.

Scholars have referred to Sweden as a country having a de facto exception in relation to euro membership.[25] The meaning, effect and consequence of such a 'de facto exception' is not further elaborated upon. However, it seems to imply that since the EU tolerates the fact that Sweden refrains from taking the steps otherwise prescribed in the Treaties with a view to adopting the euro as its currency, a de facto exception is constituted.

Rosas and Armati have discussed the issue regarding the EU institutions' laissez-faire approach towards a Member State that fulfils the economic criteria as laid out in the TFEU but refrains, nevertheless, from taking the foreseen steps towards acceding to the third stage of EMU.[26] It may prove to be a pertinent

[21] Rosas and Armati (n 19) 110.

[22] R Adler-Nissen, 'The Vocal Euro-outsider: The UK in a Two-speed Europe' (2016) 87(2) *The Political Quarterly* 245.

[23] Art 3 TEU sets out the establishment of EMU with the euro as the currency as one of the aims of the EU. Other Member States have an obligation to accede thereto once the relevant criteria are met, see notably Art 140(1) TFEU.

[24] K Inglish, 'The Union's Fifth Accession Treaty: New Means to make enlargement possible' (2004) 41 *Common Market Law Review* 937 points out that upon accession, new Member States did not transfer their monetary sovereignty, however the said States were given no possibility of opting out of the obligation to join the euro.

[25] See, eg, U Neergaard, 'ERM II' in F Amtenbrink and C Herrmann (eds), *The EU Law of Economic and Monetary Union* (Oxford, Oxford University Press, 2020) 741.

[26] Rosas and Armati (n 19) 117.

question not only as regards Sweden but also in relation to other Member States with a derogation, in that event that political resistance towards the euro project becomes rooted in those countries. Neergaard finds that '[u]ltimately the issue is related to the question as to what degree a multi-speed union is desirable or not'.[27] That seems to constitute more of a political than a legal view. Interesting as this discussion may be, it does not affect the Danish position as the sole holder of a de jure permanent derogation pursuant to EU law.

## III. CHANGES TO DENMARK'S POSITION ON THE EURO

Denmark alone can change its special position. Section E of the Edinburgh Decision explicitly states that Denmark, at any time and in accordance with Danish constitutional requirements, may inform the other Member States that it no longer wishes to avail itself of all or part of the Decision. In the case of the third stage of EMU, Protocol No 16, paragraph 2 further explicitly states that the procedure in Article 140 TFEU on accession to the third stage of EMU is only to be initiated at the request of Denmark. Should that happen, Denmark would naturally have to follow the otherwise regular procedures with a view to demonstrating its fulfilment of the required economic criteria, before accession to the third stage of EMU would be able to take place.

In such a scenario, the EU Treaties foresee the possibility that not all parts of the Kingdom of Denmark may adopt the euro as the currency. Dating back to the Maastricht Treaty, the following protocol remains applicable:

> PROTOCOL (No 17)
> ON DENMARK
>
> THE HIGH CONTRACTING PARTIES,
>
> DESIRING to settle certain particular problems relating to Denmark,
>
> HAVE AGREED upon the following provisions, which shall be annexed to the Treaty on European Union and the Treaty on the Functioning of the European Union:
>
> > The provisions of Article 14 of the Protocol on the Statute of the European System of Central Banks and of the European Central Bank shall not affect the right of the National Bank of Denmark to carry out its existing tasks concerning those parts of the Kingdom of Denmark which are not part of the Union.[28]

The Faroe Islands (the Faroes) and Greenland are self-governing entities, countries actually, within the Kingdom of Denmark. Neither is part of the EU, although Greenland enjoys Overseas Countries and Territories (OCT) status.[29] In case of the Faroes, their non-EU membership status has been in place ever

[27] Ulla Neergaard (n 25) 743.
[28] Protocol No 17 on Denmark [2012] OJ C326/288.
[29] Art 355(2) and (5)a TFEU.

since the Danish accession to the EC in 1973. Based on the outcome of a Greenlandic referendum, Greenland exited the EU on 1 February 1985, following the conclusion of a set of negotiated agreements with the other EU Member States settling the terms and conditions therefor.[30]

It is against this background that Protocol No 17 on Denmark was drafted. In the event that Denmark chooses to abolish the opt-out and adopt the euro (subject to the fulfilment of the economic criteria), the Faroes and Greenland would not be subject to such a decision by default.[31]

## A. Danish Referendum on Abolishing of the Euro Opt-Out

On 28 September 2000, a referendum was held in Denmark by which the electorate voted on a Bill approved by the Danish Parliament on Denmark's participation in the common currency, which implied the abolition of the euro opt-out.[32]

The Bill was the first of its kind. Its composition was simple: by Article 1, the Parliament approved Danish accession to the third stage of EMU, that is gave its parliamentary assent in accordance with Article 19(1) of the Danish Constitution. Article 2 enacted into Danish law relevant EU legislation adopted prior to the Danish accession to the third stage of EMU, to the extent that the EU legislation had direct effect in the Member States. Article 3 deleted the Danish derogation from the third stage of EMU as it appears in Danish law. This was done by removing the exemption from the third stage of EMU made in the listing of 'treaties, etc' in Article 4 of the Danish Act of Accession, which had been inserted to the Act at the time of the Danish ratification of the Maastricht Treaty and its approval of the Edinburgh Decision.[33] Finally, Article 4 laid out the procedure for the entry into force of the Bill.

The Bill did not regulate the issue of the Faroes and Greenland; in fact, the Bill was not applicable to them.[34] In the explanatory notes to the Bill, it was stated that should Denmark adopt the euro, the currency arrangements for the Faroes and Greenland were subsequently to be addressed. It was further added that for the euro to become the currency in these parts of the Kingdom too, a

[30] The arrangements with accompanying explanatory notes from the Danish Ministry of Foreign Affairs were forwarded to the Danish Parliament; see Markedsudvalget 1983–84, 2. samling, MKU Alm. del Bilag 43. It follows from the agreements that Greenland enjoys OCT status.

[31] It would require a special agreement; see the immediate subsection on the Danish euro referendum.

[32] Bill L288, '*Forslag til lov om Danmarks deltagelse i den fælles valuta*', Folketingstidende 1999/00, Tillæg A, col 7900.

[33] See ch 2.

[34] Reply by the Minister for Foreign Affairs to question 8 by the Europe Committee of the Parliament, Europaudvalget, samling 1999–2000, L288 – bilag 7.

special arrangement involving the relevant EU institutions and the euro Member States would be necessary.[35]

It was the provision in Article 3 of the Bill that triggered the referendum. It implied the transfer of powers to the EU within the field of the third stage of EMU in the legal sense as laid out in Article 20 of the Danish Constitution.[36] The corresponding qualified procedure for the adoption of the Bill was therefore applicable. As the prescribed five-sixths majority in the Danish Parliament did not approve Bill L 288, a referendum on its final approval followed as the next step. Interestingly, in the explanatory notes to the Bill, the Government had pledged to take the necessary steps to provide for a referendum also in the event that it would not follow from the procedure laid down in Article 20 in the Constitution, that is if the Bill were to be adopted by the prescribed qualified majority.[37] This pledge was necessary in order to honour, in all circumstances, the general commitment to hold a referendum on the abolition of any of the opt-outs, as set out in the explanatory notes to the Act on the approval of the Maastricht Treaty and the Edinburgh Decision from 1993.[38]

The electorate overturned the Bill in the subsequent referendum by 53.2 per cent to 46.8 per cent. Consequently, no changes to the special legal position of Denmark in respect of participation in the third stage of EMU were made. In other words, the opt-out on the euro remained untouched then and still is as at the time of writing.

## IV. ACTIVE DANISH PARTICIPATION IN EMU COOPERATION

Protocol No 16 sets boundaries for Denmark's participation in the economic and monetary policy of the EU in so far as Denmark remains outside of the euro, with the effect that all articles and provisions of the Treaties and the Statute of the ESCB referring to a derogation are applicable to Denmark.

In the Danish Act of Accession, an explicit exemption is made for the third stage of EMU, given that Denmark, as a consequence of the opt-out, has not conferred competence to the EU on the matter. Consequently, it follows from Danish law as well that Denmark cannot participate in the EU cooperation within the third stage of EMU.[39]

However, the Danish derogation does not extend beyond these boundaries. In other words, Denmark has a free *political* choice to decide on its participation

[35] Folketingstidende 1999/00, Tillæg A, col 7906.

[36] Justitsministeriet, 'Notat om visse forfatningsretlige spørgsmål i forbindelse med en dansk tiltrædelse af Den Økonomiske og Monetære Unions 3. fase med den fælles valuta' (2000). See Folketingstidende 1999/00, Tillæg B, col 1452.

[37] Folketingstidende 1999/00, Tillæg A, col 7906.

[38] See ch 2, section VI.B.

[39] ibid.

in matters of an economic and monetary character that *legally* fall outside the boundaries.[40]

So far and to a large extent, Denmark has pursued an approach of rather active participation in various areas of the field of economic and monetary cooperation. This stands in contrast to the approach that the UK took while an EU Member State enjoying a special legal position within cooperation on EMU, and as such may have caused confusion to some.[41]

### A. Fixed Exchange Rate

The Danish currency, *den danske krone* (the Danish crown, DKK) is pegged to the euro. Pursuing a fixed-rate policy does not exceed the boundaries set by the Danish euro opt-out. It is hardly a political surprise either.[42]

With the exception of a short period of time that ended in 1982, Denmark has since the end of the Second World War pursued a policy of using a fixed exchange rate.[43] Complying with this policy, Denmark explicitly pledged in the Edinburgh Decision to continue to participate in exchange-rate cooperation within the European Monetary System (EMS).[44] Denmark was at the time already a party to the European Exchange Rate Mechanism (ERM) under the EMS. On 1 January 1999, the EMS, including its ERM, was replaced by a new established exchange-rate mechanism, ERM II, in view of the entry into force of the euro.[45] This second version of the mechanism essentially aims to ensure that exchange-rate fluctuations between the euro and currencies of Member States that are not part of the third stage of EMU do not disrupt economic stability within the Single Market.

From the outset, Denmark has participated in ERM II. The boundaries set by and legally defined within the euro opt-out clearly do not prohibit Denmark from doing so.

According to EU law, participation in the ERM II is not mandatory for non-euro Member States. However, participation in the exchange-rate mechanism under the EMS and the fulfilment of specific criteria set out in this regard form

[40] Naturally, Denmark can only participate subject to its fulfilment of any obligation under EU law, eg those arising from the second stage of EMU.

[41] See, eg, Beukers and Van der Sluis (n 3), who find that Denmark's full participation in the Fiscal Compact (see section IV.C) is remarkable.

[42] cp for a seemingly different view, U Neergaard, '"A More United Union" and the Danish Conundrum' in AB Engelbrekt and X Groussot (eds), *The Future of Europe: Political and Legal Interaction Beyond Brexit* (Oxford, Hart Publishing, 2019) 249, 258, '[s]omehow *in spite of* the opt-out, it is noteworthy that Denmark follows a fixed-exchange-rate policy vis-à-vis the euro' (emphasis added).

[43] Reply by the Minister for Economy to the Europe Committee of the 'Folketing'; question 288, Europaudvalget (L 288 – bilag 64).

[44] Edinburgh Decision, Section B, para 3.

[45] Resolution of the European Council on the establishment of an exchange-rate mechanism in the third stage of economic and monetary union [1997] OJ C236/05.

part of the convergence criteria for joining the Eurozone.[46] ERM II may thus be regarded as a 'waiting room' for euro Members.[47] At the time of writing, the currency of Bulgaria forms part of ERM II alongside the Danish *krone*.[48] Naturally, the 'waiting room' euphemism does not apply to Denmark. At times, Denmark may be the only participant in ERM II, as was the case from 2001–04.[49] Eventually, Denmark would ideally become the sole participant, as other Member States gradually adopt the euro.

Within ERM II, a bilateral central rate vis-à-vis the euro is fixed for the currency of each participating country, with a default fluctuation band of +/− 15 per cent. However, in the case of Denmark, a much lower band of +/− 2.25 per cent was negotiated and established during the informal meeting of the Economic and Financial Affairs Council (Ecofin) on 25–27 September 1998.[50] This essentially means that the Danish currency is very closely pegged to the euro.

As already established in this study, the Danish position defined by the opt-out does not prevent Denmark from participating in fixed-exchange rate cooperation. The opposite question, however, would need to be examined, given the pledge by Denmark set out in the Edinburgh Decision and which concerns continued Danish participation in exchange-rate cooperation within the EMS.

Protocol No 16 to the EU Treaties does not repeat the pledge. However, given that the Edinburgh Decision remains in force as an instrument under international law,[51] the question could be raised as to whether Denmark, by way of the Edinburgh Decision, legally, under international law, committed itself to this particular element of its monetary policy.

Whereas the question appears to be unanswered by scholars, the following contribution is offered. Paragraph 2 of Section B of the Edinburgh Decision prescribes that Denmark, as a consequence of its euro opt-out as referred to in the first paragraph and defined in Protocol No 16, 'will retain its existing powers in the field of monetary policy according to its national laws and regulations, including powers of the National Bank in the field of monetary policy.' Being in a position of possessing powers includes, of course, the right to define but also, at a later stage, *re-define* the specific policies to pursue within these powers. The subsequent finding in paragraph 3 that Denmark 'will participate fully in the second stage of Economic and Monetary Union and will continue to participate in exchange-rate cooperation within the European Monetary System (EMS)'

[46] ibid. See also Art 140(1) TFEU and Art 3 of Protocol No 13 on the Convergence Criteria. A discussion of the perceived ambiguity on the matter is conducted by Neergaard (n 25) 742–43.

[47] Neergaard (n 25) 739.

[48] The Croatian *Kuna* was part of ERM II prior to Croatia's joining the euro on 1 January 2023.

[49] Danmarks Nationalbank, 'Monetary Policy in Denmark – 3rd edition' (Copenhagen, Rosendahls – Schultz Grafisk 2009) 57.

[50] Danmarks Nationalbank, 'Monetary Review – 4th Quarter 1998' (1998) 21. See also Usher (n 3) 305.

[51] See ch 2, notably section VII.A.i.

should therefore not necessarily be read as a deviation from a position of having retained autonomy, but simply as the laying out of a specific policy to be pursued. On the other hand, should the last provision of Section B of the Edinburgh Decision nonetheless be read as containing a binding commitment by Denmark under international law, it is observed that the commitment concerns a mechanism and means within this mechanism that have since ceased to exist, as the ERM has been replaced by a new mechanism (ERM II). On these grounds, it seems difficult to argue that the Edinburgh Decision sets any legal constraints for Denmark's monetary policy today outside of the Eurozone.

## B. Stability and Growth Pact

Alongside the long-lasting cooperation on fixed-exchange-policy, Denmark takes part in other legal arrangements within the field of EMU cooperation that have emerged since the 1990s.

One such arrangement is the Stability and Growth Pact from 1997.[52] By way of a Council Resolution and two Regulations, the Pact clarifies and expands provisions that are currently contained in Articles 121 and 126 TFEU. Notably, it regulates aspects of the Member State's fiscal policies within the framework of the so-called European Semester. The elements of the Pact have since been revised and further elaborated, notably through the adoption of the so-called 'Six-Pack' in 2011.[53] The Danish participation in the Stability and Growth Pact did not raise legal issues in relation to the opt-out, as Denmark, under the Pact, is governed by the rules laid out for countries that do not have the euro as their currency. Two of the Regulations forming part of the 'Six-Pack' regulate sanctions. The Regulations explicitly state that they apply only to Member States whose currency is the euro; it is therefore given that this part of the 'Six-Pack' does not apply to Denmark at all.[54]

## C. The Fiscal Compact

In 2012, several Member States adopted the Treaty on Stability, Coordination and Governance in the EMU (TSCG), which is also referred to as 'the Fiscal Compact'.[55] The main obligation arising from this Treaty is a commitment

[52] Resolution of the European Council on the Stability and Growth Pact [1997] OJ C236/01.

[53] The 'Six-Pack' takes its name from six legal acts, five regulations and one directive, adopted in parallel [2011] OJ L306/1, 8, 12, 25 and 33.

[54] Regulation (EU) No 1173/2011 on the effective enforcement of budgetary surveillance in the euro area [2011] OJ L306/1; and Regulation (EU) No 1174/2011 on enforcement measures to correct excessive macroeconomic imbalances in the euro area [2011] OJ L306/8.

[55] EUR-Lex, Doc 42012A0302(01), not published in the *Official Journal*.

by the participating countries legally to ensure balanced budget rules and to provide for an institutional set-up with a view to monitoring adherence to this obligation.

Rosas and Armati observe that the chosen instrument of an intergovernmental agreement outside of the EU legal order was necessitated due to opposition by the UK to the adoption of the provisions as EU law.[56] Contrary to the position of the UK, Denmark did not oppose the cooperation but chose actively to participate in the TSCG from the very outset.

Title IV of the TSCG contains certain general and final provisions. Among them are the following provisions, laid out in Article 14:

> 1. This Treaty shall be ratified by the Contracting Parties in accordance with their respective constitutional requirements. The instruments of ratification shall be deposited with the General Secretariat of the Council of the European Union ('the Depositary').
>
> …
>
> 5. This Treaty shall apply to the Contracting Parties with a derogation, as defined in Article 139(1) of the Treaty on the Functioning of the European Union, or with an exemption, as referred to in Protocol (No 16) on certain provisions related to Denmark annexed to the European Union Treaties, which have ratified this Treaty, as from the date when the decision abrogating that derogation or exemption takes effect, unless the Contracting Party concerned declares its intention to be bound at an earlier date by all or part of the provisions in Titles III and IV of this Treaty.[57]

In this way it is made explicitly clear how the TSCG becomes applicable to Denmark, including as a prerequisite that Denmark, like all other participating states, ratify it in accordance with its own constitutional requirements.

With this in mind, the Danish Ministry of Justice undertook a thorough examination of legal issues relating to Denmark's participation. The Ministry concluded that Denmark could accede to the Treaty without observing the special procedure as laid down in Article 20 of the Danish Constitution, and as such without ultimately holding a referendum. This conclusion was based on the option given in Article 14 TSCG that Denmark would accede to the Treaty with the euro opt-out being intact. In this respect, the Ministry did not find any legal issues of the TSCG that potentially could infringe the special Danish position as a country with 'an exemption' from the third stage of EMU.[58]

It was not on the cards politically to address the issue of the Danish euro opt-out at the time of the Danish accession to the TSCG, hence the assumption for the conclusion reached by the Ministry of Justice. For Denmark to be bound by

[56] Rosas and Armati (n 19) 111.

[57] EUR-lex, Document 42012A0302(01).

[58] Justitsministeriet, 'Notat om vise forfatningsretlige spørgsmål i forbindelse med Danmarks ratifikation af traktaten om stabilitet, samordning og styring i Den Økonomiske og Monetære Union (den såkaldte finanspagt)' (2012).

the Treaty, a Danish declaration to this effect was therefore required in accordance with the provision in Article 14(5) TSCG.

Accordingly, the Danish Government ratified the TSGC while at the same time declaring its intention to be bound by all the provisions in Titles III and IV of the Treaty. The Danish Government made the following addition, however, that relates to the euro opt-out:

> As a consequence of its obligations with regard to the Treaty, Denmark will not be bound by any EU legislative rules which result from subsequent implementation of Titles III and IV of the Treaty and are adopted on the basis of provisions of the Treaties on the European Union which are applicable only to those Member States which have the euro as their currency.[59]

The legal status of Denmark under EU law as a country with 'an exemption' from the third stage of EMU is not affected by Denmark's accession to the TSCG. Nothing in the TSCG legally suggests otherwise. However, certain provisions of the TSCG anticipate that they could or should be complemented by rules later to be adopted as EU law. Prominently, Article 5 TSCG explicitly stipulates that the form and content of an instituted instrument called 'partnership programmes' subsequently should be determined by EU law.

With the addition to its Declaration to be bound by the treaty provisions in Titles III and IV, which included the provisions of Article 5, Denmark simply recalled its special legal position that prevents Denmark from being bound by rules applicable only to Eurozone countries. The addition to the Declaration may thus be viewed as a precaution to help avoid misconceptions among partners about the unchanged Danish legal position under EU law, mirrored in an equally unchanged position under Danish law, both continually applicable after Denmark became bound by the TSCG.

## D. Banking Union

Banking union consists of two main elements: a Regulation on the Single Supervisory Mechanism (the SSM Regulation)[60] and a Regulation on the Single Resolution Fund (the SRM Regulation).[61] An intergovernmental agreement

[59] Declaration/Reservation by Denmark made before the General Secretariat of the Council of the European Union in its capacity as depositary, at www.consilium.europa.eu/en/documents-publications/treaties-agreements/agreement.

[60] Council Regulation (EU) No 1024/2013 of 15 October 2013 conferring specific tasks on the European Central Bank concerning policies relating to the prudential supervision of credit institutions [2013] OJ L287/63.

[61] Regulation (EU) No 806/2014 of the European Parliament and of the Council of 15 July 2014 establishing uniform rules and a uniform procedure for the resolution of credit institutions and certain investment firms in the framework of a Single Resolution Mechanism and a Single Resolution Fund and amending Regulation (EU) No 1093/2010 [2014] OJ L225/1.

supplements the SRM Regulation.[62] Furthermore, changes are made to the European Banking Authority (EBA).[63]

No political decision on whether or not Denmark should take part in banking union has been taken. A comprehensive preparatory work on the impact of possible Danish participation in banking union has nonetheless already been produced, including an assessment of possible legal challenges to which Danish participation may give rise. The Danish Ministry of Justice has concluded that Danish accession does not invoke Article 20 of the Constitution.[64] The legal analysis undertaken by the Ministry of Justice is, as always, essentially focused on whether Danish accession would imply any 'transfer of sovereignty'.[65] It may be recalled from chapter 2 that this assessment is strictly a national issue and, in the case of Denmark, strictly related to how this is understood in the context of the said Article 20 of the Danish Constitution.[66]

In relation to the special Danish position, one particular aspect deserves attention due to the prominent role that the European Central Bank (ECB) plays in banking union. Article 132 TFEU provides a general legal base for the ECB to adopt acts with a view to carrying out its tasks. The provision is, however, only applicable to Member States whose currency is the euro, in accordance with Article 139(1)(e) TFEU. The Article is thus not applicable to Denmark. The Danish Ministry of Justice observes that none of the provisions on banking union change this fact. Nor would Danish accession to banking union change the overall legal fact that Denmark remains outside of the third stage of EMU. In other words, a Danish decision to take part in banking union can be taken without having to address the legal status of Denmark as a Member State 'with an exemption' vis-à-vis the third stage of EMU – meaning, without compromising the opt-out.[67]

In statements to the press, the Danish Prime Minister indicated in 2019 that should the decision be taken that Denmark should aim at taking part in

[62] Agreement on the transfer and mutualisation of contributions to the Single Resolution Fund.

[63] Regulation (EU) No 1022/2013 of the European Parliament and of the Council of 22 October 2013 amending Regulation (EU) No 1093/2010 establishing a European Supervisory Authority (European Banking Authority) as regards the conferral of specific tasks on the European Central Bank pursuant to Council Regulation (EU) No 1024/2013 [2013] OJ L287/5.

[64] Justitsministeriet, 'Notat om hvorvidt dansk deltagelse i det styrkede banksamarbejde forudsætter anvendelse af proceduren i grundlovens § 20' (2015).

[65] See ch 2, section VII.B.

[66] cp U Neergaard, 'Euro Forbeholdet' in BE Olsen and KE Sørensen (eds), *EU-retten i Danmark* (Copenhagen, Jurist- og Økonomforbundets Forlag, 2018) 133, 152. Neergaard argues that the findings of the Danish Ministry of Justice regarding Art 20 of the Danish Constitution possibly should be reconsidered, by citing R Lastra, *International Financial and Monetary Law*, 2nd edn (Oxford, Oxford University Press, 2015) 355, who states that '[b]anking union signifies a further transfer of sovereign powers from the national to the supranational arena'.

[67] Justitsministeriet, 'Notat om hvorvidt dansk deltagelse i det styrkede banksamarbejde forudsætter anvendelse af proceduren i grundlovens § 20' (2015) 5 and 30.

banking union, such decision should be confirmed in a referendum.[68] Given that a referendum would not follow from the procedure laid out in Article 20 of the Constitution, in accordance with the conclusion reached by the Ministry of Justice, a legal basis in the form of a specific Act on holding the referendum would therefore be required. The issue of the Danish euro opt-out would in this scenario stand unaffected, and as such would continue to apply unchanged.

## V. CONCLUDING REMARKS ON THE EURO OPT-OUT

Prior to the Edinburgh Agreement, the then newly drafted Maastricht Treaty already contained provisions on a Danish opt-out from the third stage of EMU. Consequently, the issue of synchronising the legal effects of the euro opt-out that became part of the Edinburgh Decision to the development of EU law in light of the European integration process has not occurred.

Upon the entering into force of the Maastricht Treaty, Denmark immediately notified the Union that its opt-out option, provided for by the specific Protocol that formed part of that Treaty, was activated. Later, when the third stage of EMU materialised, the special position of Denmark took effect in concrete terms by preventing Denmark from becoming part of the third stage. Subsequent changes to the EU Treaties since Maastricht have required only technical adaptations to the Danish EMU Protocol under EU law.

Denmark has, vis-à-vis the EU, preserved its powers in the field of monetary policy. Put differently, Denmark has not transferred powers to the EU within this particular field of EU law pursuant to Article 20 of the Danish Constitution. As a consequence, Denmark has not adopted the euro as its currency but holds a permanent position under EU law as a country with a de jure exemption from the third stage of EMU. All articles and provisions of the Treaties and the Statute of the ESCB referring to a derogation are applicable to Denmark.

A Danish referendum on the abolition of the opt-out was held in 2000, pursuant to Article 20 of the Danish Constitution, given the element of transfer of powers to the EU that such a step would entail. Given the negative outcome of the referendum, the Danish position has been maintained. Any change to this legal position would require confirmation by a renewed Danish referendum.

Ever since the introduction of the euro in 1999, Denmark has remained a non-euro country, with the legal implications of this status as provided for in the EU Treaties. Consequently, Denmark has not participated in the many legal acts adopted as part of the third stage of monetary union. In 2017, the Danish Think Tank 'Europa' calculated that number to comprise 155 acts since 1999.[69]

[68] 'Frederiksen lover folkeafstemning, inden Danmark går ind i bankunionen' (Altinget, 17 October 2019) at www.altinget.dk.

[69] Tænketanken Europa, 'Forbeholdslandet Danmark. De mange aktiveringer af forbeholdene – og det voksende tab af suverænitet' (2017) 44.

Denmark does not take part in the deliberations of Ministers meeting as the Euro Group, nor is Denmark represented in the management structure of the ECB.[70]

Nonetheless, it would constitute a misconception to associate the impact of the special Danish position with what was the position of the UK: first, because the legal nature of the UK opt-out was broader than is the case for the Danish opt-out; and, second, because in the Danish case there is no political spill-over from the euro opt-out to other parts of economic and monetary cooperation within the EU and among EU partners outside of the EU Treaty regime. Pursuant to political choices, Denmark participates rather actively in such cooperation as falls beyond the legal boundaries of the opt-out.

In short, the Danish currency is closely pegged to the euro and Denmark is bound by essential pieces of monetary cooperation like the Fiscal Compact. Arguably, speculation against the Danish *krone* would therefore prove futile, as the ECB would actively support interventions by the Danish National Bank to ensure that fluctuations of the currency stay with the agreed limits.

For most of the years since the entry into force of the third stage of EMU, Denmark has fulfilled the convergence criteria. As part of her research, Adler-Nissen quotes the position of civil servants that Denmark probably is 'the best euro country that never was'.[71]

[70] Dashwood has argued for constitutional recognition within EU law of non-Euro Area Member States, and that concrete constitutional arrangements are needed for the appropriate ordering of the relationship between members and non-members of the Euro Area: see Dashwood (n 3).

[71] Adler-Nissen (n 22) 242.

# 5

# *Defence*

## I. INTRODUCTION

FOLLOWING A SUCCESSFUL referendum held in June 2022, the defence opt-out was abolished. With effect from 1 July 2022, Denmark no longer holds a special position within the area of defence cooperation. Nonetheless, a full discussion of this opt-out is undertaken in this chapter so that the comprehensive nature of the entire legal analysis of the Danish opt-outs is ensured. This has relevance not only in a historical sense, but also with a view to providing a contextual and comparative understanding of the other, and still in force, opt-outs.[1]

This chapter starts at the beginning, with the Edinburgh Decision, and leads from there to a discussion of how the opt-out has adapted to the evolution of the European integration process both in terms of its legal layout as well as its interpretation (see section II). A discussion of the opt-out's effects under EU law, as it unfolded prior to its abolition in the summer of 2022, will be found in section III. As will become apparent, that account can only be determined by engaging in a fairly in-depth interpretation of distinct aspects of the opt-out's scope, and in this respect also of its legal nature. This all feeds into providing an answer to the question of what the legal effects of the opt-out are. Naturally, the answer in this case would be in past tense.

An account of the legal framework that came into play regarding abolition of the defence opt-out is provided in section IV.

The chapter is rounded off with concluding remarks in section V.

## II. IMPACT ON THE DEFENCE OPT-OUT – FROM THE EDINBURGH DECISION TO EU TREATY LAW

Section C of the Edinburgh Decision on 'Defence Policy' reads as follows:

> The Heads of State and Government note that, in response to the invitation from the Western European Union (WEU), Denmark has become an observer to that

[1] On the defence opt-out, see, eg, P Koutrakos, 'Foreign policy between opt-outs and closer cooperation' in B de Witte, A Ott and E Vos (eds), *Between Flexibility and Disintegration. The Trajectory of Differentiation in EU Law* (Cheltenham, Edward Edgar Publishing, 2017) 405; and G Butler, 'The European Defence Union and Denmark's Defence opt-out: A Legal Appraisal' (2020) 25/1 *European Foreign Affairs Review* 117.

> organization. They also note that nothing in the Treaty on European Union commits Denmark to become a member of the WEU. Accordingly, Denmark does not participate in the elaboration and implementation of decisions and actions of the Union which have defence implications, but will not prevent the development of closer cooperation between Member States in this area.[2]

The first sentence refers to the fact that Denmark was an observer to the defence alliance, the Western European Union (WEU), which was created in 1954.[3] This is immediately followed by a reassurance from the Heads of State and Government that EU law did not require Denmark to become a member of that organisation. This is of importance, since Denmark had no intention of becoming a member of the WEU, even though the EU's common defence policy, as instituted by the Maastricht Treaty and in particular the layout of the then new Article J.4 TEU, was closely linked to the WEU.[4] Unlike the EU itself, the WEU was at the time an organisation with an operational capacity in the field of defence policy.

The first two paragraphs of Article J.4 TEU read as follows:

> 1. The common foreign and security policy shall include all questions related to the security of the Union, including the eventual framing of a common defence policy, which might in time lead to a common defence.
> 2. The Union requests the Western European Union (WEU), which is an integral part of the development of the Union, to elaborate and implement decisions and actions of the Union which have defence implications. The Council shall, in agreement with the institutions of the WEU, adopt the necessary practical arrangements.[5]

Not only did Article J.4 TEU in this way declare that the WEU formed an integral part of the development of the EU, it also linked the concrete decisions and actions of the EU to the WEU by prescribing that the Union was to request the WEU to 'elaborate and implement' decisions and actions of the Union with defence implications.

It was thus clear that the Maastricht Treaty designated the WEU as the organisation through which the innovation of a formal EU security and defence policy was channelled. It follows from the first part of Section C of the

[2] Denmark and the Treaty on European Union [1992] OJ C348/1.

[3] In 1948, Belgium, France, Luxembourg, the Netherlands and the UK signed the Treaty of Brussels creating the Western Union for the defence of Western Europe and with a common defence structure established in Fontainebleau, France. The Brussels Treaty was revised considerably in 1954 and the Western Union was transformed into the Western European Union (WEU), see at www.shape.nato.int/page214845116. For general discussion of the WEU, see R Haslach, 'The Western European Union: a defence organisation in search of a new role' (1991) *Europe* 17; W van Eekelen, 'The WEU is a crossroads institution' (1990) 23(3) *International Defense Review*; P Schmidt, 'The Western European Union in the 1990s: Searching for a Role' (Washington, DC, 6 May 1993) Strategic Outreach Roundtable Paper and Conference Report; S Rohan, *The Western European Union, International Politics Between Alliance and Integration* (Abingdon, Routledge, 2014).

[4] See the discussion of the Danish memorandum 'Denmark in Europe', ch 2, section IV.

[5] Treaty on European Union [1992] OJ C191/01.

Edinburgh Decision that no legal obligation for Denmark to join the WEU could be deduced from these provisions of Article J.4 TEU.[6]

The second half of Section C defines the opt-out per se, namely, that Denmark does not participate in the 'elaboration and implementation of actions and decisions of the Union which have defence implications'. It is formulated as constituting an accordingly legal effect derived from the prior-established Danish position vis-à-vis the WEU. Undoubtedly, this formulation is due to the above-mentioned fact that the WEU was entrusted with the tasks of elaboration and implementation of the Union's actions. The wording of the opt-out is thus closely modelled on the wording of Article J.4 TEU.

During the years that followed, the Danish opt-out was invoked in relation to eight legal acts adopted (or foreseen as to be adopted) by the Council pursuant to Article J.4(2) TEU.[7] At the time, legislation within this field was mostly done by way of a two-tier approach: adoption by the Council of a measure on the substance pursuant to Article J.3 TEU; followed by the adoption by the Council of a separate measure pursuant to Article J.4 TEU with the aim of implementing the former. The opt-out was invoked in relation to the 'implementing' measure, with an exception in the case of the 1996 Joint Action on anti-personnel landmines, in which instance the opt-out was invoked in relation to the main measure adopted pursuant to Article J.3 TEU by way of a reference to an anticipated follow-up measure pursuant to Article J.4 TEU. The Danish statement reads (in part) 'The Danish Government has decided that Denmark will not participate in future Council decisions on follow-up to the common action on anti-personnel landmines based on Article J.4.2. of the Treaty on European Union.'[8]

The substance of the initiatives concerned varied: for example, one related to the Great Lakes Region in Africa and foresaw the use of military means;[9] another related to initiatives to assist Albania with police matters, which did not imply military means.[10] However, at the time, such differences were of no importance in relation to the Danish opt-out. The opt-out was in all instances invoked against the background that Article J.4 formed the legal basis for the measures, and the reference in Article J.4 to the WEU, to which Denmark was

[6] The legal reading instituted by the Member States in the Edinburgh Decision seams not to have been contested by scholars.

[7] See note produced by the Danish thinktank Tænketanken Europa, 'Notat 3 November 2019'.

[8] Joint Action 96/588/CFSP of 1 October 1996 adopted by the Council on the basis of Article J.3 of the Treaty on European Union on anti-personnel landmines [1996] OJ L260/1.

[9] The implementing measures to which the opt-out applied was Council Decision 96/670/CFSP of 22 November 1996 adopted on the basis of Article J.4(2) Treaty on European Union on the elaboration and implementation of a Joint Action by the Union in the Great Lakes Region [1996] OJ L312/3.

[10] First, Council Decision 98/547/CFSP of 22 September 1998 adopted on the basis of Article J.4(2) of the Treaty on European Union on the study of the feasibility of international police operations to assist the Albanian authorities [1998] OJ L263/1; second, Council Decision 1999/190/CFSP of 9 March 1999 adopted on the basis of Article J.4(2) of the Treaty on European Union on the implementation of the joint action concerning a contribution by the European Union to the re-establishment of a viable police force in Albania [1999] OJ L63/3.

not a party, clearly seems to have been decisive. Butler claims that 'the defence opt-out has never been interpretated as to mean civilian operations (including those involving police forces) come within the scope of the defence opt-out'.[11] That is true in the sense that no interpretation took place at all at the time of the Maastricht Treaty, but the Albanian example cited above shows that the opt-out was indeed invoked in relation to a civilian police mission.

It was, at this time, left to Denmark to initiate the application of the opt-out. A testimony to this is that the opt-out generally was invoked through a statement by Denmark given in relation to the relevant measure. With a few individual variations, the statement followed the wording as issued regarding the Council Decision on the Great Lakes Region:

> In accordance with Section C of the Decision adopted at the European Council held in Edinburgh on 11 and 12 December 1992, Denmark does not participate in the elaboration and the implementation of decisions and actions of the Union which have defence implications.
>
> The Danish Government has decided that Denmark does not participate in the Council Decision requesting the WEU to elaborate and implement the action of the Union in the Great Lakes Region.
>
> In accordance with the Edinburgh decision Denmark will not prevent the development of closer cooperation between Member States in this area. Accordingly, the position indicated does not prevent the adoption of the Council Decision.[12]

The statement clarifies that not only did Denmark not participate in the elaboration and implementation of the measure (that was, as it may be recalled, left to the WEU), but also that Denmark would not participate in the measure as such. This implied that Denmark did not participate in its adaptation by the Council, an issue that was not explicitly regulated by the provision in the Edinburgh Decision. What the Edinburgh Decision did regulate, however, was a commitment by Denmark not to prevent closer cooperation by the other Member States. By recalling that and combining it with an 'accordingly' observation that the Danish position would not prevent the adoption of the measure at hand, a derogation for Denmark from the otherwise prescribed unanimity for the adaptation of the measure, in accordance with then Articles J.8(2) and J.4(3) TEU, was effectively instituted.

Interestingly, it is suggested that Denmark exercised a choice in this regard. This may well have to do with the wording of the opt-out as discussed above. However, it seems to be a rather obvious choice given that Denmark could not elaborate on and implement the decision; so why participate in its adoption? More decisive is the fact that in the Memorandum 'Denmark in Europe', a clear intention was expressed to ensure that Denmark did not participate in the so-called defence policy dimension of the Union, which involved membership of

[11] Butler (n 1) 134.
[12] Council Decision 96/670/CFSP (n 9).

WEU – as one element – and that Denmark should not participate in 'a common defence policy or a common defence' of the Union as the other element.[13] Rather than being paranoid,[14] the step taken by the Danish Government seems to be a way of ensuring that the intended scope of the opt-out was honoured.

Whereas the opt-out was consistently invoked by Denmark in relation to all legal acts with a legal basis in Article J.4, Denmark never invoked it in relation to security and defence matters being addressed in declarations and conclusions of the Union. The interpretation was clear from the outset: the opt-out related only to formally adopted legal measures.

One particular aspect of conduct had been explicitly addressed in Edinburgh. During the negotiations on the opt-out, Denmark had agreed to renounce its right according to the Treaties to exercise the rotating Council Presidency of the Union on matters related to the opt-out. This is reflected in the Second Declaration of the European Council, 'Declaration on Defence', which forms part of the Edinburgh Agreement.[15] The Danish pledge became operative during the Danish EU Presidency in 2002, when Denmark did not exercise the Presidency of the Council, including presiding over various Working Groups, within the field of the Union's security and defence cooperation. Instead, the duty was handed to Greece, which would occupy the next Presidency. As will be explored in section III.B, the Lisbon Treaty introduced a number of changes, including one to the effect that the commitment of Denmark to renounce its right to exercise the Presidency of the Union on matters falling within the scope of the opt-out became obsolete, as it was no longer a task that fell to the rotating Presidency. The Danish Minister of Defence has always participated in Council meetings, but the Minister would not take the floor on matters falling within the scope of the opt-out. This approach also continued during the time of the Lisbon Treaty.[16]

During the application of the Maastricht Treaty, the defence opt-out was solely regulated by Section C of the Edinburgh Decision. The changes to the Treaties introduced by the Amsterdam Treaty brought an end to that. Henceforward, the opt-out would find its primary legal basis within EU law.

## III. THE DEFENCE OPT-OUT AS PART OF EU LAW

### A. Impact on the Defence Opt-Out Following the Amsterdam Treaty

The Amsterdam Treaty introduced various changes to the treaty provisions on the EU's Common Foreign and Security Policy (CFSP), including the special

[13] 'Denmark in Europe', Part 2; Markedsudvalget 1992-93, MKU Alm. del bilag 70, part A.

[14] RA Wessel, *The European Union's Foreign and Security Policy. A legal Institutional Perspective* (The Hague, Kluwer Law International, 1999) 140.

[15] See ch 2, sections VI.C and VII.A.ii.

[16] Reply to parliamentary question: EUU Alm del (Europaudvalget 2021-22, L 193 – Bilag 3) – svar på spørgsmål 109.

provisions on defence cooperation.[17] Generally, the wording concerning a potential common defence was strengthened by changing it from an '*eventual* framing of a common defence policy, which might in time lead to a common defence'[18] to 'the *progressive* framing of a common defence policy, ... which might lead to a common defence'.[19] Also, the EU was no longer to send requests to the WEU but instead was to avail itself of that organisation with a view to elaborating and implementing decisions and actions of the Union that had defence implications.[20]

It is worth recalling in this respect that the issue of the emergence of EU common defence capabilities was a main driver behind the Danish defence opt-out, as articulated in the Danish Memorandum of 1992.[21]

At the same time, the Amsterdam Treaty elaborated on and clarified the issues being addressed by the EU within this field of cooperation. The then new Article 17(2) TEU thus read 'Questions referred to in this Article shall include humanitarian and rescue tasks, peacekeeping tasks and tasks of combat forces in crisis management, including peace-making.' The list represents the so-called 'Petersberg tasks'.[22]

The Danish Government had participated in the IGC prior to the Amsterdam Treaty on the basis of a negotiation mandate endorsed by the Danish Parliament.[23] On this basis, the Danish position was to ensure that all four opt-outs as defined in the Edinburgh Decision maintained their legal effects, despite changes introduced by the Amsterdam Treaty within the respective fields of cooperation. Provided that the Danish Government got reassurance that this was the case, it would not raise any objections to changes in the Treaty provisions, in accordance with the pledge made in the Edinburgh Agreement to that effect.

The assessment made on the Danish side was that the nature of the Treaty changes introduced within the field of EU's security and defence cooperation did necessitate clarification of the Danish position on non-participation as otherwise laid out in the Edinburgh Decision.[24] The Danish assessment was endorsed by the IGC, and the solution was the introduction of provisions to this effect within EU primary law. In this way, Denmark could rest reassured that the defence opt-out was maintained.

[17] CSDP in the current TEU.

[18] Art J.4 TEU.

[19] Then Art 117(1) TEU.

[20] Then Art 17(3) TEU.

[21] See ch 2, section IV.

[22] See *Glossary of Summaries*, EUR-Lex. In the current treaty the tasks are defined in Art 43(1) TEU.

[23] The Government's negotiation mandate was entitled 'Det Åbne Europe' (The Open Europe) and was endorsed by the Danish Parliament, see Folketingstidende 1995–96, Forhandlingerne, col 1040.

[24] Explanatory Notes to Bill L1 of 26 March 1998 on Danish ratification of the Amsterdam Treaty, Folketingstidende 1997-98, 2. Saml, L1, col 247.

A side-effect of the opt-out's being lifted into the EU treaty regime was that previous criticism by scholars of the fact that the special Danish position, as introduced by the Edinburgh Decision, had not been subject to ratification by the EU Member States was no longer an issue, given that all Member States ratified the Danish special position as part of the Amsterdam Treaty.[25]

The Amsterdam Treaty introduced a new Protocol, annexed to the TEC and to the TEU, bearing the title 'The Protocol on the Position of Denmark'.[26] The Protocol reflected a combined request from Denmark that not only related to the defence opt-out but also included a request for provisions to maintain the Danish position in relation to the opt-out within the AFSJ, in light of more ground-breaking changes made by the Amsterdam Treaty in that field. Part I of the Protocol regulated Denmark's position within the AFSJ;[27] part III covered Denmark's abolition of the opt-outs.

Part II, Article 6 regulated the defence opt-out. In the original version from the Amsterdam Treaty, it read as follows:

> With regard to measures adopted by the Council in the field of Articles 13(1) and 17 of the Treaty on European Union, Denmark does not participate in the elaboration and the implementation of decisions and actions of the Union which have defence implications, but will not prevent the development of closer cooperation between Member States in this area. Therefore Denmark shall not participate in their adoption. Denmark shall not be obliged to contribute to the financing of operational expenditure arising from such measures.[28]

The first sentence brought clarity to the special Danish position within defence cooperation by repeating the wording from the Edinburgh Decision that Denmark 'does not participate in the elaboration and the implementation of decisions and actions of the Union which have defence implications', while leaving out any reference to the WEU. As discussed in section II, the wording of the Edinburgh Decision could be read as making the Danish position within the Union dependent on the Danish position regarding the WEU. That would, however, be an incorrect interpretation, which the reformulation prevented.

The formulation from the Edinburgh Decision that Denmark would not prevent the development of closer cooperation between Member States in this area was duly maintained in Article 6, but the sentence following was new. It explicitly clarifies that not only did Denmark not 'elaborate and implement' the measures concerned, but also that Denmark did not participate in their *adoption* either. It implies that Denmark did not form part of otherwise prescribed decision-making procedures.[29] The Edinburgh Decision falls short of explicitly

[25] On that criticism, see ch 2.

[26] Treaty of Amsterdam amending the Treaty on European Union, the Treaties establishing the European Communities and certain related acts [1997] OJ C340/1.

[27] For a discussion of the matters falling within the AFSJ, see ch 6.

[28] Treaty of Amsterdam (n 26).

[29] That included the then new Art 23(1) TEU on abstention; in the current treaty it is Art 31(1) TEU.

saying the same, which undoubtably was to do with the fact that the wording in the Edinburgh Decision merely repeated that of Article J.4. Non-participation of Denmark in the adoption stage was, however, only a natural consequence of the opt-out; hence the use of the word 'therefore' in the Protocol. Moreover, the explicit formulation in the Protocol did not represent a novelty as regards the way in which Denmark had interpreted the scope of the opt-out pursuant to the Edinburgh Decision in light of the Danish Memorandum.[30]

The last sentence of Article 6 was also new. It clarified that Denmark was also exempt from financing aspects. It was a general exemption in its own right; it did not depend on otherwise prescribed procedures as laid out in the then Article 28(3) TEU, referring to Article 23(1) TEU.[31] This clarification was also only a natural consequence of the effects of the special Danish position.

The new Article 17(3) TEU, as drafted by the Amsterdam Treaty, maintained the formulation from the previous Article J.4 of 'decisions and actions' of the Union that have defence implications. The same wording was repeated in Article 6 of the Protocol, which, as mentioned above, repeated the wording of the Edinburgh Decision. At the beginning of Article 6, however, the term 'measures' was used. This has been read as expressing a clear intention not to limit, in a narrow and literal sense, the scope of the opt-out to 'decisions and actions' only, but instead to include all qualifying legal acts, irrespective of whether they were designated as a decision or as an action.[32]

Article 6 of the Protocol referred not only to the then Article 17 but also to Article 13(1) TEU, which was concerned with the European Council, and determined that it 'shall define the principles of and general guidelines for the common foreign and security policy, including for matters with defence implications'. Generally, this task would be fulfilled by the European Council's adoption of declarations or conclusions of a non-legal character. Nevertheless, the practice established prior to the Amsterdam Treaty, that only legal measures were covered by the defence opt-out and not declarations, conclusions, etc, would continue to be applied. This was in line with a clear Danish understanding that the opt-out had been kept unchanged after the adoption of the Amsterdam Treaty.[33] Therefore, the crucial point seems to be that Article 6 referred to measures, decisions and actions adopted by 'the Council'. On this basis, it is assumed that the reference to Article 13(1) TEU was inserted in Article 6 so as to cater for the exceptional situation when the European Council acts as 'the Council' and in such capacity adopts legal acts.

[30] See the discussion in section II.

[31] In the current Treaty it is Art 41(2) TEU that makes reference to Art 31(1) TEU.

[32] It is only by the later Lisbon Treaty that a streamlining of the various instruments within the CFSP including the ESDP (joint actions, common positions, decisions, etc) is introduced by providing for only one type – decisions. See Arts 26 and 31(1) TEU.

[33] See the written presentation by the Danish Foreign Minister of Bill L1 of 26 March 1998 on Danish ratification of the Amsterdam Treaty, Folketingstidende 1997-98, 2. Saml, L1.

Koutrakos has, on the other hand, suggested that the scope of the opt-out included 'general guidelines' adopted by the European Council.[34] Such a definition would have meant an arguably unintended expansion of the scope of the opt-out to cover non-legally binding measures too.

Shortly after the entry into force of the Amsterdam Treaty, it turned out that Articles 14 and 15 TEU formed the legal basis for concrete legal acts within the European Security and Defence Policy (ESDP) adopted by the Council, not the articles mentioned in the Danish Protocol. The interpretation of Article 6 of the Danish Protocol followed suit, that is the opt-out was consequently invoked in relation to relevant legal acts based on Articles 14 and 15 TEU. This is judged not to constitute a violation of the provisions of Article 6, as the drafters cleverly had used the terminology of 'in the field of' and not 'pursuant to' Articles 13(1) and 17, thus leaving room for the inclusion of legal acts adopted with Articles 14 or 15 TEU as their legal bases.

Another development proved of importance to the interpretation of the opt-out. Already prior to the entering into force of the Amsterdam Treaty on 1 May 1999, the policy debate on the EUs 'progressive framing of a common defence policy … [r]einforcing the European identity and its independence in order to promote peace, security and progress in Europe and in the world'[35] not only gained momentum but also resulted in a changed focus for its operational capacity. Testimony to this effect is found in the Presidency Conclusion from the meeting of the European Council in December 1998, where the European Council welcomed

> the new impetus given to the debate on a common European policy on security and defence. The European Council considers that in order for the European Union to be in a position to play its full role on the international stage, the CFSP must be backed by credible operational capabilities.[36]

In the communiqué from the North Atlantic Treaty Organization (NATO) Summit the following spring, the alliance committed itself to providing access to its capabilities and common assets for use in EU-led operations.[37] This seems to be the first such commitment to the EU from NATO.

Following the entry into force of the Amsterdam Treaty, the European Council met in Cologne in June 1999 and adopted a Declaration that defined the main objectives of what was referred to as 'the European Security and Defence Policy'. Furthermore, the EU leaders were to

> launch a new step in the construction of the European Union. To this end we task the General Affairs Council to prepare the conditions and the measures necessary to achieve these objectives, including the definition of the modalities for the inclusion

[34] Koutrakos (n 1) 407.
[35] Treaty of Amsterdam (n 26) recital 3.
[36] Presidency Conclusion, Vienna European Council, 11 and 12 December 1998, para 76.
[37] The Washington Summit Communiqué, 24 April 1999, para 10.

> of those functions of the WEU which will be necessary for the EU to fulfil its new responsibilities in the area of the Petersberg tasks.[38]

A follow-up was carried out later that same year at the Helsinki European Council, where it was agreed to build up the military capabilities necessary for EU-led military operations.[39]

The hastily emerging political developments heralded a significantly less prominent role for the WEU than otherwise prescribed in the Amsterdam Treaty, which had kept, as its default provisions, the same leading role for the WEU as instituted by the Maastricht Treaty. In the subsequent Nice Treaty, which was signed in February 2001 and entered into force two years later, the references to the WEU, including the provision on the EU's availing itself of that organisation in operational matters, were scrapped altogether from Article 17 TEU. Over the coming years, a number of the operational activities of the WEU were gradually transferred to the EU or simply ceased to be operational.[40] The WEU lived on, albeit with an amputated role, until its formal dissolution by June 2011. The EU's cooperation with NATO, on the other hand, became ever closer over the same period.

These developments influenced the interpretation of the Danish defence opt-out as laid out in the Protocol on the Position of Denmark. This is not to imply, however, that the opt-out lost its *raison d'être* just because the WEU did. As already discussed, the opt-out was directed not only towards the WEU per se but also towards the defence policy dimension that included the Union's foreign and security policy.

The fact that the WEU was no longer called upon by default to elaborate and implement measures adopted by the Council contributed to a change in the approach to the applicability of the defence opt-out. The previous automatic invocation of the opt-out, depending solely on the legal basis for a measure by the Council, which was the then Article J.4 TEU, and the compulsory role of the WEU, was replaced by an analysis of the content of each concrete measure. Although the legal base continued to play a crucial role, the prescribed 'defence implication' of a measure was to become instrumental.[41] From a legal point of view, this amended approach is deemed to be correct and necessary, with the aim of making sure that the scope of the opt-out would not go beyond its defined limits.

Before embarking on the interpretation of the opt-out's applicability, and consequently its effects as part of EU law (see section III.C), the further evolution of the layout of the opt-out that followed after the Amsterdam Treaty will be accounted for in section III.B.

[38] European Council Declaration on Strengthening the Common European Policy on Security and Defence, Annex III to the Presidency Conclusions, Cologne European Council, 3 and 4 June 1999.

[39] Known as the Helsinki Headline Goals.

[40] Bulletin 75 (Polish Institute of International Affairs, 2010).

[41] C Thorning, 'Forsvarsforbeholdet' in BE Olsen and KE Sørensen (eds), *EU-retten i Danmark* (Copenhagen, Jurist- og Økonomforbundets Forlag, 2018) 160.

### B. Impact on the Defence Opt-Out Following the Lisbon Treaty

The IGC on the Nice Treaty that followed rather quickly after the entry into force of the Amsterdam Treaty did not lead to any changes to the wording of the Danish defence opt-out as set out in the Protocol on the Position of Denmark. The Lisbon Treaty of 2008, on the other hand, introduced certain drafting changes to the Protocol provision as a consequence of amendments to and innovations in the Treaties made by the Lisbon Treaty.

One major feature of the Lisbon Treaty was the removal of the pillar structure as it had been known since the Maastricht Treaty. However, the area of the CFSP, to a large extent, maintained its intergovernmental characteristics from the old second-pillar structure.[42] An integral part of the CFSP is the ESDP, which the Lisbon Treaty renamed the Common Security and Defence Policy (CSDP). The Lisbon Treaty did introduce a number of changes with a view to strengthening cooperation within the CFSP, including in the CSDP, notably by enlarging the role of the High Representative and by the introduction of the European External Action Service (EEAS) and some new rules on speedy financing.[43] A prominent innovation was the dedicated scheme for enhanced cooperation, entitled Permanent Structured Cooperation (PESCO).[44]

The approach of the Danish side all along, during the lengthy processes of negotiation that ultimately led to the Lisbon Treaty, after the fall of the draft Constitutional Treaty, was unchanged from the position held at the IGC prior to the Amsterdam Treaty, namely, to ensure that the four Danish opt-outs, including on defence, were maintained, irrespective of the introduction of various Treaty changes.[45] On that basis, adaptations of the Protocol text were agreed.

In its updated version, the Danish defence opt-out was set out in Part II, Article 5 of Protocol No 22 on the Position of Denmark, as follows:[46]

> With regard to measures adopted by the Council pursuant to Article 26(1), Article 42 and Articles 43 to 46 of the Treaty on European Union, Denmark does not participate

[42] See Declarations 13 and 14 annexed to the Final Act of the IGC that adopted the Lisbon Treaty [2016] OJ C202/1; Arts 2(4), 24(1) and 40 TEU and Art 275 TFEU. For a critical analysis of the continuous intergovernmental character of the CFSP, see RA Wessel, 'Integration and Constitutionalisation in EU Foreign and Security Policy' in R Schütze (ed), *Globalisation and Governance: International Problems, European Solutions* (Cambridge, Cambridge University Press, 2018) 339.

[43] Nonetheless, the rules remain that expenditure originating from CSDP measures that have military or defence implications cannot be charged to the EU budget.

[44] Art 46 TEU and Protocol No 10 on permanent structured cooperation established by Article 42 of the Treaty on European Union. See, for an analysis of PESCO, among many contributions, eg, H Bribosia, 'Les nouvelles formes de flexibilité en matière de défense' in Amato, Bribosia and De Witte (eds), *Genesis and Destiny of the European Constitution* (Brussels, Bruylants 2007) 835; M Cremona, 'Enhanced cooperation and the common foreign and security and defence policy' (2009) EUI Working Papers LAW 2009/21; S Blockmans and DM Crosson, 'Differentiated integration within PESCO – clusters and convergence in EU defence' (2019) CEPS Research Report 2019/04. See also ch 7 for a discussion of PESCO as an instrument of differentiated integration.

[45] Udenrigsministeriet, 'Redegørelse til Folketinget om Lissabon-Traktaten' (2008).

[46] The whole of Protocol 22 remains intact, even though Denmark has exercised the option in Art 7 to no longer avail itself of the section on defence (see section IV); hence the subsequent discussion of

> in the elaboration and the implementation of decisions and actions of the Union which have defence implications. Therefore Denmark shall not participate in their adoption. Denmark will not prevent the other Member States from further developing their cooperation in this area. Denmark shall not be obliged to contribute to the financing of operational expenditure arising from such measures, nor to make military capabilities available to the Union.
>
> The unanimity of the members of the Council, with the exception of the representative of the government of Denmark, shall be necessary for the acts of the Council which must be adopted unanimously.
>
> For the purposes of this Article, a qualified majority shall be defined in accordance with Article 238(3) of the Treaty on the Functioning of the European Union.[47]

What is immediately apparent is the rectification of the previous ambiguity concerning the legal basis within the Treaty for measures that may fall within the scope of the opt-out. This is done in two ways. First, by adapting the cited articles to the current legal bases of the TEU: Article 26(1), which replaced the formerly cited Article 13(1), and Articles 42 and 43, which replaced the formerly cited Article 17; followed by the addition of the remaining articles of chapter 2, section 2 of the TEU on the CSDP. Second, the provision on the defence opt-out has been redrafted by replacing the wording 'in the field of' with 'pursuant to' in relation to the cited Treaty provisions. Combined, these adaptations clarify that the applicability of the opt-out, as a main rule, was limited to measures with defence implications adopted by the Council pursuant to the cited articles of the TEU only.

The aspect of financing continues to be regulated by explicit wording to ensure that Denmark would not be obligated to contribute to the financing of general expenditure related to the above-mentioned measures. This also pre-empts the situation where the Council adopts measures to administer the common costs outside of the EU budget, which, incidentally, the Council did by its adoption of the Athena Mechanism in 2011.[48] The explicit wording of the opt-out on financing makes it clear that Denmark could not take part in such measures, irrespective of whether they had a legal basis squarely within the CSDP section of the TEU.

Furthermore, the obligation for Member States provided for by Article 42(3) TEU to make military capabilities available to the Union is mirrored by the formulation inserted within the opt-out to make it clear that this obligation does

the wording is in the present tense. The prescribed legal position on defence no longer has any legal effects and the discussion thereof in section III.C is therefore in past tense.

[47] Protocol No 22 on the Position of Denmark [2012] OJ C326/299. The Protocol is annexed to the TEU and the TFEU. The changes introduced by the Lisbon Treaty to the other provisions of Protocol 22 are presented and analysed in ch 6 on the AFSJ opt-out.

[48] Council Decision 2011/871/CFSP of 19 December 2011 establishing a mechanism to administer the financing of the common costs of European Union operations having military or defence implications (Athena) [2011] OJ L343/35, which later was replaced, see text to n 89.

not apply to Denmark.[49] This is not a widening of the scope of the opt-out; on the contrary, it is arguably part of its very essence, which all along had been to ensure that Denmark did not take part in the defence dimension of the Union.

Article 42(7) TEU contains an obligation to aid and assist a Member State that is the victim of armed aggression on its territory. It is legally binding upon each Member State and constitutes a mutual obligation between the Member States. It is unique in the sense that it does not provide any role to the EU institutions, neither does it provide for any procedures to be followed by the Member States. It is therefore for the Member States to determine how the provision is to be implemented in a given case.[50]

In the subsequent Protocol to the treaties on concerns raised by Ireland vis-à-vis certain aspects of the Treaty of Lisbon,[51] the scope of Article 42(7) is clarified. Article 3 of the said Protocol reads:

> It will be for Member States – including Ireland, acting in a spirit of solidarity and without prejudice to its traditional policy of military neutrality – to determine the nature of aid or assistance to be provided to a Member State which is the object of a terrorist attack or the victim of armed aggression on its territory.

Following the terror attacks in Paris in November 2015, and at France's request, the article was invoked. At the November 2015 Council meeting, the Ministers of Defence expressed their 'unanimous and full support for France and their readiness to provide all the necessary aid and assistance'.[52] The High Representative noted that no formal decision or conclusion by the Council was required to implement Article 42(7) TEU.

Given these particularities of Article 42(7), and even though no explicit exemption was made within the definition of the scope of the opt-out undertaken in Article 5 of Protocol No 22, it is held that the provision, nonetheless, fell outside the opt-out's scope and therefore always has been binding upon Denmark. Accordingly, Denmark did form part of the unanimous support to France in 2015.

The final paragraphs of Article 5 are innovations. They are clarifications of a 'housekeeping' nature, related to the core provision that Denmark did not participate in the adoption of the relevant measures. It is explicitly laid out that, when adopting acts of the Council by unanimity or, when relevant, by qualified majority voting (QMV), Denmark – obviously – should be disregarded in the corresponding adoption procedures.

[49] The exact scope of the obligation in Art 42(3) should be seen in light of the fact that it is left to each Member State to decide on its contribution with military means. In the case of Denmark, however, no contribution at all was possible.

[50] This stands in contrast to the solidarity clause entailed in Art 222 TFEU. See text to nn 71–72.

[51] Protocol No 38 to the Treaty on European Union and to the Treaty on the Functioning of the European Union 'on the concerns of the Irish people on the Treaty of Lisbon' [2013] OJ L60/130, adopted by the IGC convened to conclude the Accession Treaty of Croatia in 2012.

[52] Document 14120/15 on the outcome of the Council meeting 16–17 November 2015, 6, available at www.concilium.europa.eu.

## C. The Effects of the Defence Opt-Out under EU Law

The opt-out essentially regulated two distinct scenarios. One related to the elaboration and adoption of concrete measures, which notably concerned concrete CSDP missions established by the adoption of Council Decisions. The other one related to implementation aspects thereof. The latter necessarily had repercussions for Denmark's participation within certain institutional and cooperation structures as well. It also affected Denmark's ability to participate in the Union's international agreements relating to CSDP measures falling within the scope of the opt-out. This subsection will address each of the two scenarios in turn.

In section III.A, it was established that ever since the opt-out became part of EU Treaty law in 1999, legal analysis on a case-by-case basis would determine whether or not the opt-out was applicable. The subsections following will shed light on various elements forming part of that analysis, including by drawing on the further provision in the opt-out stating that Denmark did not contribute financially to the operational expenditure arising from such measures.

With that said, it is clear that no particular interpretation was needed to establish that the scope of the opt-out included the provision in Article 42(2) TEU on the eventual creation of a common European defence. The provision requires that a decision to establish a common defence should be taken in accordance with the respective constitutional requirements of the Member States. In the case of Denmark, an abolition of the opt-out would have been a precondition for Denmark even to embark on this. Also, the opt-out explicitly exempted Denmark from providing military capabilities available to the Union, as foreseen in Article 42(3) TEU. Arguably, this would have been the case even without explicit reference, given the fact that such contributions ensure the Union's ability to implement its operations. These considerations had applied in relation to EU's battle groups that were established by the European Union Military Staff (EUMS) in 2004. Member States may participate on a voluntary basis, which all but Malta and Denmark have done over the years. In the case of Denmark, the opt-out clearly prevented any Danish contribution.

Given that the Danish defence opt-out formed an integral part of primary EU law, the interpretation of its scope was not an issue for Denmark alone[53] but a joint effort for the Council. One should, however, bear in mind the observation of Piris that the task of ensuring proper implementation of CFSP decisions is 'left to the goodwill of Member States, to their obligation of loyalty and thus to mutual peer pressure'.[54] In practice, the interpretation came into existence in consultations between Denmark and the Council Legal Service, with Denmark often taking a proactive role.[55]

[53] The situation was de facto different prior to the Amsterdam Treaty. See the discussion in section II.

[54] J-C Piris, *The Lisbon Treaty: A Legal and Political Analysis* (Cambridge, Cambridge University Press, 2010) 264.

[55] Butler (n 1) 128.

Notwithstanding certain competences on jurisdiction to review Member States' compliance with Article 40 TEU on the procedures and the extent of the powers of the EU institutions, as well as to rule on the legality of decisions on restrictive measures against natural or legal persons, in general, the CJEU is not competent on matters falling within the CFSP, see Article 24(1) TEU and Article 275 TFEU.[56] There is no jurisprudence on the defence opt-out from the CJEU. In his discussion of the defence opt-out, Butler remarks that the CJEU is not prevented from interpreting protocols annexed to the EU Treaties.[57] It would seem, however, to be problematic for the Court to interpret the substance of the defence opt-out as laid out in the Protocol on the Position of Denmark without at the same time interpreting the CSDP cooperation as laid out in the TEU, which the Court – at least in principle – cannot do.

### *i. Effects of the Defence Opt-Out – Elaboration and Adoption of Measures*

Advantageously, the legal method applied to determine the applicability of the opt-out would have included the examination of three elements, all of which in general should have been present for the opt-out to be applicable: the measure should be a formal legal act; it should have a legal basis as listed within the opt-out's definition; and, finally, 'defence implications' would be required as regards the measure concerned.[58]

In what follows, concrete examples are utilised to illustrate cases where the opt-out has been applicable.[59] Certain cases that have fallen outside the scope of the opt-out are discussed as well to illustrate the limitations on the scope of the opt-out's application.

First, the opt-out applied only to legal measures. Lifting of the opt-out from the Edinburgh Decision to a protocol within EU primary law caused no change to the prior reading, according to which the opt-out was considered applicable to formally adopted legal acts but not to initiatives of an essentially political nature in the form of declarations, conclusions, etc. Denmark thus took part in such policy initiatives, irrespective of whether they addressed matters with 'defence implications'.[60] Nonetheless, this did not necessarily imply that the

[56] Yet on the increasing role of the Court in matters of CFSP, see, among many contributions, eg RA Wessel, 'Legality in EU Common Foreign and Security Policy: The Choice of the Appropriate Legal Basis' in C Kilpatrick and J Scott (eds), *Contemporary Challenges to EU Legality* (Oxford, Oxford University Press, 2021) 71; C Hillion and RA Wessel, 'The Good, the Bad and the Ugly: Three Levels of Judicial Control over the CFSP' in S Blockmans and P Koutrakos (eds), *Research Handbook on EU Common Foreign and Security Policy* (Cheltenham, Edward Elgar Publishing, 2018) 65.

[57] Butler (n 1) 129, fn 39.

[58] Thorning (n 41) 161–64.

[59] For an overview of all CSDP missions, see 'EU Missions and Operations' on the webpage of the EEAS at www.eeas/europa.eu. A comprehensive overview of the 23 of them for the period 2003–09 is to be found in Piris (n 54) 269–73, box 31.

[60] As a prominent example, Denmark was a party to the Declaration on ESDP adopted by the European Council in Cologne in 1999; see section III.A.

opt-out had no bearing in these situations. Denmark's political leverage and political status within the EU and among partners were likely impacted by the fact that the defence opt-out prevented Denmark from taking part in concrete follow-up activities of CSDP policy initiatives with defence implications that otherwise had the support of Denmark.

Second, although the legal basis for a proposed measure of the Union did not in itself trigger the applicability of the opt-out, as had been the case prior to the introduction of Protocol No 22, the legal basis still formed an essential element when assessing whether the opt-out would be applicable. The wording of Article 5 of Protocol No 22 limits the measures potentially falling within its scope to those with a legal basis in the listed articles of the TEU. The further requirement was the qualitative one on 'defence implications'. That meant that a legal act adopted pursuant to another legal basis within the Treaties, as a general rule, fell outside the scope of the opt-out, irrespective of whether that legal act, one way or the other, had a link to CSDP matters and policies with defence implications.

As an example, this was the case in relation to the so-called procurement directives from 2004 and the subsequent specific directive of 2009 within the field of defence and security that amended the two first directives.[61] These directives all had legal bases within the TFEU; consequently, the Danish defence opt-out did not apply.

As a follow-up to the Union's 2016 global strategy on foreign and security policy of the EU, the Commission issued a communication on the launching of the European Defence Fund (EDF).[62] As an implementing element, the European Defence Industrial Development Programme (EDIDP) was established by the adoption of a Regulation in 2018.[63] In April 2021, the EDIDP Regulation was repealed and replaced by a new Regulation establishing the EDF.[64] Both Regulations were based on Article 173 TFEU on industrial policies, and the recent Regulation also on a number of Articles within Title XIX of the TFEU. Even though these legal acts entail elements to underpin the Union's CSDP policies in general, from a legal point of view they remain non-CSDP legal acts; hence the Danish defence opt-out was not applicable. Denmark has

[61] Directive 2009/81/EC of the European Parliament and of the Council of 13 July 2009 on the coordination of procedures for the award of certain works contracts, supply contracts and service contracts by contracting authorities or entities in the fields of defence and security, and amending Directives 2004/17/EC and 2004/18/EC [2009] OJ L216/76. Directive 2004/18/EC has since been repealed by Directive 2014/24/EU of the European Parliament and of the Council of 26 February 2014 on public procurement and repealing Directive 2004/18/EC [2014] OJ L94/65.

[62] Com(2017)295 final.

[63] Regulation (EU) 2018/1092 of 18 July 2018 of the European Parliament and of the Council establishing the European Defence Industrial Development Programme aiming at supporting the competitiveness and innovation capacity of the Union's defence industry [2018] OJ L200/30.

[64] Regulation (EU) 2021/697 of the European Parliament and of the Council of 29 April 2021 establishing the European Defence Fund and repealing Regulation (EU) 2018/1092 [2021] OJ 170/149.

never maintained an opt-out from the Union's industrial policies, nor from those on research and technological development, irrespective of the substance.

Another consequence of the prominence of the legal basis was that the use of military equipment in non-CSDP actions in general would fall outside the scope of the opt-out. As an illustrative example, a Danish military Challenger aircraft with a military crew has on several occasions been deployed to assist in border-patrolling operations under the Union's border agency, FRONTEX.[65] The legal nature of these operations was not CSDP but rather AFSJ. Consequently, the Danish defence opt-out was not applicable.[66] However, it would have been crucial for Denmark to monitor that the nature of such an operation in which Denmark took part did not change character, either to a CSDP mission per se or to a mission whereby the Danish aircraft effectively would participate in the implementation of CSDP measures with defence implications. In such scenarios, the defence opt-out would have become applicable, with the consequence that Denmark would have had to withdraw its aircraft.

The Lisbon Treaty introduced, in Part Five, Title VII of the TEU, the innovative 'Solidarity Clause'. The aim of the Clause is to ensure assistance from the Union and its Member States in the event that a Member State is the object of a terrorist attack or the victim of a natural or man-made disaster.[67] It is provided that in such situations, the Union shall mobilise all the instruments at its disposal, including the military resources made available by the Member States.[68]

Denmark envisaged that the defence opt-out potentially could be applicable in relation to Article 222(1) TFEU.[69] In Declaration No 48 to the Final Act of the Lisbon Treaty, the IGC noted that 'Denmark declares that Danish participation in actions or legal acts pursuant to Article 222 TFEU takes place in accordance with Part I and II of the Protocol on the position of Denmark'.[70]

Despite its legal basis within TFEU, the Solidarity Clause does indeed have a clear CSDP dimension to it.[71] Pursuant to Article 222(3) TFEU, the Council has adopted a Decision on the arrangements for the implementation of the Clause as far as the obligation on the Union is concerned.[72] This Decision explicitly clarifies what is not entirely clear from Article 222 itself, that in the event that a situation requires a CFSP or CSDP action, the Council should adopt a

[65] See as an example communication on 1 December 2021 on the homepage of the Danish Ministry of Defence at www.mfn.dk.

[66] The AFSJ opt-out is applicable but Denmark nonetheless participates in FRONTEX, albeit on special Schengen conditions; see ch 6, section III.B.i.

[67] Prior to the new provision, the Member States had adopted an ad hoc declaration of solidarity with Spain following the Madrid terror attacks in March 2004.

[68] Art 222(1) TFEU.

[69] The same applies to AFSJ. See ch 6, section III.A.

[70] Declaration No 48 concerning the Protocol on the position of Denmark [2012] OJ C326/355.

[71] Butler (n 1) 143.

[72] Council Decision 2014/415/EU of 24 June 2014 on the arrangements for the implementation by the Union of the solidarity clause [2014] OJ L192/53.

separate Decision on this aspect in accordance with the relevant provisions of the Treaties.[73] This in turn meant that the application of the defence opt-out would have been straightforward; Denmark would not participate in the elaboration, adoption or implementation of such a measure.

The third requirement built into the opt-out related to the qualification that a measure should have 'defence implications'. This would not necessarily be an easy conclusion to draw in every case. Measures under the CSDP may not have only a military character; there are also measures with a civilian character, or a combination of the two.[74] Piris rightly points out:

> In fact, the so-called 'defence policy' of the EU does not use only military forces and does not cover only activities usually described under this formulation. It uses a wide range of actors, among them soldiers, of course, but also policemen, judges, diplomats and so on ... The EU is the only international organisation having access to all of these tools and having the necessary means to deploy them abroad.[75]

Genuine military operations naturally have 'defence implications'; that is their very purpose. Consequently, measures establishing such operations all fell within the scope of the opt-out. The political motive behind an operation would be irrelevant; for example, it had no bearing on the applicability of the opt-out that an operation had a peacekeeping nature and/or aim. The essential element was whether the operation made military forces available to EU, including by placing such forces under EU command, with rules of engagement and/or similar military aspects, and at least with the potential to use force. That would constitute 'defence implications', which the opt-out had made the decisive element regardless of the context. Likewise, it would have no bearing that a military/defence mission may have underpinned other EU activities, including activities of a non-CSDP character, in which Denmark actively participated. As examples, the opt-out was applicable to the EU's military operation off the Somali coast (Atalanta);[76] operation ALTHEA in Bosnia and Herzegovina (BiH),[77] operation SOPHIA;[78] and the military operation in Libya.[79] These operations arguably underpinned a wider EU engagement that Denmark also actively supported, and the Danish non-participation may occasionally have appeared inconsistent from

[73] ibid recital 13.

[74] See Art 42 TEU.

[75] Piris (n 54) 268.

[76] Council Joint Action 2008/851/CFSP of 10 November 2008 on a European Union military operation to contribute to the deterrence, prevention and repression of acts of piracy and armed robbery off the Somali coast [2008] OJ L301/33 and later amendments.

[77] Council Joint Action 2004/570/CFSP of 12 July 2004 on the European Union military operation in Bosnia and Herzegovina [2004] OJ L252/10 and later amendments.

[78] Council Decision (CFSP) 2015/778 of 18 May 2015 n a European Union military operation in the Southern Central Mediterranean (EUNAVFOR MED) [2015] OJ L122/31 and later amendments.

[79] Council Decision 2011/210/CFSP of 1 April 2011 on a European Union military operation in support of humanitarian assistance operations in response to the crisis situation in Libya (EUFOR Libya) [2011] OJ L89/17.

a political point of view. However, from the legal angle, the scope of the opt-out was consistent.

On the other hand, the consistency implied that the opt-out was not made applicable to CSDP measures of a civilian character, as the clear assumption would be that such missions had no defence implications. As a rather obvious example, the opt-out was not applicable to the first EU rule-of-law operation, Eujust Themsis, which aimed to support the Georgian authorities in addressing challenges in the criminal justice system as well as to assist the Georgian Government in developing reforms.[80] Another example is the Aceh Monitoring Mission,[81] which concerned civilian monitoring of the implementation of various aspects of a peace agreement between the Government of Indonesia and the Free Aceh Movement (GAM), including decommissioning of weapons. Despite the substance, it did not change the civilian character of the mission as such; consequently, the opt-out did not apply.

Based on the above-mentioned example it is assumed that the use of military equipment such as military aircraft or vessels in a civilian CSDP rescue mission would also not in itself have triggered the opt-out. On the other hand, if the use of force was a potential part of the mission, the mission would have had an element of defence implications and the opt-out would have been applicable. In practice, examples of this sort would be plentiful, and the scope of the opt-out would have been determined on a case-by-case basis weighing all elements on the legal scales.

A particular issue would arise when a CSDP measure contained a combination of both military and civilian elements. While it was clear that the defence opt-out would only be applicable to the military elements, the complexity of a concrete measure may not necessarily allow for making a distinction between its civilian and military elements. If a distinction between military and civilian aspects was possible to achieve, Denmark would have participated in the civilian part of a measure but not the part with defence implications as a consequence of the opt-out. That was the case in relation to the Union's civilian–military supporting action to the African Union mission in the Darfur region of Sudan.[82] The civilian and military elements of this supporting action were clearly separated; each was regulated in different sections, with the civilian component being addressed in section II and the military component in section III. The first and last (IV) sections contained common provisions. Recital 25 referred to the Danish position, as set out in the opt-out, and qualified its impact by stating that 'Denmark does not participate in the implementation of Section III of this Joint

[80] Council Joint Action 2004/523/CFSP of 28 June 2004 on the European Union Rule of Law Mission in Georgia, EUJUST THEMIS [2004] OJ L228/21.

[81] Council Joint Action 2005/643/CFSP of 9 September 2005 on the European Union Monitoring Mission in Aceh (Indonesia) (Aceh Monitoring Mission – AMM) [2005] OJ L234/13.

[82] Council Joint Action 2005/557/CFSP of 18 July 2005 on the European Union civilian-military supporting action to the African Union mission in the Darfur region of Sudan [2005] OJ L188/46.

Action and therefore does not participate in the financing of military components of this supporting action.' The composition of the measure ensured that the opt-out was respected, while at the same time the effects of the opt-out were not extended beyond its scope.

Another example concerns the establishment of a European Union Satellite Centre (SATCEN).[83] The aim of the Centre was 'to provide early warning and crisis monitoring functions within the context of the Common Foreign and Security Policy (CFSP), and in particular of the European Security and Defence Policy (ESDP)'.[84] The Centre originally incorporated relevant features from the then existing WEU structures.[85] The activities were foreseen to be a combination of military and non-military ones. True to the standard practice in CSDP measures with defence implications, a reference was made to the Danish defence opt-out in the recitals. The fifth and final recital thus referred to the provision concerning the defence opt-out as laid out in Protocol No 22; but it continued as follows:

> This provision, however, does not exclude the participation of Denmark in the civilian activities of the Centre on the basis of a declared willingness of Denmark to contribute to covering the expenses of the Centre not having defence implications.

The operative part contained dedicated provisions on the position of Denmark, by which Denmark's participation in various activities of the Centre was regulated.[86] Among a number of transitional provisions, one related to a Danish voluntary financial contribution to related activities of WEU for the remaining budget year until the entering into action of the EU Satellite Centre.

In this way, the legal measure establishing the Centre contemplated the special position of Denmark by explicitly allowing for Denmark's participation in all civilian activities of the Centre. A logical add-on was an obligation for Denmark to contribute to the financing of the civilian activities, whereas this was not the case in relation to the other activities of the Centre that had defence implications. In this way, the defence opt-out was safeguarded, that is, non-Danish participation was enabled in measures with defence implications while at the same time the effects of the opt-out were not extended beyond this defined scope.

The original measure establishing SATCEN was repealed in 2014 and replaced by a Council Decision with a view to consolidating previous amendments and to repeal the no-longer-relevant transitional provisions with regard to the WEU.[87] The legal bases for this new measure were Articles 28 and 31(1)

[83] Council Joint Action 2001/555/CFSP of 20 July 2001 on the establishment of a European Union Satellite Centre [2001] OJ L200/5.

[84] ibid recital 2.

[85] ibid recital 1.

[86] ibid Art 20.

[87] Council Decision 2014/401/CFSP of 26 June 2014 on the European Union Satellite Centre and repealing Joint Action 2001/555/CFSP on the establishment of a European Union Satellite Centre [2014] OJ L188/73.

TEU, which are not among the legal bases mentioned in Article 5 of Protocol No 22 and thus generally would not provide for the application of the opt-out. Nonetheless, the opt-out continued to be applicable. The new measure repeated the special recital provision that qualified the impact of the Danish opt-out, as well as including special provisions in the operative part regulating the position of Denmark. The precedent of the prior measure on the establishment of SATCEN, including the fact that Article 28 TEU is a continuation of the former Article 14 TEU on which the original measure was based and which triggered the opt-out, combined with the fact that the essential mission and activities of the Centre have remained the same, may explain why an exception was made to a strict reading of Article 5 of the Protocol concerning the relevant legal bases of the TEU in that particular case.

In Spring 2021, the Council adopted a new, comprehensive European Peace Facility (EPF) that established a fund worth EUR 5.7 billion, financed outside of the EU budget for the seven-year period between 2021 and 2027.[88] The EPF replaced and repealed the Athena Mechanism on financing of CSDP measures with defence implications.[89] Denmark did not participate in the Athena Mechanism, which fell squarely within the scope of the opt-out.[90] The EPF also replaced the African Peace Facility (APF) that was established in light of the Cotonou Agreement with a view to supporting operations through the military forces of the partners. Denmark participated in the APF, given an assessment that its actions in the form of technical assistance and education, etc did not have defence implications of a CSDP nature.[91]

The scope of the new EPF is comprehensive, catering for operations pursuant to Article 42 TEU as well as 'assistance measures' pursuant to Article 28 TEU, which may consist of financial, technical or material support.[92] The EPF refers to the Danish opt-out in recital 26 and Article 5(4) as follows:

> In accordance with Article 5 of Protocol No 22 on the position of Denmark, Denmark does not participate in decisions on operations having defence implications adopted by the Council pursuant to Articles 42 to 44 TEU and does not contribute to the financing of these operations.

Unlike the recital in the Athena Mechanism, the references to the opt-out in the EPF fall short of declaring that Denmark does not participate in the measure.

[88] Council Decision (CFSP) 2021/509 of 22 March 2021 establishing a European Peace Facility, and repealing Decision (CFSP) 2015/528 [2021] OJ L102/14. Further financial means have since been allocated.

[89] Council Decision 2011/871/CFSP of 19 December 2011 establishing a mechanism to administer the financing of the common costs of European Union operations having military or defence implications (Athena) [2011] OJ L243/35, replaced by Council Decision (CFSP) 2015/528 of 27 March 2015 establishing a mechanism to administer the financing of the common costs of European Union operations having military or defence implications (Athena) and repealing Decision 2011/871/CFSP [2015] OJ L84/39.

[90] Council Decision (CFSP) 2015/528, recital 12.

[91] Butler (n 1) 142.

[92] Arts 1 and 4 EPF.

This way, it was left open for Denmark to continue to participate in elements within EPF not having a character as defined in the opt-out, notably the ex-APF elements, whereas the opt-out would apply in the reverse situation.[93]

Regarding the institutional framework created within the CFSP, the European Union Military Committee (EUMC) constitutes the highest military body within the Council. It is composed of the Chiefs of Defence of the Member States, who are regularly represented by their permanent military representatives.[94] Due to the opt-out, Denmark's participation in the EUMC was very limited.[95]

The Defence Agency was established by the Council in 2004 to 'support the Council and the Member States in their effort to improve the EU's defence capabilities in the field of crisis management and to sustain the ESDP'.[96] Given the very nature of the Agency, the defence opt-out was applicable. Consequently, Denmark did not take part in the elaboration and adoption of the measures establishing the Agency and its statute, etc, nor did Denmark become bound by them.[97] In light of an increasing overlap between CSDP cooperation and other policies not falling within the scope of the opt-out, not least the EDF, combined with an increased policy-developing role for the Defence Agency on such non-CSDP matters, the Danish Minster of Defence in 2018 aired a wish to seek observer status for Denmark at the Defence Agency.[98] Observer status would not in itself have violated the opt-out.[99] It should be recalled that Denmark, at the time of the Edinburgh Decision, already enjoyed observer status within the WEU, which otherwise formed a prominent part of the opt-out at the time. However, it would have been essential that potential observer status within the Defence Agency should have respected the constraints of the opt-out, notably that Denmark could not actively participate in CSDP matters with defence implications. The Council Decision on the establishment of the Agency is silent on the matter of observer status and the Danish preferences in this regard never materialised.[100]

[93] In the explanatory notes to the subsequent Bill L193 on the abolition of the opt-out (see section IV), the EPF is on the list of measures falling within the scope of the opt-out either in full or partly. This measure fell in the latter category.

[94] See the website of the EEAS at www.eeas.europa.eu/eeas/eumc_en.

[95] Udenrigsministeriet and Forsvarsministeriet, 'EUs Sikkerheds- og Forsvarspolitiske Samarbejde og det danske Forsvarsforbehold – Redegørelse', EUU Alm del (Europaudvalget 2021–22 – Bilag 416) 23.

[96] Council Joint Action 2004/551/CFSP of 12 July 2004 on the establishment of the European Defence Agency [2004] OJ L245/17.

[97] The legal basis for the 2004 Joint Action was the then Art 14 TEU, which – as explained in section III.A – was the legal basis used for CSDP actions prior to the Lisbon Treaty. The recast of the measure adopted 12 October 2015 cites the new dedicated legal bases in Arts 42 and 45 TEU. Reference to the Danish defence opt-out is made in recital 23 of Council Decision (CFSP) 2015/1835 of 12 October 2015 defining the statute, seat and operational rules of the European Defence Agency (recast) [2015] OJ L266/55.

[98] PE Rasmussen, 'Danmark ønsker observatørstatus i europæisk forsvarsagentur' (Olfi – Netavis on dansk forsvars, udenrigs og sikkerhedspolitik, 22 November 2018) at www.olfi.dk.

[99] Butler (n 1) 138.

[100] Denmark did have the opportunity to participate in a few well-defined activities of the Agency relating to industrial, research and transport policies, as these fell outside the scope of the opt-out.

The legal situation presented itself differently in relation to the Union's Coordinated Maritime Presence (CMP), which aims to build strong maritime security architecture, including in the fight against piracy at sea. In January 2021, the Council adopted conclusions launching a pilot case on the concept in the Gulf of Guinea. The concept contains both civilian and military aspects, but it does not take the form of a formal legal act. Also, military contributions of the Member States remain under national command and not under a single EU command. Danish participation would therefore not breach the provision of the opt-out regarding not being part of an EU implementing effort.[101] The opt-out did not apply.

As an innovation, the Lisbon Treaty provided for the possibility for a group of Member States to set up PESCO with a view to strengthening their cooperation in defence matters.[102] On 11 December 2017, the Council adopted a decision establishing PESCO.[103] Participating Member States agreed on an initial list of 17 projects to be undertaken as part of the Cooperation. The list was later expanded to 60 projects, and further additions will no doubt be made over time. All EU Member States took part in PESCO, with the exception of Malta and Denmark. Given the defence implications of PESCO, the Danish non-participation was not by political choice but rather a legal consequence of the opt-out.

Finally, the financial aspect should be highlighted in relation to the legal analysis undertaken to determine the scope of the opt-out. It is clear that the legal effect of the opt-out was that Denmark did not participate in the elaboration nor in the adoption of the measures concerned. The opt-out explicitly prescribed that unanimity and QMV were calculated without Denmark's vote. Partly connected to decision-making is the issue of financing, which is separately regulated within Article 5 of the Protocol. The issue is of particular importance in light of the special budget position that CSDP measures enjoy. Article 41(2) TEU provides that 'expenditure arising from operations having military or defence implications' may not be charged to the Union budget. Expenditure is borne directly by Member States according to defined distribution keys and further specific rules.

Initially, Member States adopted a purely ad hoc approach, but later the matter was institutionalised by the adoption of the afore-mentioned Athena Mechanism, with a view to facilitating and administering the financing of the common costs of CSDP operations.[104] As a legal consequence of the specific

See Udenrigsministeriet and Forsvarsministeriet (n 95) 19; as well as reply to parliamentary question: EUU Alm del (Europaudvalget 2021–22, L 193 – Bilag 3) – svar på spørgsmål 154.

[101] See further the discission in section III.C.ii on implementation.

[102] Arts 42(6) and 46 TEU. On PESCO, see references in n 44.

[103] Council Decision (CFSP) 2017/2315 of 11 December 2017 establishing permanent structured cooperation (PESCO) and determining the list of participating Member States [2017] OJ L331/57.

[104] Council Decision 2011/871/CFSP (n 48). Expenses directly related to the deployment of personnel and equipment would still to a large extent be covered directly by the participating Member States, whereas the Athena Mechanism covered common expenses.

provisions in the defence opt-out on non-Danish contribution to expenditure on CSDP measures with defence implications, Denmark neither became part of nor was bound by this measure.[105]

It was immediately clear from the provision in Article 5 that once a CSDP measure with defence implications had been adopted, Denmark would not contribute to its financing. This provision also provided guidance when the assessment was made in the first place as to whether a proposed measure had defence implication and therefore fell within the scope of the opt-out or not. If the nature of the proposed measure was considered non-chargeable to the EU budget pursuant to the specific provisions in Article 41(2) TEU, it was fair to assume that the CSDP measure had 'defence implications' within the meaning of Article 5 of the Danish Protocol as well. The converse would also hold true. While the wording of Article 41(2) TEU does not fully correspond to the wording of the opt-out, there is nonetheless a strong correlation between the two. In practice, it would most probably prove challenging to detect a difference.

### *ii. Effects of the Defence Opt-Out – Implementation Scenario*

The element in the opt-out that prohibited Denmark from participating in the implementation of measures with defence implications would in practice be an issue detached from the decision-making process. At times, such issues would arise long after a concrete CSDP measure had been adopted, or the question would emerge on a more general level detached from specific CSDP measures.

In essence, the way in which the provision is defined in the opt-out implied that Denmark could not, *by its conduct*, contribute to the implementation of the part of CSDP that had 'defence implications'. This is a rather complex issue.

Danish cooperation with military staff and set-ups within the EU structures had to respect the limits of the opt-out so as to ensure that Danish contribution did not serve to assist in the implementation of CSDP measures. That would be so in relation to existing measures, but equally with a view to future initiatives. Denmark could thus not assist in capacity-building, including training activities, etc.

In general, also as regards this aspect of the opt-out, a case-by-case interpretation would prove necessary to define the limits of its scope. The answer to the question whether a Danish contribution would have been subject to EU military command and/or to EU military rules of engagement would be a relevant consideration as part of the analysis. If the answer was 'yes', the contribution would most likely be one with 'defence implications' and thus fall within the scope of the opt-out. As mentioned in section III.C.i, the same would apply if financing was not possible via the EU budget, in accordance with Article 41(2) TEU.

[105] The Athena Mechanism has been replaced by the EPF; see text to n 89.

In practice life is complex, and answers to the above questions would not necessarily have proved decisive. In recent years, combating cyberattacks has become a new and increasingly important aspect of modern life, including within the sphere of warfare. It differs in many respects from traditional military operations but would nonetheless likely qualify as having 'defence implications' as well.[106] Even though no concrete examples have been detected, it is clear that the scope of the opt-out would have had to include such activities, with negative consequences as regards Denmark's participation.

A few scenarios and examples are offered here to illustrate the scope of the opt-out as it did unfold. As a starting point, it is underlined that the opt-out regulated Denmark's position within the EU and was applicable within an EU setting only. Consequently, it was not applicable per se to Denmark's bilateral relations with other Member States. As an example, in 2018, Denmark together with seven other Member States signed up to a French initiative entitled the European Intervention Initiative (E12), with the aim of 'creating the pre-conditions for coordinated and jointly prepared future engagements in various scenarios of military operations'.[107] If that cooperation had been lifted into EU law, or if the cooperation on a concrete basis had made available to implement CSDP operations with defence implications, it would most likely have had consequences for continuous Danish participation due to the constraints of the opt-out that such a scenario would have breached.

In the same vein, it seems prudent to assume that the opt-out would not have prevented Danish authorities from entering into cooperation arrangements regarding the leasing of equipment on a commercial basis to other Member States. That would have remained so, even in a situation when the Member State decided to make use of the leased equipment with a view to contributing to a CSDP operation with defence implications in which Denmark did not take part due to the opt-out. However, it is clear that arrangements that effectively circumvented the opt-out would have constituted a breach of it. In other words, the particular details of such arrangements would become detrimental in the assessment of whether or not the opt-out's prohibition on Danish contribution to implementing efforts would become effective.

Denmark is a founding Member of both NATO and of the UN, and has a record of being an active partner in various military operations undertaken within the framework of those organisations. It is clear that the opt-out was not applicable to the Danish position within NATO or the UN. However, should an operation be transferred and taken over by the EU, the opt-out would of course have applied to the Danish position. This was the case in relation to

[106] For a general discussion, see MN Schmitt (ed), *Tallinn Manual on the International Law Applicable to Cyber Warfare* (Cambridge, Cambridge University Press, 2013).

[107] 'Letter of Intent Concerning the Development of the European Intervention Initiative (E12)' available at www.defense.gouv.fr.

the NATO-led operations in the Balkans in 2003 and 2004, with the result that Denmark had to withdraw its military contribution.[108]

The situation could become somewhat complex in relation to cooperation arrangements between other international organisations and the EU. The opt-out restrained the flexibility of such cooperation on the part of Denmark. If military operations of the UN or NATO, to which Denmark actively contributed, were used to render support to an EU-led operation, Denmark would likely have been obliged to withdraw its contribution. The issue materialised in relation to a Danish military air contribution to the UN's operation in Mali (MINUSMA), in which instance the opt-out prohibited the Danish contribution from being redeployed to the UN mission in the Central African Republic (CAR) with the aim of assisting an EU-led military operation there.[109]

Characteristic in the circumstance described above was that the situation on the ground would have remained the same while the legal framework would have changed, and the Danish position with it. It is fair to assume that this outcome would not always have been clear to international partners and/or would likely have caused political challenges, and in any case it would have caused practical challenges for the ongoing operation. The reverse situation, where the EU provides assistance to a NATO- or UN-led operation in which Denmark participated, would not have raised issues in relation to the opt-out, as long as Denmark continued its engagement unaffected under NATO or UN command.

From time to time, international agreements are entered into among partners with a view to regulating and easing implementation of commitments otherwise taken. Even though such agreements themselves were not EU measures, the opt-out set boundaries for the participation of Denmark if they related to CSDP measures that fell within the opt-out.

Agreements of the above-mentioned nature have been concluded among Member States with a view to regulating issues on immunities and privileges for EU agencies like the Defence Agency[110] and the Satellite Centre,[111] which themselves are all established by CSDP measures with (partly) defence implications. However, the additional intergovernmental agreements on immunities, etc essentially regulate substance of a civilian nature. Moreover, they do not impose an obligation on Denmark as such. This likely explains why the provision in the opt-out requiring Denmark not to participate in the implementation of CSDP measures with defence implications was not considered applicable. Consequently, Denmark is a party to the agreements.

[108] Udenrigsministeriet and Forsvarsministeriet (n 95) 12.

[109] Thorning (n 41) 167.

[110] Decision of the representatives of the Governments of the Member States, meeting within the Council, of 10 November 2004 on the privileges and immunities granted to the European Defence Agency and to its staff members.

[111] Decision of the Representatives of the Governments of the Member States, meeting within the Council, of 15 October 2011 on the privileges and immunities granted to the European Union Institute for Security Studies and the European Union Satellite Centre, and to their bodies and staff.

The situation seemed to have been more complex in relation to the 'Status of Forces Agreement' (EU SOFA), agreed to in November 2003 by the Member States. The EU SOFA concerns

> the status of military and civilian staff seconded to the institutions of the European Union, of the headquarters and forces which may be made available to the European Union in the context of the preparation and execution of the tasks referred to in Article 17(2) of the Treaty on European Union, including exercises, and of the military and civilian staff of the Member States put at the disposal of the European Union to act in this context.[112]

A corresponding agreement is the NATO SOFA. However, unlike the NATO activities falling within the scope of the NATO SOFA, it is quite clear that Denmark would not have been part of (most of) the EU activities with which the EU SOFA concerns itself, given their 'defence implications'. Bearing that in mind, Denmark made the following statement in connection with the signature of the Agreement in 2003:

> When signing this Agreement, Denmark recalled the Protocol on the position of Denmark annexed to the Treaty on the European Union and the Treaty establishing the European Community. Danish approval of the Agreement will take place in observance of that Protocol, and any reservation or declaration which Denmark may have to make in this connection shall be limited to the scope of part II of the said Protocol and shall in no way prevent the entry into force of the Agreement and the full implementation of it by the other Member States.[113]

Noticeably, the wording in the opt-out, that 'Denmark will not prevent the other Member States from further developing their cooperation in this area', was given particular attention by Denmark in this case. The commitment by itself could not have overruled the essence of the opt-out that left Denmark out of CSDP measures with defence implications, including not participating in their implementation. However, it played a role when the concrete scope of the opt-out was defined, as indicated in the Danish statement reproduced above. The final article of the EU SOFA provides for its approval by all Member States as a prerequisite for it to enter into force. True to the obligation under the opt-out not to prevent CSDP cooperation among the other Member States, Denmark did ratify the EU SOFA in 2016. As at the time of the signature, Denmark recalled the opt-out in connection with ratification as well. In a declaration (explanatory note), Denmark pointed to the limits set by the defence opt-out for Denmark to enter into potential sub-agreements envisaged by the SOFA[114]

[112] Agreement between the Member States of the European Union … (EU SOFA) [2003] OJ C321/6.
[113] ibid, 'Statement by Denmark'.
[114] Art 9 of the EU SOFA relates to the deploying of personnel, including troops, military equipment and the setting up of military headquarters on the territories of the participating Member States according to prior, separate agreements with the Member States concerned. It seems likely that Denmark would not have been able to enter into such agreements due to the constraints of the opt-out.

on the deploying of troops and setting up of headquarters in Denmark. The explanatory note reads:

> Upon approval of this Agreement, Denmark recalls Protocol No 22 on the position of Denmark annexed to the Treaty of Lisbon according to which Denmark does not participate in the elaboration and the implementation of decisions and actions of the Union which have defence implications. It is noted that this Agreement shall respect Denmark's status under Protocol No 22. This, inter alia, limits the scope of the possible agreements, referred to in Part III of this Agreement, that Denmark can undertake.[115]

What Denmark effectively stated was that Danish ratification ensured the entry into force of the SOFA, but the SOFA would in practice not have much effect in or for Denmark due to the opt-out.

Finally, the opt-out had repercussions for Danish participation in the international agreements within CFSP, as provided for in Article 37 TEU.

As regards the CSDP part, such agreements are mostly concluded as part of the implementation of the Union's operations and missions. In the event that such missions had defence implications and consequently fell within the scope of the opt-out, Denmark would not be a party. The same applied if an international agreement regulated matters with defence implications in a more generic sense. As an example, Denmark did not participate in the military training mission in the CAR due to the opt-out.[116] Consequently, Denmark also did not participate in the agreement between the Union and CAR on the status of the mission, which was adopted pursuant to Article 37 TEU. Reference to the Danish opt-out is made in recital 5 of the Council Decision.[117] There seems to have been some inconsistency, however, with regard to making reference to the Danish opt-out in relevant Article 37 Council Decisions. Denmark did not take part in the Union's military training mission in Mali (EUTM Mali),[118] and Denmark did not take part in the subsequent status agreement with Mali pursuant to Article 37 TEU.[119] The Danish opt-out is duly reflected in both cases. However, no reference is made to the position of Denmark in the Union's later agreement with

[115] Council Secretariat Homepage at www.consilium.europa.eu/en/documents-publications/treaties-agreements/ratification/?id=2003102&partyid=DK&doclanguage=en.

[116] Council Decision 2016/610 of 19 April 2016 on a European Union CSDP Military Training Mission in the Central African Republic (EUTM RCA) [2016] OJ L104/21.

[117] Council Decision 2016/1791 of 12 July 2016, on signing and conclusion on behalf of the Union of the agreement in the form of Exchange of Letters between the European Union and the Central African Republic on the status of the European Union CSDP Military Training Mission in the Central African Republic [2016] OJ L274/31.

[118] Council Decision 2013/34/CFSP of 17 January 2013 on a European Union military mission to contribute to the training of the Malian Armed Forces (EUTM Mali) [2013] OJ L14/19. Recital 11 makes reference to the Danish opt-out.

[119] Council Decision 2013/178/CFSP of 25 February 2013 on the signing and conclusion of the Agreement between the European Union and the Republic of Mali on the status in the Republic of Mali of the European Union military mission to contribute to the training of the Malian Armed Forces (EUTM Mali) [2013] OJ L106/1. Recital 5 makes reference to the Danish opt-out.

Switzerland on that country's participation in the EUTM Mali.[120] Regardless, Denmark could not have participated in that agreement due to the opt-out.[121] If an Article 37 agreement concerned a mission or operation with no defence implication, the issue of the defence opt-out would, naturally, not have arisen.

## IV. ABOLITION OF THE DEFENCE OPT-OUT

Mirroring Section E of the Edinburgh Decision, Article 7 of Protocol No 22 states as follows:

> At any time Denmark may, in accordance with its constitutional requirements, inform the other Member States that it no longer wishes to avail itself of all or part of this Protocol. In that event, Denmark will apply in full all relevant measures then in force taken within the framework of the European Union.[122]

This standing option for Denmark to decide to abandon its special position either in part or in full is a one-way street. Once exercised, Denmark cannot reinstall its former special position.

In Spring 2022, a broad section of the Danish political parties entered into a political agreement on Danish security policy.[123] As part thereof, the parties agreed that the time was right to make use of the sovereign right for Denmark to abolish the defence opt-out. The parties called for a referendum on the matter, to be held on 1 June 2022.

This was the first time that a date for a referendum concerning Denmark's relations with the EU had been announced before the legal basis for such a referendum had been established.[124] In order to make sure that all necessary legislation was in place in due time, the Government swiftly proceeded by tabling two Bills before the Parliament. One concerned the abolition of the opt-out as such, and the other established the legal basis for holding the required referendum.

[120] Council Decision 2014/293/CFSP of 15 April 2014 on the signing and conclusion of the Agreement between the European Union and the Swiss Confederation on the participation of the Swiss Confederation in the European Union military mission to contribute to the training of the Malian Armed Forces (EUTM Mali) [2014] OJ L151/16.

[121] It had no practical implications whether Denmark was regarded as being part of the agreement or not, since Denmark was not part of the EUTM Mali.

[122] Protocol No 22 on the Position of Denmark [2012] OJ C326/299.

[123] The agreement is entitled 'National Compromise' (in Danish: '*nationale kompromis*'), which incidentally corresponds to the popular name for the Memorandum adopted by Danish parties in 1992 relating to the Maastricht Treaty (see ch 2). The two documents should not be confused.

[124] In total, eight Danish referenda on EU matters had occurred prior to the one on defence cooperation: on the accession to the EC, on the European Common Act 1986, on the Maastricht Treaty/Edinburgh Decision (the second referendum), on the Amsterdam Treaty and on the Patent Court (all with a positive outcome); and referenda with a negative outcome on the Maastricht Treaty (the first referendum), on the abolition of the euro opt-out and on changing the AFSJ opt-out to an opt-in. On the last of these, see ch 6.

The first Bill was short, with only one operational article, which stated that Denmark participates in all parts of Title V, Section 2 of the TEU (CSDP).[125] By the adoption of the Bill, the Danish Parliament gave its required assent, in accordance with Article 19 of the Constitution, for the Government to make use of the option in Article 7 of Protocol No 22 to inform the other Member States that Denmark no longer would avail itself of Part II of the Protocol that regulates the defence opt-out. By doing so, the opt-out would cease to apply, with the intended consequence that Denmark would participate fully in all aspects of CSDP cooperation.

The second Bill on holding a referendum on the first Bill as and when adopted, was a necessity given the conclusion reached by the Danish Ministry of Justice that the particular procedure set out in Article 20 of the Constitution was not applicable.[126] The referendum could therefore not in any circumstance be based on Article 20.[127] In line with its previous conclusions, notably in relation to Denmark's ratification of the Lisbon Treaty, the Ministry of Justice had thus found that the particularities of the CFSP, including CSDP, are such that it is *not* left to the Union to exercise legislative, administrative or judicial authority with direct effect in Denmark; nor is it left to the Union to act on behalf of Denmark in international relations.[128] The latter notably follows an examination of the nature of agreements pursuant to Article 37 TEU, to which Denmark would become party following an abolition of the opt-out. Since such agreements are concluded by the Union and not the Member States, no issue arises with regard to Article 20 of the Danish Constitution.

The referendum Bill was modelled after the 1993 Bill on the Danish referendum on the Edinburgh Decision and the Maastricht Treaty. As such, the parliamentary consent given by the Parliament's adoption of the main Bill on the abolition of the opt-out was carved out and put up for a referendum, in accordance with Article 42 of the Constitution. In this way, the referendum was legally binding pursuant to the Constitution.[129]

The result of the referendum was an overwhelming confirmation of the adopted Bill with 66.9 per cent voting in favour and 33.1 per cent against. The Bill was thus approved and, upon receiving Royal Assent, entered into force. Accordingly, the Government informed the other Member States in writing of the new Danish position, being that Denmark 'no longer wishes to avail itself'

[125] Bill L193 of 3 May 2022; Folketingstidende, saml 2020–21, Tillæg A, L193.

[126] Justitsministeriet, 'Notat om hvorvidt en ophævelse af det danske forsvarsforbehold forudsætter anvendelse af proceduren i grundlovens § 20' (2022).

[127] It should be recalled that even a referendum pursuant to Art 20, when applicable, is only the last resort, in the event that the prescribed qualified majority for the adoption of the Bill is not met.

[128] For the criteria to examine pursuant to Art 20 of the Constitution, see the judgment of the Danish Supreme Court in *Maastricht* UfR U.1998.800. See ch 2, section VII.B.

[129] Bill L194 of 3 May 2022; Folketingstidende, saml 2020–21, Tillæg A, L194. On the model, see the discussion in ch 2, section VII.B on the 1993 Bill on the Danish referendum on the Edinburgh Decision and the Maastricht Treaty.

of Part II of Protocol No 22, which covers the defence opt-out.[130] Formally, it is a Communication between the contracting parties to the Treaties (the Member States). In practice, the High Representative and the Council Secretariat, including the Legal Service, were equally informed and involved, with a view to ensuring the application of all relevant measures for Denmark. The Danish Foreign Minister handed over the Article 7 letter to the High Representative during a small ceremony in Brussels in late June 2022.[131]

The provisions of Part II of the Protocol ceased to take effect from 1 July 2022: the opt-out on defence was effectively abolished. At the time, seven active CSDP operations fell within the scope of the opt-out and a total of 38 legal measures were in force within the domain. Most of those related to concrete operations, but five concerned general cooperation issues related to the European Defence Agency, PESCO, the Satellite Centre, the EPF, and the Military Planning and Conduct Capability (MPCC).[132]

The special provision in Article 31(1) TEU allows for a Member State to abstain in a vote on a decision pursuant to the CFSP chapter of the TEU. When combined with a formal declaration in which the Member State qualifies its abstention, the Member State is not obliged to apply the decision. In general, the special provision in Article 31(1) has only been invoked on rare occasions.[133] The Article 31(1) abstention was applicable to Denmark in relation to its accession to the existing measures pursuant to Article 7 of Protocol 22.[134] Denmark did not make use of it. Consequently, 36 of the 38 measures identified became applicable to Denmark from the date of the Article 7 Communication. Denmark's participation in the Defence Agency as well as PESCO did not follow automatically, as this could only happen in accordance with the specific procedures and requirements governing the Agency and the permanent structured cooperation.[135] Upon request from Denmark and after the completion of all required procedures, Denmark joined both areas of cooperation in the early Summer of 2023.

In the absence of its special excluding position, Denmark gained the right to contribute actively with military staff and equipment, etc to the ongoing operations of which Denmark became part from the date of the Article 7 Communication. However, no obligation to do so exists for any Member State, including Denmark. Instead, it is a separate issue for each Member State

[130] See the wording of Art 7 of Protocol No 22.

[131] The event was widely reported in the Danish media. A copy of the letter would be filed with the Danish Foreign Ministry and, it must be assumed, with the Council Secretariat too.

[132] A table of the measures as of 1 March 2022 is produced as part of the explanatory notes to Bill L193 (n 125).

[133] For a discussion of Art 31(1) TEU in a broader context, see RA Wessel and V Szép, *The Implementation of Article 31 of the Treaty on European Union and the Use of Qualified Majority Voting: Towards a more effective Common Foreign and Security Policy?* (Strasbourg, European Parliament, 2022).

[134] See the explanatory notes to Bill 193 (n 125).

[135] Participation in PECSO and the Defence Agency takes place on a voluntary basis.

to decide on according to their respective national procedures. In the case of Denmark, any such active commitments from the Danish Government can only be undertaken in consultation with the Parliament pursuant to Article 19(2) of the Danish Constitution.[136]

## V. CONCLUDING REMARKS ON THE DEFENCE OPT-OUT

As a formal part of EU cooperation, the CSDP was in its infancy in the early years of the Maastricht Treaty.[137] Arguably, the wording of the Treaty provision in Article J.4 TEU lacked the sophistication to cater for the differences in substance of CSDP cooperation. In any case, and regardless of the substance concerned, the implementation was channelled through the military alliance of the WEU. Against this background, the opt-out was applicable to all eight CSDP measures that occurred. This was a logical approach, seen from a legal point of view.

A more particular drafting of the Treaty provisions on CSDP was introduced by the Amsterdam Treaty and has since been further elaborated by later Treaty changes. At the same time, practice on the implementation side of the CSDP shifted too. The WEU was rather quickly phased out, both de facto and de jure, and closer cooperation between EU and NATO emerged alongside a transfer of tasks from the WEU to the EU, with a view to building up the EU's own capabilities.[138] Later, instruments were adopted to facilitate the financing of CSDP activities outside of the EU budget.

The opt-out followed suit in two ways: by becoming part of EU primary law; and by being subject to an interpretation that reflected the complex nature of the CSDP.

The Amsterdam Treaty lifted the opt-out into the EU treaty regime in the form of provisions set out in a specific Protocol, with the aim of ensuring an unbroken Danish position from the Edinburgh Decision of non-participation in the defence policy dimension of the Union, which in concrete terms was translated into non-Danish participation in the elaboration, adaptation, financing and implementation of decisions and actions of the Union with defence implications. Some 10 years later, the Protocol provisions underwent

[136] It is observed that none of the measures that Denmark became part of following the abolition of the opt-out required implementation in national Danish law given their special CSDP character, including being non-legislative acts.

[137] The 1986 Single European Act (entered into force 1987) had vaguely included a reference to foreign policy cooperation (no mention of defence) but it was the Maastricht Treaty that introduced the matter, including defence as one part of the three-pillar structure of the EU.

[138] See, for a contemporary point of view, RA Wessel, 'The EU as Black Widow: Devouring the WEU to Give Birth to a European Security and Defence Policy' in V Kronenberger (ed), *The European Union and the International Legal Order – Discord or Harmony?* (The Hague, TMC Asser Press, 2001) 405.

amendment as part of the Lisbon Treaty, to cater for the further changes introduced to the treaties.

In light of European integration within the CSDP, the adaptation of the opt-out has, consequently, been somewhat pronounced. The aim all along was to maintain the scope of the opt-out as originally defined in the Edinburgh Decision, while at the same time ensuring that the scope was not expanded outside its legally defined borders. The reason for this was the fact that Denmark did not request a change to its special position at any of the IGCs that occurred. The position of Denmark was therefore locked to the definition found in the Edinburgh Decision. The changes to the opt-out were all *adaptations* and not changes to the *scope* of the opt-out.[139]

It is observed that the original version of the opt-out in the Edinburgh Decision included provisions to safeguard Denmark's position as a non-member of the WEU. That part was never included in the provisions on the opt-out under EU law, as the WEU quickly faded and subsequently was dissolved.

It is clear that the defence opt-out was not generic but rather set within a legal frame with a relatively limited and well-defined scope. The need for a comprehensive, concrete analysis of CSDP measures and issues related to such measures, with a view to ascertaining the applicability of the opt-out, was a reflection of the complexity of the CSDP cooperation and not so much of the opt-out itself. Importantly, as Butler rightly observes, 'there has been a steady line of interpretation that Denmark and the Council Legal Service has followed to ensure the defence opt-out is applied correctly', and that 'its legal interpretation has prevailed over any subsequent political considerations given its compulsory application in given circumstances'.[140]

Non-CSDP measures, as well as CSDP measures of a civilian character, fell outside the scope of the opt-out. That may well have given rise to particular challenges in practice and in political life, as the importance of the distinction between military and civilian and between CSDP and non-CSDP cooperation would not always have the same relevance for other stakeholders as it had for Denmark in light of the opt-out.

The implications of the opt-out were twofold: first, Denmark was not part of the decision-making process and did not become bound by measures resulting from it; second, Denmark could not by its conduct participate in the implementation of such measures either concretely or more indirectly by offering support and assistance, including by engaging in training activities, etc that underpinned CSDP initiatives with defence implications. It is observed that it was not so much an issue of activating the opt-out as such by way of a statement or in any other way; the opt-out simply applied when the criteria were met.[141]

[139] Butler (n 1) 126.
[140] ibid 149–50.
[141] See Reply to parliamentary question: EUU Alm del (Europaudvalget 2021-22, L 193 – Bilag 3) – svar på spørgsmål 106.

While it is obvious that the opt-out regulated Denmark's position within the EU and not beyond, it was important to be vigilant in relation to cooperation arrangements between the EU and other organisations, as the opt-out had implications for Denmark's participation should activities shift from, say, NATO to the EU side. The same would be the case in connection with intergovernmental defence cooperation among Member States, including Denmark, that took place outside of the EU Treaties.

During the Danish Presidency of the EU in 2002, Denmark renounced its right to exercise the Presidency of the Council on defence matters. Denmark thus honoured the commitment undertaken in the Edinburgh Agreement.[142] The Danish commitment later became obsolete due to the changed role of the rotating Presidency introduced by the Lisbon Treaty.

Finally, it is noted that the legal nature of the opt-out ever since the Edinburgh Decision provided for an absolute exclusion of Denmark from participating directly as well as indirectly in CSDP activities with defence implications. Whereas the EU, on an intergovernmental level, may enter into agreements with non-Member States on their participation in concrete CSDP initiatives, and even PESCO, such agreements could not be entered into with Denmark, as it would have conflicted with the essence of the opt-out and effectively hollowed out its content. Consequently, and, as will be explored in chapter 6, unlike the situation on the AFSJ, it was not an option to mitigate the effects of the defence opt-out by way of so-called parallel agreements or other models whereby Denmark would be treated as if it were a third state.[143]

In summary, the legal effects of the defence opt-out were on the face of it quite simple: Denmark was legally barred from taking part at all in the EU's formally adopted CSDP initiatives with defence implications, including by participating in their implementation. To the naked eye, it may have seemed confusing that Denmark participated in the Defence Fund and actively contributed to FRONTEX with military aircraft, without that raising any issues with respect to the defence opt-out; at the same time, Denmark would have had to withdraw from an ongoing military operation in the field if it changed character from a NATO to an EU operation. In 2017, the Danish thinktank, *Tænketanken Europa*, made the following observations: 'It seems counterproductive that Denmark cannot pursue Danish interests in both NATO and the EU … It seems paradoxical that Denmark is willing to participate militarily under FRONTEX, but not under defence policy.'[144] Butler pointed to an impact of the opt-out both on the part of Denmark, in the form of loss of influence, and on the part of the EU, in the form of less impact of the European Defence

[142] Denmark and the Treaty on European Union [1992] OJ C348/1, Annex II.
[143] On 'parallel agreements' as well as other mitigating instruments see ch 6.
[144] Tænketanken Europa, 'Forbeholdslandet Danmark. De mange aktiveringer af forbeholdene – og det voksende tab af suverænitet' (2017) 25–26 (author's own translation).

Union when not all Member States stand ready to defend it.[145] These were all perfectly genuine points of a political nature. However, the legal nature of the defence opt-out, as defined by the Edinburgh Decision and upheld through the Protocol to the EU Treaties, left Denmark with no room for discretion.

The only way that the political logic could prevail would be by seeking popular approval for abolition of the opt-out. This is what happened in June 2022. Based on a set of Danish legislation specifically adopted for the occasion, a referendum was held, and its positive outcome allowed the Danish Government to invoke Article 7 of Protocol No 22 on the Position of Denmark. Addressed to the Member States, Denmark formally renounced Part II of the Protocol, with the effect that the defence opt-out ceased to apply as of 1 July 2022. Denmark has since applied the relevant EU measures then in force, although its participation in the Defence Agency and PESCO began only once completion of the necessary procedures had occurred in the early Summer of 2023. Denmark participates in all subsequent areas of cooperation within the field according to the ordinary rules and procedures as laid down in the Treaties. The new, ordinary position of Denmark is irreversible: there is no mechanism to reinstall the defence opt-out.

[145] Butler (n 1) 118.

# 6

# *Area of Freedom, Security and Justice*

## I. INTRODUCTION

THE LEGAL NATURE of EU cooperation within the Area of Freedom, Security and Justice (AFSJ) has undergone major changes since the Maastricht Treaty.[1] The evolution has greatly impacted on the effects of the Danish AFSJ opt-out.[2] The evolution has taken place in several stages. This will all be explored and explained in a systematic way in section II to ascertain how the European integration process has affected the opt-out, as well as with a view to establishing, in section III.A the effects of the opt-out in EU law. Different ways identified to mitigate certain effects of the opt-out will then be explained and discussed in section III.B. This discussion will disclose why such ways have proved legally possible in relation to this particular opt-out as opposed to those discussed so far in this book.

The AFSJ opt-out in particular has raised legal issues of an external nature. These are examined in section III.C. As a consequence of the particularity of this opt-out's nature, the question of a potential conversion from an opt-out to

[1] On AFSJ matters in general, see, among many contributions, I Gade et al, *Det Politimæssige og Strafferetlige Samarbejde i Den Europæiske Union* (Copenhagen, Jurist- og Økonomforbundets Forlag, 2005); C Ladenburger, 'Police and Criminal Law in the Treaty of Lisbon. A New Dimension for the Community Method' (2008) 4(1) *European Constitutional Law Review* 20; S Peers, 'In a world of their own? Justice and Home Affairs Opt-Outs and the Treaty of Lisbon' (2008) 10 *Cambridge Yearbook of European Legal Studies* 383; S Peers, 'Legislative Update: EU Immigration and Asylum Competence and Decision-Making in the Treaty of Lisbon' (2008) 10 *European Journal of Migration and Law* 219; S Peers, *EU Justice and Home Affairs Law*, vols I and II (4th edn, Oxford, Oxford University Press, 2016); AR Servent and F Trauner (eds), *The Routledge Handbook of Justice and Home Affairs Research* (Abingdon, Routledge, 2017).

[2] On differentiated integration within AFSJ in general, see, eg, T Kostakopoulou, 'The Area of Freedom, Security and Justice and the European Union's Constitutional Dialogue' in C Barnard (ed), *The Fundamentals of EU Law Revisited: Assembling the Impact of the Constitutional Debate* (Oxford, Oxford University Press, 2007) 152; F Trauner, 'Increased Differentiation as an Engine for Integration? Studying Justice and Home Affairs' in G Falkner (ed), *The EU's Decision Traps: Comparing Policies* (Oxford, Oxford University Press, 2011) 145; C Matera, 'Much Ado About the Opt-outs? The Impact of Variable Geometry in the AFSJ on the EU as a Global Security Actor' in S Blockmans (ed), *Differentiated Integration in the EU From the Inside Looking Out* (Centre for European Policy Studies 2014) 75; JS Vara and E Fahey, 'Transatlantic relations and the operation of AFSJ flexibility' in S Blockmans (ed), *Differentiated Integration in the EU From the Inside Looking Out* (Brussels, Centre for European Policy Studies, 2014) 103; S Peers, 'Differentiated integration and the Brexit process in EU Justice and Home Affairs' in Servent and Trauner (eds) (n 1).

an opt-in has arisen. This topic will be discussed in the penultimate section III.D of this chapter. Furthermore, an assessment of how such a conversion may take place from a legal point of view provides input to the overall question on how to legislate for changes to the special Danish position.

Concluding remarks in relation to this opt-out are provided in the ultimate section IV.

## II. IMPACT ON THE AFSJ OPT-OUT – FROM THE EDINBURGH DECISION TO EU TREATY LAW

It may be recalled that the structure of the Union as created by the Maastricht Treaty was one of three pillars, with the first pillar containing the traditional EU cooperation, often referred to as the 'communitarian cooperation' given its supranational character. The second pillar contained the foreign and security policy, including defence, and was of a purely intergovernmental character. The then Title VI of the TEU made up the third-pillar cooperation on Justice and Home Affairs (JHA), the name given to AFSJ cooperation at the time. This cooperation was essentially also of an intergovernmental character.[3]

On this basis, Section D of the Edinburgh Decision on 'Justice and Home Affairs' has the following wording:

> Denmark will participate fully in cooperation on Justice and Home Affairs on the basis of the provisions of Title VI of the Treaty on European Union.[4]

Section D seems to be nothing more than a statement of the obvious for an EU Member State, namely, that 'Denmark participates fully'. Clearly, it did not in itself establish a special position for Denmark in relation to the cooperation as it unfolded according to the provisions introduced by the Maastricht Treaty. Consequently, Section D had, at the time, no legal impact on Danish participation in AFSJ (JHA) cooperation. However, within that apparently obvious statement laid a dormant opt-out, ready to be awakened should the character of the AFSJ (JHA) cooperation change.

Such a change was already an in-built possibility under the Treaty. Article K.9 TEU provided for a so-called 'pillar-jump', whereby actions under the intergovernmental third-pillar cooperation could be transferred by way of a unanimous decision of the Council to the communitarian first pillar, thereby changing the character of the cooperation from intergovernmental to supranational.[5]

[3] A few special features were applicable to the third pillar that did not apply to the second pillar, like a joint right of initiative between the Commission and the Member States.

[4] Denmark and the Treaty on European Union [1992] OJ C348/1.

[5] The subsequent European integration process led to a discontinuation of this Article. A number of provisions, which today are called 'passerelle clauses', persist in the current Treaties and provide mechanisms for introducing changes of a very specific nature, notably by allowing a shift from

In the Danish Memorandum prior to the Edinburgh Decision,[6] the Danish politicians had made it clear that Denmark was happy to continue to cooperate within the JHA field on the existing intergovernmental basis, but would not be prepared to transfer sovereignty to the EU on this area of cooperation. As discussed in chapter 2, the issue of delegating powers vested in the Danish authorities to international authorities – popularly known as transfer of sovereignty – is regulated by Article 20 of the Danish Constitution. It was clear that the potential invoking of Article K.9 TEU would indeed trigger Article 20.[7] Bearing that in mind, Section D of the Edinburgh Decision should be read as if 'only' was inserted in relation to the refence made to Title VI measures, since Denmark would *not* fully participate in a non-intergovernmental version of the cooperation.

Elholm correctly mentions that the main point governing the Danish position on AFSJ was Danish resistance towards supranational cooperation and consequently 'transfer of sovereignty' from Denmark to the EU on the matter.[8] Elholm also emphasises an apparent Danish political wish to maintain unanimity.[9] That may have been an additional Danish preoccupation; however, as the Danish Ministry of Justice has repeatedly stated on various occasions, the issue of changing voting procedure from unanimity to QMV does not in itself constitute a 'transfer of sovereignty' within the legal understanding of Article 20 of the Danish Constitution.

In the second unilateral Declaration by Denmark that forms part of the Edinburgh Agreement, Denmark recalled that its constitutional requirements should be observed in relation to a potential 'pillar jump' in accordance with Article K.9. The requirements referred to are the procedures laid out in Article 20 of the Constitution, which potentially includes a referendum. Given the way in which the Edinburgh Decision was to form part of Danish national legislation in relation to Denmark's ratification of the Maastricht Treaty, it is posited in chapter 2 that holding a referendum would have been mandatory for Denmark in any case in such a scenario, as Danish involvement in an Article K.9 situation would have challenged the commitment in Section D of the Edinburgh Decision to Danish participation within AFSJ on an intergovernmental level only.[10]

Moreover, as discussed and concluded in chapter 2, it is tempting to speculate that by this Declaration, Denmark indicated a potential political willingness to participate in a 'pillar-jump' in principle, with the consequence that the opt-out

unanimity to QMV. Within the AFSJ, a special passerelle clause is found in Art 81(3) TFEU on family law with cross-border implications.

[6] 'Denmark in Europe', Markedsudvalget 1992–93, MKU Alm del bilag 70, part A.

[7] See ch 2, section VII.B.

[8] T Elholm, 'Det retlige forbehold og strafferetten' in BE Olsen and KE Sørensen (eds), *EU-Retten i Danmark* (Copenhagen, DJØF's Forlag, 2018) 87, 88–89.

[9] ibid.

[10] The procedure laid out in Art 20 of the Danish Constitution only prescribes a referendum as a last resort if a defined qualified majority is not present in the Danish Parliament. See ch 2.

would then be partly abolished, provided that the relevant Danish procedures were successfully observed at such a stage. The issue of a 'pillar-jump' pursuant to Article K.9 did not materialise. Instead, the matter was addressed in the IGC that led to the Amsterdam Treaty.

The Amsterdam Treaty transferred one major part of the AFSJ cooperation from the third to the first pillar. A new Title IV within the TEC contained provisions on communitarian cooperation on visa, asylum, immigration and border control, as well as on judicial cooperation in civil matters.

As it turned out, in the IGC leading to the Amsterdam Treaty the Danish Government was in no position to show willingness in principle to change the Danish opt-out. The Government negotiated on the basis of a parliamentary mandate that called for all of the Danish opt-outs to be maintained.[11]

Given the major changes to the AFSJ cooperation that the Amsterdam Treaty would introduce, a solution had to be found for the Danish Government to adhere to its mandate and maintain the special Danish position while at the same time honouring the commitment in the Edinburgh Agreement not to prevent closer cooperation between the other Member States. Addressing at the same time issues relating to upholding the defence opt-out in light of changes to that area of cooperation, also introduced by the Amsterdam Treaty, a comprehensive solution was found by way of the introduction of the Protocol on the Position of Denmark. The new Protocol stipulated and regulated the two opt-outs as part of EU primary law.[12]

The Danish Ministry of Justice had concluded that Article 20 of the Danish Constitution was applicable in relation to the Danish ratification of the Amsterdam Treaty, as a number of elements in the new Treaty required the transfer of powers to the EU.[13] The Danish ratification was exercised on the basis of a positive outcome of an Article 20 referendum, held on 28 May 1998, on the ratification Bill adopted by the Danish Parliament. However, the ratification Bill did not transfer powers to the EU within the AFSJ. Rather, and as a consequence of the opt-out maintained, the ratification Bill inserted in Article 4 of the Danish Act of Accession, which regulates powers that may be exercised by the EU institutions according to the Treaties, an explicit exemption for AFSJ first-pillar matters.[14] By ratifying the Amsterdam Treaty, it was thus explicitly

[11] Explanatory Notes to Bill L2, Folketingstidende 1997–98, 1. saml, col 247. The same applied to the defence opt-out (see the discussion in ch 5).

[12] For Protocol No 5 on the Position of Denmark annexed to the Treaty establishing the European Community and to the Treaty on European Union see Treaty of Amsterdam amending the Treaty on European Union, the Treaties establishing the European Communities and certain related acts [1997] OJ C340/1. In its current version, it is Protocol No 22, which is discussed in detail in section III. The provisions in the Protocol on the defence opt-out are addressed in ch 5.

[13] Justitsministeriet, 'Justitsministeriets redegørelse af 6 oktober 1997 om visse forfatningsretlige spørgsmål i forbindelse med Danmarks ratifikation af Amsterdam-Traktaten' (1997).

[14] A similar exemption had already been provided for in the Danish Act of Accession by the time of the ratification of the Maastricht Treaty, to cater for the opt-out from the third stage of EMU; see the discussion in ch 2, section VII.B.

clear from the Danish legislation that the transfer of powers from Denmark to the EU did not include AFSJ cooperation.

Effectively, the Amsterdam Treaty had provoked the Danish AFSJ opt-out to emerge from the chrysalis of the Edinburgh Decision. The opt-out was activated and given effect in both EU law and Danish national law.

Some 10 years later, the Lisbon Treaty completed the transfer of the remaining part of the AFSJ, that is police cooperation and judicial cooperation in criminal matters, from intergovernmental to supranational cooperation. This was because the Lisbon Treaty terminated the third pillar altogether. Consequently, the entire AFSJ is currently regulated in Title V of Part Three of the TFEU. In the IGCs prior to the conclusion of the Lisbon Treaty, including the one on the failed Constitutional Treaty, the question of abolition of the opt-out was not included in the negotiations by the Danish Government; on the contrary, once again, the issue was one of ensuring its continuation. The changes introduced by the Lisbon Treaty to the AFSJ cooperation therefore necessitated adaptations of the opt-out provisions within the Protocol to that effect.[15]

The combined effects of the opt-out in EU law, from Amsterdam to Lisbon, will be explored in section III.

## III. THE AFSJ OPT-OUT AS PART OF EU LAW

### A. The Effects in EU Law of the AFSJ Opt-Out

The current Protocol on the Position of Denmark, as last updated by the Lisbon Treaty, contains in Parts I and III the specific provisions on the Danish position within the AFSJ.[16] The core provisions are found in the first articles, which in the current version, following the changes made by the Lisbon Treaty, read as follows:

> *Article 1*
>
> Denmark shall not take part in the adoption by the Council of proposed measures pursuant to Title V of Part Three of the Treaty on the Functioning of the European Union. The unanimity of the members of the Council, with the exception of the representative of the government of Denmark, shall be necessary for the decisions of the Council which must be adopted unanimously.

[15] The Nice Treaty had also introduced certain changes to the decision-making procedures within the AFSJ, but this had no consequence for the Danish opt-out as regulated in the Protocol on the Position of Denmark. The Nice Treaty had left police and judicial cooperation in criminal matters within the third pillar.

[16] Protocol No 22 on the Position of Denmark [2012] OJ C326/299. The Protocol is annexed to the TEU and the TFEU. Part II contains the provisions on the defence opt-out (discussed in ch 5) and Part IV contains provisions on the abolition of the provisions and, regarding the AFSJ parts only, on changes to the provisions. The latter is discussed in section III.D of this chapter.

> For the purposes of this Article, a qualified majority shall be defined in accordance with Article 238(3) of the Treaty on the Functioning of the European Union.
>
> *Article 2*
>
> None of the provisions of Title V of Part Three of the Treaty on the Functioning of the European Union, no measure adopted pursuant to that Title, no provision of any international agreement concluded by the Union pursuant to that Title, and no decision of the Court of Justice of the European Union interpreting any such provision or measure or any measure amended or amendable pursuant to that Title shall be binding upon or applicable in Denmark; and no such provision, measure or decision shall in any way affect the competences, rights and obligations of Denmark; and no such provision, measure or decision shall in any way affect the Community or Union acquis nor form part of Union law as they apply to Denmark. In particular, acts of the Union in the field of police cooperation and judicial cooperation in criminal matters adopted before the entry into force of the Treaty of Lisbon which are amended shall continue to be binding upon and applicable to Denmark unchanged.
>
> *Article 3*
>
> Denmark shall bear no financial consequences of measures referred to in Article 1, other than administrative costs entailed for the institutions.[17]

The provisions are not easily read or understood. Peers found that they undoubtedly qualified as the winner of 'major awards' for the worst-drafted new treaty provisions, alongside the ones in Protocol No 21 on the British/Irish position.[18] This is, at least partly, a regrettable side-effect of an updated legal text that has to reflect changes made to other parts of the Treaties.[19]

In a nutshell, the opt-out means that Denmark does not take part in the adoption of, nor is Denmark bound by, any measures pursuant to the AFSJ Title of the TFEU, including international agreements concluded by the Union pursuant to that Title as well as rulings of the CJEU on measures pursuant to the same Title V. Also, Denmark is not bound by any of the AFSJ treaty provisions themselves. Denmark does not contribute financially to the measures concerned, although administrative costs of the institutions are exempted. The latter is owing to the fact that Denmark, just like any Member State, naturally contributes to the institutions in general.

The effect of the special Danish position on the AFSJ is one of a proper opt-out from a defined part of EU cooperation. It offers no room for policy choices or discretion; rather, the clear and unavoidable effect is that Denmark cannot take part in AFSJ measures, and consequently such measures cannot become binding upon Denmark. The Danish AFSJ opt-out thus differs fundamentally from the Irish, and formerly also British, position pursuant to Protocol No 21,

[17] Protocol No 22 (n 16).

[18] Peers, 'In a World of Their Own?' (n 1) 383.

[19] This author personally participated in the so-called Piris Group that undertook the final drafting of the Lisbon Treaty and can testify to the immense time pressure, which left no room for recast drafting attempts.

which allows for active policy choices with the effect that the default position, which is similar to the opt-out situation, is revoked. This matter is explored further in section III.D.

As in the case of the defence opt-out, the AFSJ opt-out relates to legal measures only. The opt-out has not been made applicable in relation to policy documents like Declarations and Conclusions, including comprehensive work programmes like the Tampere and the later Stockholm programmes adopted by the European Council by way of conclusions.[20]

Except for adaptations, the main elements of this part of the Protocol originate from the version found in the Amsterdam Treaty. It provides the legal definition of the scope of the opt-out, which relates to both provisions and to measures adopted pursuant to legal bases within a defined area of the Treaty. Unlike the defence opt-out, there is no qualification concerning which AFSJ legal acts fall within the scope of the opt-out and which do not; they all do. Conversely, this implies that issues that may be considered as judicial cooperation in civil matters, like consumer protection or matters concerning insurance, which are not regulated within Title V of Part Three of the TFEU, fall outside the scope of the opt-out, hence Denmark participates fully.[21] The legal basis for a measure defines the position of Denmark.

Denmark's position in relation to legal acts that have dual or multiple legal bases both within and outside of Title V is addressed in Declaration 48, annexed to the final Act of the Lisbon Treaty, in the following way:

> The Conference notes that with respect to legal acts to be adopted by the Council acting alone or jointly with the European Parliament and containing provisions applicable to Denmark as well as provisions not applicable to Denmark because they have a legal basis to which Part I of the Protocol on the position of Denmark applies, Denmark declares that it will not use its voting right to prevent the adoption of the provisions which are not applicable to Denmark …[22]

The Declaration is based on the premise that in such cases, Denmark participates in the adoption of the measure but will not be bound by the part that is based on a Title V legal basis, that is the part that regulates AFSJ matters.

In the same Declaration, another specific issue is addressed, namely the Danish position vis-à-vis the Solidarity Clause pursuant to Article 222 TFEU. It reads:

> Furthermore, the Conference notes that on the basis of the Declaration by the Conference on Article 222, Denmark declares that Danish participation in actions or legal acts pursuant to Article 222 will take place in accordance with Part I and Part II of the Protocol on the position of Denmark.[23]

[20] Presidency Conclusion of the Tampera European Council Meeting, 15–16 October 1999.
[21] PA Nielsen, 'Det retlige forbehold og civilretten' in Olsen and Sørensen (eds) (n 8) 80.
[22] Declaration No 48 concerning the Protocol on the position of Denmark [2012] OJ C326/355.
[23] ibid.

Essentially, it means that any existing AFSJ measure forming part of a concrete response pursuant to the Clause – naturally – does not include the participation of Denmark; nor will Denmark be able to participate in or be bound by any new AFSJ measures that may be called for as part of a response.[24]

The main effect of the opt-out as defined in Protocol No 22 is that Denmark does not participate in *decision-making*. As a consequence, the opt-out makes it explicit that the Danish vote is not included in the relevant decision-making procedures. Although not overtly clear from the wording itself, Denmark does, on the other hand, take part in *decision-shaping*. In the explanatory notes to the ratification Bill on the Amsterdam Treaty, the Danish Government clarified that although Denmark could not ultimately participate in the adoption of the relevant AFSJ measures, Denmark would remain at the negotiating table with the aim of airing its views during deliberations.[25] No Danish pledge similar to the one given with regard to the defence opt-out, to vacate the rotating Presidency of the Council on AFSJ matters, was ever made. This has to do with the difference in the nature of the two opt-outs.

The nature of the Danish AFSJ opt-out is not absolute in the same sense as the opt-out on defence. Given the point of departure set out in the Edinburgh Decision, it is clear that the opt-out relates to the form of cooperation (supranational cooperation) but not to a legally binding cooperation on AFSJ matters per se, as long as it is done on an intergovernmental level. This opens up space for special legal constructions, with a view to mitigating, in some instances and under special conditions, the effect of the AFSJ opt-out that otherwise would leave Denmark outside all AFSJ cooperation. This is explored in section III.B.

At this stage, it should be noted that although the political weight of Danish views aired within the Council as part of the decision-shaping process is challenged by the fact that Denmark cannot take part in the ultimate decision-making, the Danish contribution may nonetheless be of political and practical relevance, given that subsequent mitigating solutions on the matters at hand will indeed include Danish participation.

### *i. The Effects in EU Law – Particularities Regarding Visa Policy*

Ever since the Amsterdam Treaty, the AFSJ opt-out has contained one specific modification concerning certain aspects of visa policy. In the current version it constitutes a separate Part III of the Protocol, as a new addition, although

[24] Such a general call has indeed followed, see Council Decision 415/2014/EU of 24 June 2014 on the arrangements for the implementation by the Union of the solidarity clause [2014] OJ L 192/53, Art 5. The issue of the Solidarity Clause relating to Part II (defence) of the Protocol on the position of Denmark is discussed in ch 5, section III.C.i.

[25] Explanatory Notes to Bill L2, Folketingstidende 1997-98, 1. saml, 247.

the wording of the single Article is unchanged from its original version, as follows:

> *Article 6*
>
> Articles 1, 2 and 3 shall not apply to measures determining the third countries whose nationals must be in possession of a visa when crossing the external borders of the Member States, or measures relating to a uniform format for visas.[26]

The modification brings Denmark out of the opt-out situation; hence Denmark has always participated fully in these particular visa elements within the AFSJ. The reason for this is that the two policy issues mentioned – the country list and the uniform format for visas – at the time of the Maastricht Treaty were regulated pursuant to the then Article 100C TEC and therefore as ordinary 'communitarian' cooperation outside of the intergovernmental third pillar to which the Edinburgh Decision, Section D referred. Consequently, these two issues did not form part of the (dormant) AFSJ opt-out of Edinburgh. From a Danish legal perspective, the Article 20 procedure pursuant to the Danish Constitution was observed in relation to the Danish ratification of the Maastricht Treaty. The issue of transfer of powers from Denmark to the EU on the two particular matters was handled as an integral part thereof.[27]

By the time of the Amsterdam Treaty, the issue in relation to these particular provisions was not one of activation of the dormant opt-out from the Edinburgh Decision as a consequence of the changes introduced to the AFSJ cooperation. The opposite was the case: this was an issue regarding the preservation of their status as falling outside the scope of the opt-out. This was achieved by inserting the above-cited provision into the Protocol on the Position of Denmark.

The legal scope of the opt-out did not change as a consequence of the Lisbon Treaty. The effects, however, were expanded, given that the Lisbon Treaty did away with the third-pillar construction. The demolition of the third pillar did not happen overnight; rather, the coming into force of the Lisbon Treaty initiated a process of termination of the third-pillar cooperation.

A dedicated Protocol on transitional provisions forming part of the Lisbon Treaty concerns itself with general aspects of the matter.[28] The Protocol entails a provision that preserves

> the legal effects of the acts of the institutions, bodies, offices and agencies of the Union adopted on the basis of the Treaty on European Union prior to the entry into force of the Treaty of Lisbon … until those acts are repealed, annulled or amended in implementation of the Treaties. The same shall apply to agreements concluded between Member States on the basis of the Treaty on European Union.[29]

[26] Protocol No 22 on the Position of Denmark [2012] OJ C326/299.
[27] On Danish ratification of the Maastricht Treaty, see ch 2, section VII.B.
[28] Protocol No 36 on Transitional Provisions [2008] OJ L115/322.
[29] ibid Art 9.

The preservation of the legal effects pursuant to the above-mentioned provision was accompanied by another provision that explicitly regulated for continued limitation of the powers of the Commission and the CJEU regarding Member States' non-compliance with obligations under the existing intergovernmental acts in the fields of police and criminal justice; however, this limitation was only upheld for the duration of a transitional period of five years from the entry into force of the Lisbon Treaty, provided that the intergovernmental acts had not been amended pursuant to the new Treaty provisions in the meantime.

In this regard, the IGC invited the institutions to see to the adoption of new legal acts pursuant to the Lisbon rules with a view to amending or replacing the third-pillar acts on police and criminal law within the five-year period mentioned in the Protocol.[30]

The issue is of relevance to Denmark's position. During the time prior to the Lisbon Treaty, a number of legal measures had been adopted within the fields of police and judicial cooperation in criminal matters. Given their intergovernmental character as third-pillar instruments, Denmark participated fully therein.

While the transitional Protocol contains provisions on the continuous special position of the UK and Ireland after the expiration of the transitional period,[31] it makes no reference to the Danish situation. Instead, this particular issue is addressed in Protocol No 22 on the Position of Denmark. A new, last sentence in Article 2 of the Protocol was inserted by the Lisbon Treaty. It stipulates as follows:

> In particular, acts of the Union in the field of police cooperation and judicial cooperation in criminal matters adopted before the entry into force of the Treaty of Lisbon which are amended shall continue to be binding upon and applicable to Denmark unchanged.[32]

The additional provision in the Danish Protocol may be read as meaning that the said acts would continue to be binding and applicable on an intergovernmental level and with the upholding of limited infringement powers of the Commission and the Court. Nonetheless, following the entry into force of the Lisbon Treaty, it turned out that the precise implication of the provision could be, and in fact was, read in a different way. In reply to questions from Scrutiny Committees of the Danish Parliament, the Danish Ministry of Justice produced a note that reflected on the matter. The Ministry concluded that the consensual legal reading as shared by the Council Legal Service and other Member States was that acts adopted before the entry into force of the Treaty of Lisbon, which are repealed and/or replaced by new acts falling

[30] Declaration No 50 concerning Article 10 of the Protocol on transitional provisions [2012] OJ C326/356.

[31] Protocol No 36 (n 28) Article 10(4)–(5).

[32] Protocol No 22 (n 26).

within the scope of the opt-out, in principle would continue to apply to Denmark. However, this starting point may be deviated from, as the other Member States may decide that a repealed or replaced act no longer shall apply to Denmark if the new act otherwise becomes inapplicable to the other Member States. In addition, if Denmark remains the only Member State still bound by a third-pillar act on police and criminal justice cooperation that is based on the principle of mutual recognition, or which establishes the legal basis for existing EU bodies (agencies), such an act will in practice have no effect in relation to Denmark.[33]

This reading means that Denmark is excluded from continuous cooperation based on the pre-Lisbon third-pillar *acquis*. Effectively, this outcome limits the scope of the statement-like provision of the Edinburgh Decision that Denmark will participate fully in AFSJ cooperation of an intergovernmental nature. It is clear, however, that it is not for Denmark to define whether such a cooperation exits or not.

Another policy change of the Lisbon Treaty concerned the protection of personal data, the character of which also necessitated reflection in the Danish Protocol. This is done through the insertion of a provision annexed to Article 2. It reads:

> *Article 2a*
>
> Article 2 of this Protocol shall also apply in respect of those rules laid down on the basis of Article 16 of the Treaty on the Functioning of the European Union which relate to the processing of personal data by the Member States when carrying out activities which fall within the scope of Chapter 4 or Chapter 5 of Title V of Part Three of that Treaty.[34]

This provision mirrors the one inserted on the same occasion as Article 6a of Protocol No 21 on the position of the UK and Ireland in respect of the AFSJ. The provision does not represent an extension of the Danish opt-out (nor of the position of UK and Ireland); rather, it provides clarity that Denmark will not be bound by rules that relate to measures falling within the scope of the opt-out. The opposite would have made no sense.

## B. Mitigating Solutions to the Effects of the AFSJ Opt-Out

### i. *Mitigating Solutions – Schengen*

A significant contribution to the European integration process accomplished by the Amsterdam Treaty was the integration into the EU legal framework of the

[33] Reply to parliamentary question: EUU Alm del (Europaudvalget 2015–16, L29) – svar på spørgsmål 2. Identical reply provided to the Scrutiny Committee on Justice and Legal Affairs.

[34] Protocol No 22 (n 26).

Schengen Agreement of 1985 on the abolition of border checks, and its further elaboration and expansion by the Convention of 1990.[35]

Denmark was party to the existing intergovernmental Schengen cooperation outside of EU law.[36] The year 2001 is sometimes referred to as the year of Danish membership of Schengen.[37] However, that year does not relate to the Danish Schengen accession but represents the time of activation of abolition of the internal border checks in Denmark upon Danish fulfilment of the procedures and criteria laid down within the Schengen rules.

Given its incorporation into the EU Treaties by the Amsterdam Treaty, Denmark faced a challenge, as the opt-out by default would be applicable to the part of the Schengen rules determined to have a legal basis in the then Title IV of the TEC. Papagianni argued that Denmark, as a contracting party to the Schengen Agreement,

> was willing to participate in a cooperation concerning the establishment of an 'area without internal frontiers', [however] it contested, mainly for internal political reasons, the transfer of such a competence to the community level. It opted instead for the maintenance of such cooperation within the intergovernmental sphere.[38]

That is correct as long as it is kept in mind that this was the only option for the Danish Government, as long as the opt-out was in force; and, as previously mentioned, it was not at all on the cards to put the abolition of the opt-out up for a referendum by the time of the Amsterdam Treaty.

As part of the Amsterdam Treaty, a Protocol had been drafted on the integration of the Schengen rules into EU law that in part addressed the Danish position,[39] but the principle and forward-looking solution were set out in the Danish opt-out Protocol.[40] The current version of this solution, which includes a few technical adaptations following the Lisbon Treaty, is worded as follows:

> 1. Denmark shall decide within a period of six months after the Council has decided on a proposal or initiative to build upon the Schengen *acquis* covered by this Part, whether it will implement this measure in its national law. If it decides to do so, this measure will create an obligation under international law between Denmark and the other Member States bound by the measure.

[35] For a short overview of the history of the Schengen cooperation, see '35 years since the signing of the Schengen Agreement' (2000) at www.concilium.europa.eu. See also E Wagner, 'Integration of Schengen into the Framework of the European Union' (1998) 25 *Legal Issues of European Integration* 1. Ch 7 contains a brief discussion of the element of differentiated integration ingrained in the Schengen cooperation itself.

[36] Act L 418 of 10 June 1997 on Danish accession to the Schengen Convention.

[37] See Elholm (n 8) 102.

[38] G Papagianni, *Institutional and Policy Dynamics of EU Migration Law* (Leiden, Martinus Nijhoff Publisher, 2006) 30.

[39] Art 3 of Protocol No 3 Integrating the Schengen Acquis into the framework of the European Union, annexed to the Treaty on European Union and the Treaty establishing the European Community [1997] OJ C340/93. In the current version it is Protocol No 19 [2015] OJ C326/1.

[40] Protocol No 22 (n 26). In the current version of the Schengen integration protocol following the Lisbon Treaty, its provision on Denmark simply refers to the rules laid out in Protocol No 22.

2. If Denmark decides not to implement a measure of the Council as referred to in paragraph 1, the Member States bound by that measure and Denmark will consider appropriate measures to be taken.[41]

In a Danish context, the solution is popularly labelled as 'the Schengen Technicality'.[42] In law, it would be wrong to refer to the Danish position as an opt-in, since Denmark does not become party to measures that build upon the Schengen *acquis* but rather to their content.[43] It is achieved by Denmark's implementation of the content of the Schengen measure into its national law. This is also the case when the measure in question takes the form of an EU Regulation. It is possible for Denmark to do so precisely because the measure is not binding upon Denmark under EU law.[44] The legal obligation that is constituted pursuant to the Schengen Technicality is intergovernmental and is binding as such between Denmark and the other Member States – not the Union.

The Schengen Technicality is not a deviation from or a modification of the opt-out that, as explained in section III.A, relates to the supranational form of AFSJ cooperation but not to Danish cooperation on AFSJ per se. Shaw nonetheless found the Danish position to be somewhat 'perverse'.[45] Given the legal effects of the opt-out, arguably the construction of the Schengen Technicality proved the only way to keep Denmark within Schengen.

In practice, the difference between a supranational and an intergovernmental legal obligation is probably marginal. Legally, however, it implies that the infringement procedures of the Commission and CJEU are not applicable. Furthermore, the Danish Supreme Court has rejected a request for a referral for a preliminary ruling by the CJEU in a Danish court case concerning the interpretation of rules originating from a Schengen measure implemented in Danish law pursuant to the Schengen Technicality. The Supreme Court pointed to the non-supranational character of the Danish participation in the Schengen *acquis* and found on that background the lack of a right or an obligation to make a referral to the CJEU by a Danish court pursuant to Article 267 TFEU.[46] It is therefore clear that the legal construction of the Schengen Technicality implies that judicial control by the CJEU is excluded.[47]

[41] ibid Art 4.

[42] In Danish '*Schengen teknikaliteten*', referred to as such, for example, in the explanatory notes to Bill L29 of 12 November 2015 on changing the Danish position vis-à-vis the AFSJ opt-out. See further section III.D.

[43] In section III.D, legal definitions of an opt-out and an opt-in respectively are proposed and discussed.

[44] It is recalled that EU law prohibits the transposition of regulations into national legislation.

[45] J Shaw, 'The Treaty of Amsterdam: Challenges of Flexibility and Legitimacy' (1998) 4(1) *European Law Journal* 77.

[46] Ruling of 2 May 2018 in Case 251/2017, A mod Rigspolitiet.

[47] A Ott, 'EU Constitutional Boundaries to Differentiation: How to Reconcile Differentiation with Integration?' in A Ott and E Vos (eds), *Fifty Years of European Integration: Foundations and Perspectives* (The Hague, TCM Asser Press, 2009) 116.

Vedsted-Hansen points to another consequence of the intergovernmental character of the obligations established by the Schengen Technicality, namely, that the EU Charter most likely is not applicable.[48] Although the Schengen Technicality as such forms part of EU treaty law, the non-EU law construction established pursuant to the Technicality indeed points to non-application of the Charter.

The Schengen Technicality does not necessarily leave Denmark in any favourable position. The provision is clear: Denmark is left to make a decision on implementing in national law all Schengen measures adopted by the other Member States to avoid facing 'appropriate measures'. The decision of Denmark to implement a Schengen measure does not cover future changes, recasts, etc. A new and separate decision by Denmark pursuant to the Schengen Technicality would then be necessary to avoid the said 'appropriate measures', which ultimately would imply termination of Denmark as a Schengen State. Therefore, the room for manoeuvre for Denmark after the adaptation of a Schengen measure by the other Member States is in practice non-existent as long as Denmark aims to remain a full Schengen State. That has indeed been the aim all along. As already mentioned, at times, Denmark participates actively in the deliberations within the Council on draft Schengen measures as the outcome also affects Denmark in a rather direct way, even though Denmark is excluded from participating in the adoption of the measure. To date, Denmark has implemented all Schengen measures according to the provisions of the Schengen Technicality. Consequently, the scope of 'appropriate measures' has not been tested.

As prescribed in the provision itself, the Schengen Technicality is invoked simply by a formal notification from Denmark to the Council that Denmark avails itself of Article 4 of Protocol No 22. Without further procedures or follow-up arrangements, a legally binding agreement is constituted between Denmark and the other EU Member States that are bound by the adopted Schengen measure, that is 'Schengen members'. The construction remains legal in its entirety.[49]

The limited scope of the Schengen Technicality to create international law obligations between Denmark and other Member States was explicitly addressed in relation to the EU Schengen association by Switzerland and Liechtenstein, respectively. Separate bilateral agreements on Schengen relations between Denmark and those countries were thus prescribed in the respective agreements with the EU and they were subsequently entered into.[50]

[48] J Vedsted-Hansen, 'Det retlige forbehold og personers mobilitet' in Olsen and Sørensen (eds) (n 8) 128.

[49] For a seemingly different view, see Wagner (n 35) 40. Wagner describes the Danish position on Schengen as a sort of '"legal opt-out" and a "political opt-in"'.

[50] Agreement of 28 April 2005 between Denmark and Switzerland, Retsinformation BKI nr 15 24/05/2011. The bilateral agreement is foreseen in Art 13 combined with preambular provision 11 of Agreement between the European Union, the European Community and the Swiss Confederation on the Swiss Confederation's association with the implementation, application and development of

Bilateral Schengen agreements between Denmark and Norway and Iceland, respectively, are absent. Unlike Switzerland and Liechtenstein, the two Nordic countries were prior parties to the Schengen regime and became associated with the integration of the Schengen *acquis* into the framework of the EU by way of a separate agreement,[51] which has a dedicated legal basis in the Schengen integration protocol.[52] The agreement stipulates that the original intergovernmental protocol on Denmark's Schengen accession[53] remains applicable.[54]

The European Border and Coast Guard Agency (FRONTEX) is established by a Regulation that builds upon the Schengen *acquis*. The position of Denmark is referred to in recital 125 as follows:

> In accordance with Articles 1 and 2 of Protocol No 22 on the position of Denmark annexed to the TEU and to the TFEU, Denmark is not taking part in the adoption of this Regulation and is not bound by it, or subject to its application. Given that this Regulation builds upon the Schengen acquis, Denmark shall, in accordance with Article 4 of that Protocol, decide within a period of six months after the Council has decided on this Regulation whether it will implement it in its national law.[55]

As is customary, Denmark acted accordingly and notified its positive decision. True to the provisions of the Schengen Technicality, no special arrangements for Denmark's participation in FRONTEX are foreseen. This stands in contrast to the situation applicable to the associated Schengen States. In their case, specific arrangements between the respective associated Schengen States and the EU provide for rules on their participation in the work of FRONTEX, including provisions on financial contributions and staffing.[56] The Danish Schengen Technicality is applicable in relation to the specific EU measures that conclude the foreseen arrangements with the associated Schengen States, and as such ensures the participation of Denmark in those arrangements.[57]

the Schengen acquis [2008] OJ L053/ 52. Similarly, and on the same basis, a bilateral agreement was concluded between Denmark and Lichtenstein on 17 June 2011.

[51] Agreement concluded by the Council of the European Union and the Republic of Iceland and the Kingdom of Norway concerning the latter's association with the implementation, application and development of the Schengen acquis [1999] OJ L176/36.

[52] Protocol No 3 (now 19) (n 39) Art 6.

[53] Protocol, signed in Luxembourg on 19 December 1996, on accession of the Government of the Kingdom of Denmark to the Agreement on the gradual abolition of controls at their common borders signed at Schengen on 14 June 1985 and its related declaration.

[54] Agreement [Iceland and Norway] (n 51) Art 2(1), in particular Annex A, Part 2, no 11.

[55] Regulation (EU) 2019/1896 of the European Parliament and of the Council of 13 November 2019 on the European Border and Coast Guard and repealing Regulations (EU) No 1052/2013 and (EU) 2016/162 [2019] OJ L295/1.

[56] ibid recitals 121–124.

[57] eg Council Decision 2010/490/EU of 26 July 2010 on the conclusion, on behalf of the Union, of the Arrangement between the European Community, of the one part, and the Swiss Confederation and the Principality of Liechtenstein, of the other part, on the modalities of the participation by those States in the European Agency for the Management of Operational Cooperation at the External Borders of the Member States of the European Union [2010] OJ L243/2, recital 4.

The participation by the Member State, Denmark, in an EU agency, FRONTEX, on the basis of provisions of its national law, combined with a legal obligation under international law between Denmark and the other Member States, truly constitutes a unique legal construction.

Upon the instigation, notably, of the UK, the CJEU has had the opportunity to address the question of the correct classification of a measure as a 'Schengen measure'.[58] The Court has ruled that it is a matter based on 'objective factors which are amenable to judicial review, including in particular the aim and the content of the act'.[59] That reasoning was applicable by analogy to what applies in relation to the choice of the legal basis of an EU measure, and the Court has referred to its established case law in this respect. Moreover, the Court added that since it is by analogy only, its finding is 'limited by the specific nature of the closer cooperation applicable to the Schengen *acquis*, which means that the system as a whole of which that *acquis* forms part must also be taken into account'.[60] The Court continued by stating that

> when classifying a measure as falling within an area of the Schengen acquis or as a development of that acquis, the need for coherence of that acquis, and the need – where that acquis evolves – to maintain that coherence, must be taken into account.[61]

The designation of a measure as Schengen or not has consequences for Member States that enjoy special positions, albeit with a different outcome. Put squarely, if a measure is considered to constitute a development of the Schengen *acquis*, Ireland remains out, as it cannot use the opt-in mechanism pursuant to Protocol No 21. Formerly, the same applied to the UK.[62] For Denmark, on the other hand, the situation is the reverse, as Denmark is brought on board due to the Schengen Technicality in Article 4 of Protocol No 22.

### *ii. Mitigating Solutions – Parallel Agreements*

The Schengen Technicality is a treaty-based provision that mitigates the effect of the opt-out with a view to ensuring continued Danish participation as a full Schengen State, albeit on a non-privileged, special legal footing. Otherwise, the opt-out leaves Denmark outside all other AFSJ cooperation of a legally binding nature.[63]

[58] Case C-77/05 *United Kingdom of Great Britain and Northern Ireland v Council of the European Union* ECLI:EU:C:2007:803; and Case C-482/08 *United Kingdom of Great Britain and Northern Ireland v Council of the European Union* ECLI:EU:C:2010:631.

[59] Case C-77/05 (n 58) para 79.

[60] Case C-482/08 (n 58) para 46.

[61] ibid para 48.

[62] There is a modification, as Ireland is (and the UK was) party to a part of the Schengen *acquis* not directly related to the principal objective on the abolition of checks on persons at the common borders of the Member States. The opt-in is applicable to that part. Protocol No 19 on the Schengen integration contains a number of detailed provisions on the position of Ireland and (formerly) the UK as well.

[63] With the exception of the minor visa issues that falls outside the scope of the opt-out. See section III.A.i.

Denmark may choose, if it so wishes, to align its national policies and regulations with EU standards and other EU legal measures within the AFSJ that regulate particular subject matter through harmonisation of legal definitions, producers, penalty levels, etc. Denmark has indeed chosen to do this in certain areas of the AFSJ, for example within judicial cooperation in criminal matters,[64] while choosing another path on other matters, notably relating to migration.[65]

The situation is different in the event that EU regulation relates to the concept of mutual recognition, or in cases when EU institutions have been empowered to exercise authority. Denmark cannot by unilateral alignment of national laws obtain the effects of such EU regulation, notably the rights and obligations it establishes, should Denmark so wish. As long as the opt-out is in force, it would require a special arrangement to reach such an outcome.[66]

Following the entry into force of the Amsterdam Treaty in 1999, several new EU legal acts were rather quickly adopted within the AFSJ on judicial cooperation in civil matters, as well as on asylum and migration. That included measures on matters that previously had been regulated pursuant to the intergovernmental regime of the Maastricht Treaty, and as such with the participation of Denmark. Due to the AFSJ opt-out, Denmark was now left out of the new communitarian measures, without that being a reflection of a sudden change of Danish policy vis-à-vis the matters concerned.[67]

After consulting with the Danish Parliament, the Danish Government approached the Commission to sound out the possibilities for mitigating this outcome with regard to six identified legal acts; four within judicial cooperation in civil matters[68] and two within asylum policies.[69] Denmark essentially argued that even though it was legally not able to participate in the EU measures due to the opt-out, it was not in the interest of either Denmark or the EU for Denmark to be left out of the legally binding cooperation on these matters altogether.[70]

[64] Elholm (n 8) 93.

[65] ibid 121.

[66] R Adler-Nissen and T Gammeltoft-Hansen, 'Straitjacket or Sovereignty Shield? The Danish Opt-Out on Justice and Home Affairs and Prospects after the Treaty of Lisbon' [2010] *Danish Foreign Policy Yearbook* 145.

[67] Nielsen (n 21) 80.

[68] Council Regulation (EC) No 1346/2000 of 29 May 2000 on insolvency proceedings [2000] OJ L160/1; Council Regulation (EC) No 1347/2000 of 29 May 2000 on jurisdiction and the recognition and enforcement of judgments in matrimonial matters and in matters of parental responsibility for children of both spouses [2000] OJ L160/19; Council Regulation (EC) No 1348/2000 of 29 May 2000 on the service in the Member States of judicial and extrajudicial documents in civil or commercial matters [2000] OJ L160/37; Council Regulation (EC) No 44/2001 of 22 December 2000 on jurisdiction and the recognition and enforcement of judgments in civil and commercial matters [2001] OJ L12/1.

[69] Council Regulation (EC) No 343/2003 of 18 February 2003 establishing the criteria and mechanisms for determining the Member State responsible for examining an asylum application lodged in one of the Member States by a third-country national [2000] OJ L50/1; Council Regulation (EC) No 2725/2000 of 11 December 2000 concerning the establishment of 'Eurodac' for the comparison of fingerprints for the effective application of the Dublin Convention [2000] OJ L316/1 (popularly referred to as 'The Dublin Regulation' and 'Eurodac', respectively).

[70] Abolition of the opt-out was considered a political no-go in Denmark.

The solution suggested was to associate Denmark closely with the said EU measures through agreements between Denmark on the one side and the EU on the other, binding the parties under international law; a solution that exploratory consultations at an expert level between the Commission and Denmark had found to constitute a legally possible way out.[71]

After lengthy consideration, the Commission responded favourably to the general idea of establishing such Agreements between the EU and Denmark. Upon a proposal from the Commission, in 2003 the Council subsequently adopted Decisions on authorising the Commission – extraordinary – to negotiate *three* agreements with Denmark in all, covering *four* of the six AFSJ measures requested by Denmark. The Danish request for agreements on the Insolvency Proceedings Regulation, as well as on the Brussels II Regulation, was dismissed by the Commission on the ground of insufficient interest in such agreements on the side of the EU.[72]

It was thus clear that even though it was considered, in principle, to be a legally sound option, there were nonetheless limits. Moreover, it was unequivocally clear that Denmark possessed no right to become associated to the *acquis* falling within the scope of the opt-out. The Commission's main considerations were as follows:

> After in-depth discussions, the Commission accepted to negotiate parallel agreements with Denmark, provided that the following conditions were fulfilled: Such a solution would have to be of an exceptional nature and for a transitional period only, the participation of Denmark in the Community regime would have to be fully in the interests of the Community and its citizens and the requirements imposed on Denmark would have to be identical to those imposed on all Member States, so as to ensure that rules with the same content are applied in Denmark and in the other Member States.[73]

The Commission referred to the agreement with Denmark as a 'parallel agreement' – terminology alien to the Treaties. While it is not clear which party invented that term, it is clear that the agreement on the EU side is concluded in accordance with the Treaty rules on the conclusion of EU agreements with a third country, meaning that the agreements are third-country agreements under EU law. Despite its Member State status, Denmark is in this specific circumstance treated as a third country.

From a Danish legal viewpoint, a parallel agreement is considered an ordinary intergovernmental agreement binding under international law, the conclusion of which requires parliamentary assent according to Article 19 of

[71] See Memorandum from the Danish Ministry of Justice, Justitsministeriet, 'Samarbejdet om retlige og indre anliggende – en analyse af EU-lovgivningen omfattet af retsforbeholdet' (2015) 29.

[72] ibid 30.

[73] Proposal for a Council Decision concerning the signing of the Agreement between the European Community and the Kingdom of Denmark extending to Denmark the provisions of Council Regulation (EC) No 1348/2000 on the service in the Member States of judicial and extrajudicial documents in civil or commercial matters, COM/2005/0146 final.

the Danish Constitution. Neither of the parallel agreements transfers powers to the EU in accordance with the legal understanding pursuant to Article 20 of the Constitution. Consequently, the procedure therein, including ultimately the holding of a referendum, is not applicable.

Upon completion of the negotiations, as well as the respective procedures for their conclusion, the parallel agreements entered into force in the years that followed: the one on the so-called Dublin and Eurodac Regulations on 1 April 2006;[74] and the two agreements on the Regulations within judicial cooperation on civil matters on 1 July 2007.[75]

The main content of the three parallel agreements is largely the same. Denmark's rights and obligations correspond as far as possible to those of the other Member States that derive them from the EU measures. In the case of Denmark, however, it is not the measures themselves that apply but the provisions of the measures; they are made applicable through national implementation in Denmark, and they apply under international law in Denmark's relations with the Union or, as it may be, the other participating States, depending on the content of the provisions concerned. This follows the same concept as is known from the Schengen Technicality. The reason why it is legally possible for Denmark to implement in national law provisions of an EU Regulation is due to the fact that Denmark does so not pursuant to EU law, as it is not applicable to Denmark, but as part of a legal obligation under international law.

Corresponding to what equally follows pursuant to the Schengen Technicality, the parallel agreements make it clear that changes to the underlying EU measures, as well as implementing measures pursuant to them, do not become binding upon Denmark. The agreements set a timeframe within which Denmark may decide to implement nationally the content of any such amendments or implementing measures and inform the Commission accordingly. Once implementation has taken place, a follow-up notification by Denmark creates a mutual obligation under international law between Denmark and the EU, and constitutes as such an amendment annexed to the parallel agreement. If, on the other hand, Denmark were to choose not to implement changes or implementing measures, the default position would be that the parallel agreement in question would be terminated. That outcome is avoided only if the parties (EU and Denmark) decide otherwise. The procedure for reaching such a decision is not laid down. The issue has not occurred, as Denmark has chosen to implement changes in all cases.

[74] Agreement between the European Community and the Kingdom of Denmark on the criteria and mechanisms for establishing the State responsible for examining a request for asylum lodged in Denmark or any other Member State of the European Union and 'Eurodac' for the comparison of fingerprints for the effective application of the Dublin Convention [2006] OJ L66/38.

[75] Agreement between the European Community and the Kingdom of Denmark on jurisdiction and the recognition and enforcement of judgments in civil and commercial matters [2005] OJ L299/62; and Agreement between the European Community and the Kingdom of Denmark on the service of judicial and extrajudicial documents in civil or commercial matters [2005] OJ L300/55.

International agreements concluded by the EU on matters falling within the scope of the EU Regulations concerned will not be applicable to Denmark. Consequently, Denmark is left to arrange bilateral agreements entered into in coordination with the EU to close the gaps. On the other hand, Denmark has excluded itself from entering into international agreements on its own initiative on matters falling within the scope of the EU rules in question.

With regard to the inclusion of Norway and Iceland in the Dublin/Eurodac regime, the issue of the relation to Denmark was specifically regulated in the agreement between the EU and the two countries.[76] According to Article 12 of the agreement, Denmark may request to participate in the agreement, in which case the conditions for such participation shall be determined by the Contracting Parties, acting with the consent of Denmark. Given that this request was indeed made by Denmark, a protocol to the EU's agreement with Norway and Iceland to this effect has been adopted.[77]

On the question of jurisdiction, the parallel agreements make the CJEU competent both with a view to the interpretation of the parallel agreements as well as in relation to issues of non-compliance with the agreements. Moreover, the concept of preliminary rulings is extended to cover the parallel agreements, that is Danish courts shall make referrals to the CJEU 'whenever under the same circumstances a court or tribunal of another Member State of the European Union would be required to do so in respect of the Dublin II Regulation and the Eurodac Regulation'.[78] Furthermore, Danish courts are obliged, when interpreting the parallel agreements and as such de facto the underlying EU measures, to take due account of the rulings contained in the case law of the Court in this respect. These provisions of the parallel agreements on preliminary rulings stand in contrast to the legal situation pursuant to the Schengen Technicality.

Interestingly, the parallel agreements also contain an explicit provision allowing for the Danish Government to submit observations in cases referred to the CJEU by a court or tribunal of a Member State for a preliminary ruling concerning the interpretation of any provision of the EU Regulations to which the parallel agreements relate.[79] This provision may be read as an exception from an otherwise general exclusion of Denmark from doing so in cases regarding preliminary rulings relating to the interpretation of EU measures falling within the scope of the opt-out. That, however, is not the case. Often Denmark would lack legal and political interest in such cases, as the legal acts in question are not

[76] Agreement between the European Community and the Republic of Iceland and the Kingdom of Norway concerning the criteria and mechanisms for establishing the State responsible for examining a request for asylum lodged in a Member State or in Iceland or Norway [2001] OJ L093/40.

[77] Protocol to the Agreement between the European Community and the Republic of Iceland and the Kingdom of Norway concerning the criteria and mechanisms for establishing the State responsible for examining a request for asylum lodged in a Member State or in Iceland or Norway [2006] OJ L57/16.

[78] See, eg, Art 6(1) of the Dublin/Eurodac parallel agreement (n 74).

[79] See, eg, Art 6(4) of the Dublin/Eurodac parallel agreement (n 74).

binding on Denmark due to the opt-out, which then leads Denmark to refrain from engaging in such cases before the Court. However, no elements within the opt-out suggest that Denmark generally is excluded from the provisions of the Treaties on the rights of any Member State to submit observations before the Court also in cases on the interpretation of legal acts falling within the scope of the opt-out. Denmark summitted observations in a case for a preliminary ruling referred to the Court from the Belgian *Cour Constitutionnelle* on the interpretation of the Passenger Name Record (PNR) Directive.[80] That Directive has its legal basis in Title V of Part Three of the TFEU so consequently Denmark did not take part in its adoption, neither is Denmark bound by it or subject to its application due to the opt-out.[81] However, Denmark has very deliberately adopted a national act on PNR that largely corresponds to the provisions of the PNR Directive. The preliminary ruling of the Court on the interpretation of the Directive would therefore also influence the way in which Denmark nationally legislates on the matter, with a view to maintaining close alignment with the EU Directive. That is why it makes good sense that Denmark summitted observations in this particular case. The right for Denmark to make the submission was not brought into question.

The parallel agreements contain an asymmetry with regard to the jurisdiction on compliance. Whereas the Commission may bring cases before the Court against Denmark, the opposite is not the case. Denmark may appeal to the Commission in cases of alleged non-compliance by a Member State with its obligations under the agreements.

Finally, the parallel agreements contain a clause on their termination that simply prescribes that this may happen at the request of either side, and that, in any case, the agreements will cease to operate in the event that Denmark abolishes the opt-out. This is as close as the agreements come to having the otherwise required 'transitional character' (see the criteria laid down in the Proposal for a Council decision by the Commission, as reproduced earlier in this section on parallel agreements).

Thym has argued that the agreements with Denmark circumvent the provision for Denmark to abolish the opt-out.[82] Arguably, the Commission did consider the aspect of the option for Denmark to abolish the opt-out before it nonetheless formulated its restrictive yet positive position on the agreements.

No new parallel agreements have since been concluded,[83] nor have any changes been made to the existing parallel agreements. In a single case

[80] Case C-817/19 *Ligue des Droit Humains* ECLI:EU:C:2022:491.

[81] Recital 40 of Directive (EU) 2016/681 of the European Parliament and of the Council of 27 April 2016 on the use of passenger name record (PNR) data for the prevention, detection, investigation and prosecution of terrorist offences and serious crime [2016] OJ L119/132.

[82] D Thym, 'Supranational Differentiation and Enhanced Cooperation' in R Schütze and T Tridimas (eds), *Oxford Principles of European Union Law*, vol I (Oxford, Oxford University Press, 2018) 847, 864 fn 137. Erroneously, reference is made to Protocol No 15 and not Protocol No 22.

[83] Regarding Danish association to Europol and Eurojust, see section III.B.iii.

concerning the Dublin/Eurodac agreement, a need to *supplement* the original parallel agreement materialised in light of a recast of the Eurodac Regulation. The Commission considered that the part of the recast Regulation that provided for the transfer of information for law-enforcement purposes was not covered by the parallel agreement, as the law-enforcement element constituted a new purpose in relation to the original Eurodac Regulation.[84]

In light thereof, in 2013 Denmark requested a supplementary parallel agreement to be negotiated, to which the EU side agreed. The Commission requested that negotiations with Denmark be made in tandem with the EU's negotiations on the matter with Norway, Iceland, Liechtenstein and Switzerland (the associated countries). This delayed the process of concluding the supplement to the parallel agreement with Denmark, which otherwise was considered by the Commission to be a formality.[85] A protocol to the parallel agreement on Dublin/Eurodac was therefore only concluded some six years later.[86] Upon completion of the necessary procedures, it entered into force on 13 May 2019.

With the point of departure in case law from the CJEU on the interpretation of the Dublin Regulation in light of the Charter of Fundamental Rights,[87] Vested-Hansen discusses whether the Charter is applicable in relation to the parallel agreement on Dublin/Eurodac, reaching an affirmative conclusion.[88] It is, however, questionable whether that is so, given that Denmark, through the parallel agreements, does not implement EU law but rather an obligation under international law. Vedsted-Hansen rightly points out that it is mostly a theoretical question, given that Denmark is bound by the corresponding provisions of the European Convention on Human Rights, and he highlights that Denmark, pursuant to the specific provisions of the parallel agreement, is bound to apply relevant case law from the CJEU on the interpretation of the Charter.[89]

The concept of 'parallel agreements' has not been applied to Member States other than Denmark.[90] A 'parallel agreement' whereby the Union enters into an

[84] Justitsministeriet, 'Samarbejdet om retlige og indre anliggender – En analyse af EU-lovgivning omfattet af retsforbeholdet' (Copenhagen, Rosendahls Schultz Grafisk, 2015) 30.

[85] ibid.

[86] Council Decision (EU) 2019/836 of 13 May 2019 on the conclusion of the Protocol to the Agreement between the European Community and the Kingdom of Denmark on the criteria and mechanisms for establishing the State responsible for examining a request for asylum lodged in Denmark or any other Member State of the European Union and 'Eurodac' for the comparison of fingerprints for the effective application of the Dublin Convention regarding access to Eurodac for law enforcement purposes [2019] OJ L138/3.

[87] See Case C-411/10 *N.S v Secretary of State for the Home Department* and Case C-493/10 *M.E and others v Refugee Applications Commissioner and Minister for Justice, Equality and Law Reform* ECLI:EU:C:2011:865.

[88] Vedsted-Hansen (n 48) 116–17.

[89] ibid.

[90] Reply to MEP parliamentary question of 27 November 2015, reference: P-013534/2015, in which it is further stated that '[t]he other agreements concluded between the EU and a Member State all concern specific situations where an agreement with the EU is concluded because that Member State has a special relationship with a territory which is not part of the EU'.

international agreement on alignment to the *acquis* with a Member State with a special position is thus a very specific spill-off from the Danish AFSJ opt-out, and as such a unique addition to EU law-making.

### *iii. Mitigating Solutions – Other Agreements*

The EU's law enforcement agency (Europol) was established in 1998.[91] Europol supports the national authorities in their work to prevent and combat organised crime, including terrorism, and it supports mutual cooperation among the national authorities in this regard. In 2002, this EU cooperation was further enhanced by the establishment of another agency dedicated to the judicial cooperation in criminal matters (Eurojust).[92] Given their intergovernmental status at the time, Denmark participated fully in these agencies.

Following the entry into force of the Lisbon Treaty, the legal foundations of the two agencies were reformed, with the consequence that the previous third-pillar instruments were repealed and replaced by legislative acts pursuant to the relevant provisions of the Treaties, which now fell within the scope of the opt-out.[93] A broadly-shared political assessment similar to the one that prompted the parallel agreements emerged in Denmark, namely, that Denmark should seek to remain as closely associated to the agencies while at the same time continuing to maintain its opt-out.

The mutual solution found in these two cases was an innovative development of the parallel agreements. Instead of agreements with the EU as such, and negotiated with the Commission, cooperation agreements were negotiated and ultimately adopted directly between Denmark and the two agencies.[94] The one on Europol entered into force in 2017,[95] and the one on Eurojust in 2019.[96] Despite their character as directly-adopted cooperation agreements, the Council, having regard to the opinion of the European Parliament, either

[91] Council Act of 26 July 1995 drawing up the Convention based on Article K.3 TEU on the establishment of a European Police Office (Europol Convention) [1995] OJ C316/1, entered into force 1 October 1998.

[92] Council Decision 2002/187/JHA of 28 February 2002 setting up Eurojust with a view to reinforcing the fight against serious crime [2002] OJ L63/1.

[93] Regulation (EU) 2016/794 of the European Parliament and of the Council of 11 May 2016 on the European Union Agency for Law Enforcement Cooperation (Europol) and replacing and repealing Council Decisions 2009/371/JHA, 2009/934/JHA, 2009/935/JHA, 2009/936/JHA and 2009/968/JHA [2016] OJ L135/53; and Regulation (EU) 2018/1727 of the European Parliament and of the Council of 14 November 2018 on the European Union Agency for Criminal Justice Cooperation (Eurojust), and replacing and repealing Council Decision 2002/187/JHA [2018] OJ L295/138.

[94] Denmark had been included in the list of third States with which Europol should conclude agreements by Council Decision 2009/935/JHA of 30 November 2009 determining the list of third States and organisations with which Europol shall conclude agreements [2009] OJ L325/12.

[95] Agreement on Operational and Strategic Cooperation between the Kingdom of Denmark and the European Police Office at www.Europol.europa.eu.

[96] Agreement on Criminal Justice Cooperation between Eurojust and the Kingdom of Denmark at www.Eurojust.europa.eu.

authorised (Europol) or approved (Eurojust) the agreements.[97] The matter of jurisdiction of the CJEU followed the model under the parallel agreements.

As in the case of the parallel agreement, Denmark is treated as if it were a third country.[98] The cooperation agreements contain detailed provisions on how Denmark and the agencies are to cooperate, including provisions on financial contributions from Denmark, all with an aim of ensuring cooperation 'to a level at least equivalent to that of third countries with which such agreements have been concluded'.[99] Whereas the rights and obligations of Denmark may thus correspond to those of third countries, they do not fully match those of a Member State. Notably, within Europol, Danish police no longer have the same access to Europol's database (EIS), the repercussions of which cause some political debate in Denmark.[100] In the case of Eurojust, the agreement grants Denmark a seat similar to that of a Liaison Prosecutor appointed to Eurojust by third countries that have signed a cooperation agreement. The Danish representatives act as observers without voting rights within the governing structures. Denmark has, however, maintained its access to Eurojust's information systems, and may exchange data and evidence in criminal investigations and prosecutions in the context of cases registered at Eurojust.[101]

Denmark has not requested a cooperation agreement with the European Public Prosecutor's Office (EPPO),[102] given a general reluctance from the Danish political side towards the EPPO.[103]

Prior to the establishment of the European Asylum Support Office (EASO),[104] Denmark participated in practical cooperation on asylum issues among the Member States. Given that a main purpose of the EASO is to build on and strengthen such cooperation, there was general agreement among Member States that Denmark should maintain its engagement to the extent possible. The solution in this case was found by granting Denmark the status of observer to the EASO through a provision of the Regulation establishing the Office.[105]

In any event, Denmark itself has taken the lead role in proposing initiatives to accommodate Denmark has in this regard.

[97] See the references in the recitals to the respective agreements.

[98] Curtin finds that the agreement is of a 'peculiar nature', with Denmark as an 'assumed third country', see D Curtin, 'Brexit and the EU Area of Freedom, Security, and Justice: Bespoke Bits and Pieces' in F Fabbrini (ed), *The Law & Politics of Brexit* (Oxford, Oxford University Press, 2017) 185.

[99] Recital 3 of the Europol cooperation agreement (n 95).

[100] Elholm (n 8) 100, fn 23.

[101] Q & A Eurojust's cooperation with Denmark at www.eurojust.europa.eu.

[102] Council Regulation (EU) 2017/1939 of 12 October 2017 implementing enhanced cooperation on the establishment of the European Public Prosecutor's Office ('the EPPO') [2017] OJ L283/1.

[103] Elholm (n 8) 101.

[104] Regulation (EU) No 439/2010 of the European Parliament and of the Council of 19 May 2010 establishing a European Asylum Support Office [2010] OJ L132/11. The current regulation is Regulation (EU) 2021/2303 of the European Parliament and of the Council of 15 December 2021 on the European Union Agency for Asylum and repealing Regulation (EU) No 439/2010 [2021] OJ L 468/1.

[105] Regulation (EU) No 439/2010 (n 104) recital 23 and Art 48.

## C. Effects of the AFSJ Opt-Out within EU External Relations Law

It is clear from Article 2 of Protocol No 22 that no measure adopted pursuant to Title V of Part Three of the TFEU, and no provision of any international agreement concluded by the Union pursuant to that Title, is binding upon or applicable in Denmark; moreover, no such provision or measure shall in any way affect the competences, rights and obligations of Denmark. In other words, as an effect of the opt-out, Denmark is not part of the EU's external cooperation within the AFSJ.

The conclusion of an agreement between the EU and a third country purely on AFSJ matters would necessarily require a legal basis within the AFSJ part of the TFEU, with the consequence that Denmark would not be party to the Council Decisions on the signature and conclusion, and would naturally not be bound by the agreement itself.[106]

In such a situation, it is not uncommon that the parties make reference to the special position of Denmark and point to the desirability of a bilateral agreement on the same terms as the EU's agreement, to be entered into by the third country concerned and Denmark.[107]

On the other hand, it is equally clear that an international commitment of the EU entered into by way of a Council Decision with a legal basis *not* within Title V of Part Three of the TFEU falls outside the scope of the opt-out and as such is adopted with full Danish participation. In this case, the Council Decision, and by that the international agreement, becomes binding on Denmark pursuant to EU law.

However, a third scenario may emerge in which the Union's accession to an agreement with a third country or an international organisation is based on legal bases that fall both within and outside Title V. In such a scenario, the Council Decision would need to be split in two: there will be non-Danish participation in the part based within Title V but full Danish participation in the other part, which becomes binding upon Denmark and by way of which Denmark becomes bound under EU law by the part of the international agreement that is non-AFSJ.[108]

[106] See, eg, Council Decision of 7 October 2010 on the conclusion of the Agreement between the European Community and the Islamic Republic of Pakistan on the readmission of persons residing without authorization [2010] OJ L 287/50, recital 8.

[107] See, eg, the Joint Declaration to the EU/Pakistani readmission agreement, Agreement between the European Community and the Islamic Republic of Pakistan on the readmission of persons residing without authorization [2010] OJ L287/52. The Joint Declaration reads 'Joint Declaration concerning Denmark: The Parties take note that this Agreement does not apply to the territory of the Kingdom of Denmark, nor to nationals of the Kingdom of Denmark. In such circumstances it is appropriate that Pakistan and Denmark conclude a readmission agreement in the same terms as this Agreement.'

[108] See the explanatory notes to Bill L29 of 8 October 2015, 'Forslag til lov om omdannelse af retsforbeholdet til en tilvalgsordning', Folketingstidende, saml 2015–16, L29, discussed in section III.D.

Not only is this model made necessary by the fact that the legal bases contain different and incompatible procedures for the adoption of a Council Decision – one with and one without Danish participation[109] – it is also necessary with a view to ensuring that the opt-out is respected in both the negative and positive sense; Denmark is not bound, under EU law, by the AFSJ part of the agreement, but on the other hand Denmark is bound by the part of the agreement that does not fall within the AFSJ. If the latter were not the case, the effect of the opt-out would incidentally have been widened beyond its legal scope as defined in Protocol No 22.[110]

As ever, the legal basis for the Union's measures remains essential when determining the applicability of the opt-out. It is settled case law of the CJEU that the choice of legal basis for any EU measure must rest on objective factors that are amenable to judicial review, and that these include the aim and content of the measure in question.[111] Furthermore, the Court has on several occasions ruled on the issue of legal bases as being ancillary to other legal bases with a broader scope. A centre-of-gravity test of the legal measure concerned proves decisive. It should be observed that the centre of gravity of the EU measure may differ from the centre of gravity of the international agreement itself, given that the EU measure may have a narrower scope than the international agreement in the event that parts thereof fall outside of the (exercised) EU's external competence. An example is the Council Decision on the signing, on behalf of the Union, of a Framework Agreement on Partnership and Cooperation with the Republic of the Philippines.[112] The Council had included specific legal bases on the AFSJ, transport and environment, alongside the more general legal bases on the common commercial policy as well as development cooperation. This approach was challenged by the Commission before the CJEU, which ruled in favour of the Commission. The Court found it apparent that the provisions of the Agreement relating to the AFSJ, transport and environmental issues did not contain obligations 'so extensive that they may be considered to constitute objectives distinct from those of development cooperation that are neither secondary nor indirect in relation to the latter objectives'.[113] The effect of the Court's ruling, which eliminated the AFSJ legal basis from the Council Decision, was that Denmark, along with the UK and Ireland, became bound by the Council

[109] See to that effect Case C-658/11, *European Parliament v Council of the European Union* ECLI:EU:C:2014:2025, para 57; and Case C-180/20 *European Commission v Council of the European Union* ECLI:EU:C:2021:658, para 34.

[110] Opinion 1/19 *Istanbul Convention* ECLI:EU:C:2021:198. For a further discussion of this Opinion, see text to nn 147–50 and 169–72.

[111] Case C-411/06 *European Commission v European Parliament and Council of the European Union* ECLI:EU:C:2009:518, para 45.

[112] Council Decision 2012/272/EU of 14 May 2012 on the signing, on behalf of the Union, of the Framework Agreement on Partnership and Cooperation between the European Union, of the one part, and the Republic of the Philippines, of the other part [2012] OJ L134/3.

[113] Case C-377/12 *European Commission v Council of the European Union* ECLI:EU:C:2014:1903, para 59.

Decision and consequently bound under EU law by the Union's agreement with the Philippines.

With a view to ascertaining the applicability of Protocol No 22 on the Position of Denmark, as well as the special position of Ireland and (formerly) the UK pursuant to Protocol No 21 in relation to EU's international agreements, the Court has clarified that 'it is the legal basis for a measure ... which determines the protocols to be applied, and not vice versa'.[114]

The nature of the EU's competence pursuant to the Treaties determines the nature of the external agreement. On matters enjoying exclusive EU competence, the so-called EU-only model is a legal necessity; on the other hand, a mixed agreement is a legal necessity if it also entails issues over which the EU holds no competence at all. In the event of shared competence, the Member States may choose to exercise their competence through the EU and thus opt for an EU-only agreement; if not, the mixed agreement model is used.[115]

The agreement between the EU and the Philippines is a mixed agreement, meaning that the EU and its Member States stand jointly as parties on one side. Had it been an EU-only agreement, the parties would have been the Union alone on the one side and the third country, the Philippines, on the other.

Mixed agreements have the advantage that no gap in the relationship between Denmark and the third country is created in the event that the AFSJ opt-out is applicable. Denmark participates in the AFSJ part of such an international agreement on an intergovernmental basis in the role of an independent contracting party. The other EU Member States are bound by the AFSJ part of the agreement concerned by virtue of the EU, and as such are bound by EU law.

In relation to the UK Withdrawal Agreement[116] (WA) and the EU's Trade and Cooperation Agreement (TCA) with the UK,[117] the Supreme Court of Ireland requested the CJEU to give a preliminary ruling in connection with the execution in Ireland of two arrest warrants issued by the British judicial authorities. Essentially, the referring court asked if the provisions of the two agreements relating to the arrest warrant regime were applicable to Ireland, having regard to their AFSJ content and as such Protocol No 21, which had not been invoked in relation to the WA and the TCA.

[114] Case C-137/12 *European Commission v Council of the European Union* ECLI:EU:C:2013:675, para 74.

[115] See, eg, Opinion 1/19 *Istanbul Convention* (n 110).

[116] Agreement on the withdrawal of the United Kingdom of Great Britain and Northern Ireland from the European Union and the European Atomic Energy Community [2020] OJ L29/7. On Brexit and the AFSJ, see Curtin (n 98) and M Kendrick, 'Brexit the Ultimate Opt-out: Learning the Lessons on Differentiated Integration' (2022) 7(3) *European Papers* 1211.

[117] Trade and Cooperation Agreement between the European Union and the European Atomic Energy Community, of the one part, and the United Kingdom of Great Britain and Northern Ireland, of the other part [2021] OJ L149/10. On the TCA, see, eg, J Larik and RA Wessel, 'The EU–UK Post-Brexit Trade Agreement: Forging Partnership or Managing Rivalry?' in A Cygan and A Łazowski (eds), *Research Handbook on Legal Aspects of Brexit* (Cheltenham, Edward Elgar Publishing, 2022) 122.

The EU's two agreements with the UK are based on Article 50 TEU and Article 217 TFEU, respectively. Neither of the agreements has any legal basis within Title V of Chapter Three of the TFEU to which Protocol No 21 relates. Therefore, the essential question for the Court was to establish whether the choice of legal basis that did not include Article 82(1) TFEU was legally appropriate. If so, would it then also be correct that Protocol No 21 remained non-applicable?

In a nutshell, the Court reaffirmed both aspects.[118] While the Court refers to its settled case law that the applicability of Protocol No 21 (and Protocol No 22) depends on the legal basis of a measure and not vice versa, the Court's subsequent analysis revolves around the centre-of-gravity test.[119] On this basis, the Court confirms the legal basis of Article 50 TEU and of Article 217 TFEU, respectively. Neither of these legal bases fall within the scope of Protocol No 21 and thus the Protocol is not applicable, the result being that both agreements are binding upon Ireland.

In his View in Opinion 1/19, *Istanbul Convention*,[120] Advocate General Hogan had made the following observation on the applicability of Protocols 21 and 22:

> I would point out that the application of those protocols depends on the *content* of the act in question and not on the legal bases adopted. Consequently, whatever the answer given by the Court to the first question, where the Union intends to exercise powers under those protocols, account must be taken of them.[121]

This point by Advocate General Hogan was not followed by the Court. With the Court's subsequent rulings concerning the UK agreements, any doubt about the detrimental role of the legal basis for the applicability of Protocols 21 and 22 was eradicated.

Regarding the TCA, the Court explicitly highlights its wide scope, the context of its adoption, and the unequivocal declarations by the institutions and the Member States in this regard. The Court then continues by saying:

> [T]he inclusion in that agreement, alongside rules and measures falling within many other areas of EU law, of provisions falling within Title V of Part Three of the TFEU forms part of the general objective of that agreement, which is to establish the basis for a broad relationship between the Parties, within an area of prosperity and good neighbourliness characterised by close and peaceful relations based on cooperation, respectful of the Parties' autonomy and sovereignty.[122]

[118] Case C-479/21 PPU, *Governor of Cloverhill Prison and Others* ECLI:EU:C:2021:929, notably para 47 (legal basis determines the applicability of Protocol No 21 and not vice versa), paras 54–56 (Art 50 TEU correct sole legal basis for the WA) and paras 63–69 (Art 217 TFEU correct sole legal basis for the TCA).

[119] See A Engel, 'Op-Ed: The New EAW Regime Upheld by the Court of Justice – An Olive Branch Extended to the UK?' *EU Law Live* (2021).

[120] View of AG Hogan in Opinion 1/19 *Istanbul Convention* (n 110).

[121] ibid fn 71 (emphasis added).

[122] Case C-479/21 PPU (n 118) para 67.

Moreover, the Court dismisses the suggestion that the TCA pursues objectives of a character that would require any additional legal bases to the general Article 217 TFEU.[123]

Advocate General Kokott found it of importance, in relation to both the WA and the TCA, that Ireland had made use of the opt-in pursuant to Protocol No 21 regarding the arrest warrant, with the consequence that the inclusion of the matter of extradition in the two agreements with the UK did not impose any new obligations on Ireland.[124]

In its judgment, the Court also makes reference to this issue, but only in relation to the WA. Following the conclusion by the Court that Article 50 TEU is the correct and sole legal basis for the WA, the Court remarks that the addition of the relevant AFSJ legal basis of the TFEU to that agreement would only have given rise to uncertainty. The Court reasons as follows:

> [B]ecause of the resulting applicability of Protocol (No 21), Ireland, which had chosen to be bound by the European Arrest warrant regime, including with regard to the United Kingdom, would be treated as if it had never participated in it.[125]

In relation to the TCA, the Court was silent on the matter of the Irish opt-in to the arrest warrant, which may lead one to assume that the Court did not find it relevant in that context.[126]

It seems prudent to read the Court's ruling to imply that Denmark is also bound by the two agreements with the UK given the similar scope of Protocols Nos 21 and 22, and given that the prior exercise by Ireland of its opt-in option vis-à-vis the arrest warrant was not decisive for the Court's conclusion on the crucial issue of legal basis and the non-application of Protocol No 21.

It remains unclear whether the explicit reference by the Court to the context, scope and unequivocal declarations of all parties behind the TCA has a particular bearing on the Court's conclusion that the correct legal basis for the TCA is Article 217 TFEU alone. It may not be ruled out that the Court in this way indicates that the conclusion might not necessarily be the same should the issue occur in different circumstances.[127]

The two agreements with the UK are both in the form of EU-only agreements. From an EU law perspective, in this author's opinion, at least the TCA could have been concluded as a mixed agreement given its elements of shared competence. Had it been a mixed agreement, ratification by all EU Member States individually according to national procedures would have been required. This scenario was avoided by the Member States' opting for an EU-only model, which arguably was a very deliberate choice.

[123] ibid, para 68.

[124] View of AG Kokott in Case C-479/21 PPU *Governor of Cloverhill Prison and Others* ECLI:EU:C:2021:899, point 58 and 74. On the opt-in model in general, see discussion in subsection III.D.

[125] Case C-479/21 PPU (n 118) para 55.

[126] cp Engel (n 119).

[127] ibid, where Engel seems not to share this reading.

Whereas the TCA causes no legal predicament, it is not common practice to conclude broad international agreements pursuant to Article 217 TFEU as EU-only agreements. The Stabilisation and Association Agreement (SAA) from 2016 between the EU and Kosovo based on Article 217 TFEU was, nonetheless, also concluded as an EU-only agreement.[128]

In the SAA, note was taken of the UK/Irish position, as well as the position of Denmark. It was noted that in the event that the parties, within the framework of the Agreement, were to enter into specific agreements on AFSJ matters, or in the event that any subsequent EU-internal measures were to be adopted pursuant to the AFSJ title of the TFEU to implement the Agreement, Protocols Nos 21 and 22 would be applicable.[129] Due to the pure opt-out nature of the Danish position pursuant to Protocol No 22, this would mean that Denmark could not become a party thereto and would not be bound by such measures.

No corresponding provision on the position of Ireland and Denmark appears in either of the Union's agreements with the UK. The issue of implementing measures within the field of the AFSJ has materialised on a few occasions. The Union has adopted Council Decisions regarding extension of interim periods defined by the TCA during which the UK may derogate from certain obligations within the AFSJ field as otherwise regulated by the TCA.[130] The Council Decisions have a legal basis in the Council Decision on the conclusion of the TCA,[131] as well as legal bases within the TFEU, including Article 87(2) that falls within Title V of Part Three. The Council notes in a recital in both Decisions that 'Denmark and Ireland are bound by [the relevant part of the TCA] by virtue of Decision (EU) 2021/689 and are therefore taking part in the adoption and application of this Decision, which implements the Trade and Cooperation

[128] Council Decision (EU) 2016/342 of 12 February 2016 on the conclusion, on behalf of the Union, of the Stabilisation and Association Agreement between the European Union and the European Atomic Energy Community, of the one part, and Kosovo, of the other part [2016] OJ L71/1. The legal basis of Art 37 TEU was added alongside Art 217 TFEU to the Council Decision on the conclusion of the Agreement.

[129] ibid, last recital.

[130] Council Decision (EU) 2021/2293 of 20 December 2021 on the position to be taken on behalf of the Union in the Partnership Council established by the Trade and Cooperation Agreement with the United Kingdom regarding the extension of the derogation from the obligation to delete passenger name record data of passengers after their departure from the United Kingdom [2021] OJ L458/514; and Council Decision (EU) 2021/1729 of 24 September 2021 on the position to be taken on behalf of the European Union in the Specialised Committee on Law Enforcement and Judicial Cooperation established by the Trade and Cooperation Agreement between the European Union and the European Atomic Energy Community, of the one part, and the United Kingdom of Great Britain and Northern Ireland, of the other part, regarding the extension of the period referred to in Article 540(3) of that Agreement during which DNA profiles and fingerprints can be exchanged with the United Kingdom [2021] OJ L345/36.

[131] Council Decision (EU) 2021/689 of 29 April 2021 on the conclusion, on behalf of the Union, of the Trade and Cooperation Agreement between the European Union and the European Atomic Energy Community, of the one part, and the United Kingdom of Great Britain and Northern Ireland, of the other part, and of the Agreement between the European Union and the United Kingdom of Great Britain and Northern Ireland concerning security procedures for exchanging and protecting classified information [2021] OJ L149/2.

Agreement/TCA'.[132] In other words, despite the Council Decision's reference to Article 87(2) TFEU, the opt-out was not triggered.

The TCA with the UK is in many respects one of a kind, and the issues regulated by the implementing measures are technical in character. Nonetheless, it is fair to observe that the approach taken by the Council vis-à-vis the position of Denmark and Ireland deviates from a stricter reading of the protocols as expressed in the Kosovo case, according to which also an implementing measure with a legal basis within the AFSJ part of the Treaty would lead to their applicability.

One final and general aspect of the effects of the opt-out remains to be addressed in relation to its interaction with external relations of the Union. While it is an explicit legal effect of the AFSJ opt-out that it does not in any way affect the competences, rights and obligations of Denmark, the question arises whether the opposite holds true: does the special Danish position impact the character of the Union's external competence? This matter has been addressed on several occasions before and by the CJEU.

One such occasion occurred in relation to the scope of the ERTA (European Road Transport Agreement) doctrine,[133] which was addressed in Opinion 1/13 *Convention on the Civil Aspects of International Child Abduction* in relation to an inter-institutional dispute on who – the EU or the Member States – should accept the accession of third countries to the Hague Convention on Child Abduction.[134] The core issue was whether the EU held exclusive competence on the matter pursuant to the ERTA doctrine. The Court confirmed that this was the case.

What is of particular interest, albeit not visible when reading the Opinion itself, is that the issue of the Danish AFSJ opt-out was addressed during the deliberations leading to the Court's Opinion.

Denmark is a party to the Hague Convention, but due to its AFSJ opt-out, Denmark is not a party to nor is it bound by the secondary EU law forming the grounds for the Union's exclusive competence.[135] During the proceedings, the Court asked the parties the following question, for a written answer on possible implications owing to the Danish AFSJ opt-out:

> The Danish Government, as well as the other parties, are requested to clarify – in light of Opinion 1/03 of February 7, 2006 (Rec p-I-1145) – the possible impact on the present case of the fact that, in accordance with Protocol No 22 on the position

[132] Council Decision (EU) 2021/2293 and Council Decision (EU) 2021/1729 (n 130) recitals 14 and 12, respectively.

[133] Case 22/70 *Commission v Council (ERTA)* ECLI:EU:C:1971:32.

[134] Opinion 1/13 *Convention on the Civil Aspects of International Child Abduction* ECLI:EU:C:2014:2303.

[135] Council Regulation (EC) No 2201/2003 of 27 November 2003 concerning jurisdiction and the recognition and enforcement of judgments in matrimonial matters and the matters of parental responsibility, repealing Regulation (EC) No 1347/2000 [2003] OJ L338/1. The regulation makes several references to the Hague Convention.

of Denmark, annexed to the EU and FEU Treaties, this Member State is not participating in the adoption of measures in the area of freedom, security and justice and therefore that it did not participate in the adoption of regulation No 2201/2003 and it is not bound by it.[136]

This author has previously accounted for the Danish response as follows:

> The position of Denmark was as short as it was clear: The special position of Denmark had no bearing at all on the issue. Denmark, for which this author acted as agent, pointed to the legal effect of the provisions in Protocol No 22 which exempted Denmark from the Union's legal measures on freedom, security and justice, cf Part Three, Title V, TFEU. Uniquely, Denmark has not conferred powers to the EU within the said area of cooperation, and therefore has maintained its full national competence, including its external competence. In light hereof, the legal assessment of whether the Union carries exclusive external competence or not, in relation to The Hague Convention, has no bearing regarding the legal position of Denmark. Equally, the legal position of Denmark has no bearing on the assessment of the nature of the external competence, the EU may or may not have in the field under review. In other words, were the Court to be of the position (which it was) that an exclusive external EU competence existed, it would have bearings on the legal position of the Member States, with the exception of Denmark.
>
> The Commission, the Council and the Parliament, as well as a small handful of other Member States that had submitted written replies to the Court's question all came to the same conclusion as Denmark.[137]

Advocate General Jääskinen argued that the request for an Opinion should be declared inadmissible as far as Denmark was concerned, apparently due to the special position of Denmark.[138] This could be read as implying that the Advocate General was of the view that the EU's exclusive competence would have no bearing for Denmark due to the effect of the Danish opt-out.[139] The Court did not entertain the opinion of the Advocate General on this aspect. In fact, despite having explicitly asked the parties for their views, the Court did not mention the issue of the Danish opt-out at all in the Opinion. This in turn may indicate that the Court did not dispute the concordant observations of the parties that the special position of Denmark indeed had no bearing on the matter of the implied external competence of the EU.

[136] Question of the Court of 17 March 2014 for written answer (author's own translation from French).

[137] C Thorning, 'The ERTA Doctrine Post-Lisbon: *Opinion 1/13* (Convention of the Civil Aspects of International Child Abduction)' in RA Wessel and G Butler (eds), *EU External Relation Law: The Cases in Context* (Oxford, Hart Publishing, 2022)745, 753.

[138] View of AG Jääskinen in Opinion 1/13 *Convention of the Civil Aspects of International Child Abduction* ECLI:EU:C:2014:2292, point 106.

[139] ibid point 48, which deals with the issue of an agreement's being 'envisaged', under Art 218(11) TFEU. The AG states 'the request for an opinion is, I believe, admissible in so far as it relates to the European Union's competence to express its position on the declarations of acceptance which, on the date when the request was submitted, had not yet been deposited by the Member States *other than the Kingdom of Denmark*' (emphasis added).

Prior to Opinion 1/13, the issue of the special Danish position had been raised in relation to Opinion 1/03 *Lugano Convention.*[140] The issue at that time was whether it had any bearing on the nature and scope of the EU's external competence that a parallel agreement on the relevant Regulation 44/2001 ('Brussels I') had been entered into by the EU and Denmark.[141] The answer was in the negative.[142] Thym argues that the Court should have clarified that the EU institutions are under an obligation, in line with Article 327 TFEU, to ensure that the Union's agreements with third states do not bind Denmark.[143]

Shortly after Opinion 1/13 was delivered, the issue of the special Irish position pursuant to Protocol No 21 was raised by Ireland during the proceedings that led to Opinion 2/15 *Singapore Free Trade Agreement* on the nature of EU's competence to enter into a free-trade agreement with Singapore.[144] Given that no legal basis within the AFSJ was in play, the Court found Protocol No 21, and Protocol No 22 for that matter, to be irrelevant to the procedure.[145] Denmark had argued for that result.[146] The ruling of the Court only confirms the determining nature of the legal basis in relation to the applicability of both Protocols 21 and 22.

In relation to the EU's accession to the Istanbul Convention, the issue of the special positions of both Ireland and Denmark surfaced once again in relation to Opinion 1/19 *Istanbul Convention.*[147] Denmark had not submitted observations but, as in the case of Opinion 1/13, chose to participate in the oral hearing to plead along lines similar to those used in the proceedings on the Hague Convention.

In its Opinion 1/19 *Istanbul Convention*, the Court refers to the submission of the Council, which had stated that the application of the Danish opt-out Protocol No 22 did not give rise to any particular difficulty in the case.[148] That was not to imply that Protocol No 22 was not applicable; it was indeed. Pursuant to the Protocol, Denmark had not participated in the adoption of the Council Decision on the signature of the Istanbul Convention; and similarly, Denmark was not expected to participate in the EU Council Decision on the conclusion that was foreseen to be based purely on AFSJ legal bases within Title V of Part Three of the TFEU. In the eyes of the Council (and Denmark), that was a straightforward outcome posing no difficulties.

The situation of Ireland, however, was potentially different, given that Ireland, pursuant to Protocol No 21, had opted into certain EU internal AFSJ

[140] Opinion 1/03 *Lugano Convention* ECLI:EU:C:2006:8.
[141] On parallel agreements, see section III.B.ii.
[142] See Thorning (n 137) fn 37.
[143] Thym (n 82) 857, fn 80.
[144] Opinion 2/15 *Singapore Free Trade Agreement* ECLI:EU:C:2017:376.
[145] The Court referred to its established position in Case C-137/12 (n 114) paras 74 and 75.
[146] Opinion 2/15 *Singapore* (n 144) para 218.
[147] Opinion 1/19 *Istanbul Convention* (n 110).
[148] ibid para 313. See also para 142.

measures covered by the Istanbul Convention. Those measures were thus applicable to Ireland, while at the same time Ireland had chosen not to opt into other relevant AFSJ measures, which consequently were not applicable to Ireland. On that basis, the Council had split its decisions on the signature and conclusion of the Istanbul Convention into two: one relating to measures that Ireland had opted into, and as such with the participation of Ireland in its adoption; and the other one relating to measures without Irish participation and in which Ireland would not take part. Naturally, Denmark was not to take part in either.

The Court clarified two issues. First, and contrary to the arguments of both Ireland and the Council, that the scope of Protocol No 21 should be considered in its entirety, leaving no room for Ireland to participate in some but not all parts of the conclusion of the agreement on the side of the EU as far as the AFSJ content was concerned.[149]

Second, the Court established that Article 336 TFEU was applicable as legal basis for the EU measure concerned alongside a number of AFSJ legal bases within Title V of Part Three of the TFEU. That triggered a situation that gave rise to 'an objective need to divide a measure concluding an envisaged agreement into two or more decisions'.[150] Accordingly, the Court found an objective need to divide the Council measure on concluding the agreement into two separate measures, allowing for Denmark (and Ireland) not to participate in the conclusion of the agreement on the side of the EU in so far as it related to the external competences of the EU pursuant to the AFSJ legal bases of the Treaty. Conversely, both countries should participate in the conclusion as far as the non-AFSJ part was concerned.

## D. Legal Differences between Opt-Out and Opt-In

As already explained, the effect of the position of Denmark on the AFSJ makes it legally impossible for Denmark to participate in the adoption of the measures concerned, Denmark is not able to become bound by the measures as such pursuant to EU law, and Denmark is exempted from contributing financially to their execution. Special legal constructions adopted to mitigate certain impact situations following these legal effects have been discussed, which have revealed that the legal constructions have not altered this fundamental effect of the special Danish position under EU law. Essentially, the Danish position within the AFSJ embeds the definition of a legally binding opt-out.

Curtin finds that '[o]pt-outs refer to the unwillingness or inability of a Member State to participate in an EU policy where it is assumed that all Member States will join'.[151]

[149] The dismissal by the Court of the ERTA effect is discussed further in the text to nn 169–72.

[150] Opinion 1/19 *Istanbul Convention* (n 110) para 332. The Court makes specific reference to Protocol No 22 in para 334.

[151] D Curtin, 'From a Europe of Bits and Pieces to a Union of Variegated Differentiation' in P Craig and G de Búrca (eds), *The Evolution of EU Law*, 3rd edn (Oxford, Oxford University Press, 2021) 373, 378.

A generic legal definition of an opt-out within primary law is proposed as taking the following form:[152]

> Opt-out within EU primary law: A derogation from a defined part of EU Law with the effect that the Member State concerned is excluded from taking part in and becoming bound by the defined part of EU Law. No political choices from either side can change this position on a case-by-case basis. The only political choice remaining is to abrogate the opt-out once and for all.[153]

As discussed in chapter 4 on the euro, a politically tolerated position of non-participation has been referred to as a de facto opt-out. Such a situation is legally classified as an act of non-enforcement of the EU rules and falls outside the proposed definition of an opt-out proper.

The position of Denmark stands in contrast to the Treaty-based position within the AFSJ enjoyed by Ireland and (formerly) the UK pursuant to Protocol No 21. Whereas the starting point according to Protocol No 21 is the same as under Protocol No 22, that is the Member State concerned is not participating in and not becoming bound by the measures in question, Protocol No 21 is characterised by entailing a legal basis that provides for the repealing of these effects. Ireland in such a situation thus finds itself on the same legal footing under EU law as all other Member States not holding a special position. The exercise of a political choice by Ireland is required to trigger this outcome. This is, squarely put, the definition of the opt-in position. This finding contradicts that of Matera, who equates the position of Denmark with that of the UK/Ireland by stating that '[w]hile the model chosen by the UK and Ireland differs formally from that in Denmark, the result is the same: the three countries abstain from the policies that make up the AFSJ by way of opt-out'.[154]

Put in generic terms, the definition of a permanent opt-in at the level of primary law is proposed to take the following form:

> Opt-in within EU primary law: A derogation from a defined part of EU Law with the default effect that the Member State concerned does not take part in and will not become bound by the defined part of EU Law; however, the Member State retains the option, on a case-by-case basis, unilaterally to repeal the derogative effect.

Although the proposed definitions of an opt-out, on the one hand, and an opt-in, on the other hand, are formulated generically, this is not to suggest that

[152] On specific opt-outs within *secondary law*, see T Duttle et al, 'Opting out from European Union legislation: the differentiation of secondary law' (2017) 24(3) *Journal of European Public Policy* 406.

[153] For another definition of, seemingly, an opt-out, see F Schimmelfennig and T Winzen, *Ever Looser Union. Differentiated European integration* (Oxford, Oxford University Press, 2020) 4. The definition adopts this wording: 'We speak of differentiated integration – as opposed to uniform integration – when the legally valid rules of the EU, codified in European treaties and EU legislation, exempt or exclude individual member states explicitly from specific rights or obligations of membership in the EU.'

[154] C Matera 'Much Ado About the Opt-Outs? The Impact of Variable Geometry in the AFSJ on the EU as a Global Security Actor' 75, in S Blockmans (ed), *Differentiated Integration in the EU From the Inside Looking Out* (Brussels, Centre for European Policy Studies, 2014).

permanent opt-outs and opt-ins, as part of primary law, are widely held by Member States; rather the opposite is the case.[155] Moreover, the opt-in model as defined above is currently in force through Protocol No 21 only; consequently, it only relates to the position of one Member State, Ireland, and only in relation to the AFSJ.

As part of the Lisbon Treaty, Denmark gained *the option* to change the Danish opt-out position on the AFSJ to the UK/Ireland style of an opt-in. It was done by inserting a new provision to this effect in Part IV of Protocol No 22 on the Position of Denmark. The provision states that the possibility to convert to the opt-in model is without prejudice to the option on the abolition of the opt-out altogether, which has been part of the Protocol since the Amsterdam Treaty and dates back to the Edinburgh Decision.[156]

The reason for providing Denmark with the option to change its special position to the opt-in model is given in the recitals to Protocol No 22, as updated by the Lisbon Treaty. Here the High Contracting Parties remark that a continuation (post the Lisbon Treaty) of the legal regime originating in the Edinburgh Decision would significantly limit Denmark's participation in important areas of cooperation and that it is 'in the best interest of the Union to ensure the integrity of the AFSJ acquis'. It is fair to speculate that the underlying reason is based on an assessment of the grim prospect of Denmark's wanting to abolish the opt-out altogether, as this would lead to Denmark's becoming part of the entire AFSJ *acquis*, including measures within politically sensitive areas such as migration and asylum. Hence, the reasoning that it would be better to allow Denmark the possibility to participate – under EU law – in as much as possible of the *acquis* through the opt-in model.

Should Denmark decide to avail itself of the option to convert the opt-out to an opt-in, the provisions of the current Protocol No 22 would simply be replaced by a set of provisions set out in an annex to the same Protocol. These provisions mirror the ones in Protocol No 21, with the necessary adaptations, notably with a view to catering for the fact that Denmark is a full Schengen State.

Once exercised, the choice for Denmark to change its special position cannot be undone. There is thus no provision allowing for Denmark to go back to the opt-out model once the conversion to the opt-in model has been executed.

The High Contracting Parties had welcomed Denmark's expressed intention to avail itself of the conversion option 'when possible, in accordance with its constitutional requirements'.[157] In 2015, the Danish Government decided to

[155] See ch 7 for a brief general discussion of differentiated integration. A Member State's choice not to join an initiative with other Member States that takes place *outside* of the EU legal order, eg the Banking Union, is clearly not an 'opt-out' as it is understood and defined here.

[156] Protocol No 22 on the Position of Denmark (n 26) Art 8. The provision to abolish the provisions of the Protocol altogether is found in Art 7.

[157] Protocol No 22 (n 26) recital 4.

exercise the option. To this end, a Bill was tabled and later approved by the Danish Parliament.[158]

The explanatory notes to the Bill outline in some detail the opt-in mechanism and its legal effects, as understood by the Danish Government and building on the precedence from Protocol 21. On this basis, the following main points are highlighted.[159]

First, the opt-in model provides the Member State, Denmark and Denmark alone, with the choice to opt in to a concrete AFSJ measure on a case-by-case basis. It may be done at one of two different stages: (i) either at the proposal stage of an AFSJ measure, whereby Denmark becomes part of the decision-making process; or (ii) alternatively, Denmark may await the adoption of a measure and decide to opt in at a later stage. In any case, the exercise of the opt-in choice is irreversible from the time of its notification. The legal effects are that in such a scenario, the relevant provisions of the Treaties shall apply to Denmark.[160] Should Denmark choose not to make an active choice to opt in at all, the default position, as known from the opt-out situation, remains and Denmark would not become part of nor bound by the particular AFSJ measure and bear no financial costs of the measure in question.[161]

Second, the right to opt in to a particular measure is in principle unconditional. However, there are certain specific rules to ensure that Denmark will not eventually hold a decisive no-vote at the time of adopting the measure.[162] Obviously this is only relevant for an opt-in at the proposal stage. It goes hand in hand with the general commitment by Denmark not to let its special position prevent the other Member States from further developing their cooperation within an area falling within the scope of the special Danish position. Moreover, provisions within the Annex to Protocol No 22 prescribe that Article 331(1) TFEU, on conditions to participate in enhanced cooperation, applies *mutatis mutandis* in relation to a post-adoption opt-in decision, that is the situation when the opt-in is exercised in relation to an already adopted measure and not already at the proposal stage. These rules constitute a slight modification to the general principle that Denmark has an unconditional right to opt in at its own will. However, it is noted that the corresponding provision on the *mutatis mutandis* applicability of Article 331(1) TFEU in Protocol No 21, with regard to the UK and Ireland, has never been invoked in practice.

Third, the opt-in relates to a concrete measure at hand, and would not be binding on the Danish position if and when that measure is amended. A number of provisions regulate the situation in the event that Denmark were to decide not

[158] Bill L29 of 8 October 2015, 'Forslag til lov om omdannelse af retsforbeholdet til en tilvalgsordning', Folketingstidende, saml 2015–16, L29.

[159] See also Peers, 'In a World of Their Own?' (n 1).

[160] Protocol No 22 (n 26) Annex, Art 8.

[161] ibid Annex, Art 9.

[162] ibid Annex, Art 3(2).

to opt into an amended proposal, essentially with a view to ensuring the integrity and operability of the instrument of EU law at stake.[163]

Fourth, Denmark's participation in the Schengen cooperation would be maintained under the opt-in model. The six-month reflection period awarded to Denmark to make its choice to adhere to adopted Schengen rules is maintained, as is the provision on facing 'appropriate measures' if Denmark decides not to adhere to new Schengen provisions.[164] The change in legal terms would be that in the opt-in scenario, Denmark would indeed opt into the measures that constitute a further development of the Schengen *acquis* and thus bind Denmark as EU law, and not, as is presently the case, constitute a legal obligation between Denmark and the other Schengen States under international law. Denmark would of course also have the choice to exercise the opt-in decision at the proposal stage of a Schengen measure. As a deviation from the general rule, such an opt-in would be considered binding not only for the proposed measure at hand, but also for any future proposals aiming to build upon that measure as far as the new proposal also builds upon the Schengen *acquis*.[165] The conversion provision within Article 8 of Protocol No 22 specifically regulates that existing Schengen measures, which until a potential conversion have been binding on Denmark as obligations under international law pursuant to the existing Schengen Technicality, automatically would be regarded as having been opted into by the time of the conversion, and as such would become binding upon Denmark as Union law six months after the date of the formal conversion.[166]

Fifth, an opt-in cannot be done *en bloc* as regards future measures within a section of AFSJ cooperation but only in connection with concrete measures, including proposals. The opt-in choice would thus be exercised on a case-by-case basis and, as the predominant rule, without prejudice to later amendments and new proposals. However, politically, the choice may be indicated in advance. In relation to the Lisbon Treaty, Ireland declared its firm intention to exercise its opt-in right with a view to taking part in AFSJ measures 'to the maximum extent it deems possible', and 'in particular, participate to the maximum possible extent in measures in the field of police cooperation'.[167] In relation to the possible Danish conversion of the opt-out to the opt-in in 2015, a majority of the political parties in the Danish Parliament had entered into comprehensive political agreements that determined which existing AFSJ measures to opt into, as well as determining the Danish approach to future opt-ins, including a specific

[163] ibid Annex, Art 5.

[164] ibid Annex, Art 6(1)–(2).

[165] ibid Annex, Art 6(2).

[166] ibid Annex, Art 8(2).

[167] Declaration 56 by Ireland on Article 3 of the Protocol on the position of the United Kingdom and Ireland in respect of the area of freedom, security and justice annexed to the Final Act of the Intergovernmental Conference which adopted the Treaty of Lisbon, signed on 13 December 2007 [2016] OJ C202/335.

pledge to hold a referendum should a future government wish for Denmark to opt into measures within the EU's asylum cooperation.[168]

Sixth, in relation to measures opted into, the legal effects would be that they become binding upon Denmark under EU law in the EU internal context. It would be reasonable to assume that the same would be the case in relation to EU's external competences, as defined by the general rules under EU law, including the implied powers of the ERTA doctrine. The Court has to some extent addressed the matter in Opinion 1/19 *Istanbul Convention*.[169] Advocate General Hogan argued for an understanding, which he essentially summarised as follows:

> [I]n so far as Ireland has agreed to be bound by certain acts of Union legislation, it could not then proceed to conclude a convention or other international agreement which would undermine the effectiveness of that same legislation. The converse, however, is not true. The fact that it has agreed to be bound by those EU legislative instruments does not mean that Ireland then would be obliged to take part in the adoption of an act concluding a convention relating to the area covered by Part Three, Title V of the TFEU. Any such conclusion would be contrary to the clear wording of Protocol No 21.[170]

This author was as puzzled by the second part of these findings as was Chamon, who found that the view of Advocate General Hogan seemingly disregarded the nature of the ERTA effect.[171] Falling short of referring to the above-mentioned point in the Advocate General's view, but nonetheless referring to his findings in the preceding points 186 to 189, and following an intensive systematic reading of Protocol No 21, the Court seemingly agreed with Advocate General Hogan. Although the Court did not explicitly state so, essentially it dismissed an ERTA effect for Ireland of AFSJ measures that Ireland had opted into.[172] As the potential Danish model for an opt-in mirrors the one from Protocol No 21, the same would be applicable to Denmark.

The very essence of the opt-in is that it provides for the possibility for Denmark to cooperate on a supranational level within the AFSJ pursuant to EU law. Such a step would constitute a deviation from Section D of the Edinburgh Decision and therefore require confirmation in a referendum in Denmark.[173] Moreover, such a change in the legal position of Denmark would trigger the Article 20 procedure of the Constitution.[174]

[168] The agreements formed part of the explanatory notes to Bill L29 (n 158).

[169] Opinion 1/19 *Istanbul Convention* (n 110).

[170] View of AG Hogan in *Istanbul Convention* (n 120) point 190.

[171] M Chamon, 'Op-Ed: AG Hogan's Opinion in Avis 1/19 regarding the Istanbul Convention' *EU Law Live* (2021).

[172] Opinion 1/19 *Istanbul Convention* (n 110) paras 321 to 327.

[173] See discussion in ch 2, section VII.B.

[174] Ministry of Justice Memorandum of 28 June 2008; 'Justitsministeriet, Notat om forholdet mellem grundlovens § 20 og en omdannelse af det danske forbehold om retlige og indre anliggender' (2008).

The adoption of Bill L29 in 2015 by the Danish Parliament did not meet the requirements for a qualified majority pursuant to Article 20. The Government proceeded by calling a referendum on the adopted Bill based on the procedure in Article 20. This referendum took place on 3 December 2015, and it resulted in the rejection of the Bill by 53.1 per cent 'no' to 46.9 per cent 'yes'. On that basis, the status quo was maintained, that is, the opt-out as defined in Protocol No 22 was upheld and not replaced by the provisions for an opt-in as set out in the Annex.

The provision in Article 8 of Protocol No 22 allowing conversion to the opt-in model, as laid down in the Annex, remains valid. Denmark may therefore at any time in the future choose, once again, to initiate the internal procedures needed to convert to the opt-in model.

## IV. CONCLUDING REMARKS ON THE AFSJ OPT-OUT

The AFSJ opt-out was somewhat peculiar in its original version in the Edinburgh Decision, as it did not, at the time, institute any special position for Denmark. Peers quite rightly has formulated it in this way:

> The non-participation of Denmark in JHA matters did not begin, as is often thought, when a Decision of the Heads of State and Government (known as the Edinburgh Decision) was adopted in 1992 to attempt to persuade Danish voters to support the Maastricht Treaty.[175]

Nevertheless, the Edinburgh Decision set a boundary for Danish participation in AFSJ matters by locking it at an intergovernmental level only, irrespective of progress in the European integration process. Consequently, the evolution of the AFSJ cooperation that gradually, in two stages, fully abandoned the intergovernmental stage has impacted greatly on the material scope of the opt-out.

The dormant opt-out of the Edinburgh Decision was initially activated and given effect as a consequence of the Amsterdam Treaty. With a view to achieving this activation, including by providing it with legal effects under EU law, the introduction of specific provisions within EU primary law was introduced as an integral part of the Amsterdam Treaty.

At the time of the Amsterdam Treaty, the material scope or, put differently, the matters of substance within the AFSJ affected by the activated opt-out, covered roughly half of the AFSJ cooperation, as the Amsterdam Treaty did not change the intergovernmental nature of the other half regarding cooperation on police and criminal-justice matters. The process of 'communitarisation' of the AFSJ cooperation was completed by the Lisbon Treaty. Consequently, the entire

[175] S Peers, *EU Justice and Home Affairs Law*, vol I: *EU Immigration and Asylum Law*, 4th edn (Oxford, Oxford University Press, 2016) 33.

area of AFSJ cooperation has since fallen within the material scope of the opt-out, with one minor modification on visa policies due to particularities dating back to the Maastricht Treaty.[176]

Whereas the material scope of the opt-out has undergone a fundamental evolution, the legal scope has remained unchanged throughout. The legal boundaries set by the opt-out continue to prevent Danish participation in supranational AFSJ cooperation. Consequently, Denmark does not take part in the adoption of, nor is Denmark bound by, any measures pursuant to the AFSJ title of the TFEU, and Denmark is not bound by the AFSJ treaty provisions themselves. Denmark does not contribute financially to the measures concerned.

The above position is complemented by a fact that, to the naked eye, may appear to be a contradiction in terms, namely, that Denmark in certain instances nonetheless takes part in cooperation on the matter of substance concerned. The reason why this is a legal possibility lies in the nature of the opt-out as defined in the Edinburgh Decision. Unlike the opt-out on defence, the AFSJ opt-out was clearly formulated as an opt-out from a form of cooperation and not from the cooperation per se. This has made it possible, through inventive legal solutions, to mitigate certain impacts of the opt-out, notably on Schengen. As another prominent example, Member State Denmark participates rather uniquely in the EU's border agency, FRONTEX, on terms equivalent to the participation of a third country. Likewise, in relation to the so-called parallel agreements, as well as the few other agreements on very carefully defined AFSJ measures, from an EU law point of view, Denmark is treated as if Denmark were a third country even though it is not.[177]

With regard to external relations on the AFSJ, it is clear from the case law of the CJEU, at least indirectly, that the Danish AFSJ opt-out has no effect on the issue of the external competence of the EU. This includes the question of whether this competence is mixed or exclusive.

There is a clear difference between the opt-out, which Denmark holds pursuant to Protocol No 22, and the opt-in provided for in Protocol No 21, and which regulates the position of Ireland (and formerly the UK). Pursuant to the former, Denmark cannot become part of, nor be bound by, the EU measures concerned with effects under EU law, whereas the opposite is the case for Ireland pursuant to the latter. The opt-in model thus gives the holding Member State, on a case-by-case basis, a free political choice to repeal the legal effects corresponding to the opt-out. It is observed that the measures established to mitigate the effects of the Danish AFSJ opt-out, like the Schengen Technicality and the three parallel agreements, are all characterised by their not altering or eliminating the legal effects of the opt-out. Consequently, they do not represent an 'opt-in' for Denmark in the defined legal sense of this notion.

[176] Art 6 of Protocol No 22 (n 26).

[177] Vedsted-Hansen (n 48) 130–31, wonders whether the popular, political understanding corresponds to the legal reality.

The Lisbon Treaty provided Denmark with an option to convert the opt-out into an opt-in, but it did not in itself change the Danish opt-out; on the contrary, it maintained it.[178] Therefore, application of the special procedure laid out in Article 20 of the Danish Constitution did not materialise in this respect in relation to the Danish ratification of the Lisbon Treaty.[179] Only a later, separate decision to make use of the option to convert the opt-out model to the opt-in model would trigger the Article 20 procedure, given that only from such point in time would a deviation be instituted from the established position of non-Danish participation in the AFSJ at the supranational level.

An adopted Bill on the conversion of the opt-out into the opt-in model was put up for such an Article 20-generated referendum in 2015; it was rejected. Effectively, the Danish electorate rejected the idea of providing the Danish Government with the choice to participate, on a case-by-case basis, in AFSJ matters, even though that choice would have been exercised in collaboration with the Danish Parliament in accordance with specific political agreements in this respect,[180] as well as the general and time-tested parliamentary procedures for the participation of any Danish Government in the Council. The bare option of supranational cooperation within the AFSJ depending on the will of a majority at the Danish Parliament seemingly did not appeal to the majority of the Danish electorate. The outcome therefore maintained the status quo on the special Danish position on the AFSJ.

[178] For an arguably less nuanced description, see Nielsen (n 21) 77.

[179] Nor was Art 20 of the Constitution applicable in any other respect. Consequently, no Danish referendum was held as part of the approval procedure of the Danish ratification of the Lisbon Treaty.

[180] See the explanatory notes to the conversion Bill.

# 7

# *Reflections on Differentiated Integration in General*

## I. INTRODUCTION

IN ONE OF its early ground-breaking judgments, the CJEU underlined the importance of the unity of EU law by stating that 'the executive force of Community law cannot vary from one state to another … without jeopardizing the attainment of the objectives of the Treaty'.[1] Nonetheless, it has not prevented the ever-evolving development of differentiated integration.[2]

The general issue of differentiation within the European integration process has received extensive scholarly attention, including from theoretical as well as practical points of view, and often in the form of normative contributions from political scientists and legal scholars alike.[3]

[1] Case 6/64 *Costa v ENEL* ECLI:EU:C:1964:66.

[2] B de Witte, A Ott and E Vos (eds), *Between Flexibility and Disintegration. The Trajectory of Differentiation in EU Law* (Cheltenham, Edward Edgar Publishing, 2017) 9.

[3] See, eg, A Stubb, 'A Categorization of Differentiated Integration' (1996) 34(2) *Journal of Common Market Studies* 283; A Kölliker, 'Bringing together or driving apart the union? Towards a theory of differentiated integration' (2001) 24(4) *West European Politics* 125; B de Witte, D Hanf and E Vos (eds), *The Many Faces of Differentiation in EU Law* (Antwerp, Intersentia, 2001); A Ott and E Vos (eds), *Fifty Years of European Integration: Foundations and Perspectives* (The Hague, TMC Asser Press, 2009); D Thym, '"United in Diversity" – The Integration of Enhanced Cooperation into the European Constitutional Order' (2010) 6(11) *German Law Journal* 1746; J-C Piris, *The Future of Europe. Towards a Two-Speed EU?* (Cambridge, Cambridge University Press, 2011); CB Jensen and JB Slapin, 'Institutional hokey-pokey: the politics of multispeed integration in the European Union' (2012) 17 *Journal of European Public Policy* 779; M Avbelj, 'Differentiated Integration – Farewell to the EU-27?' (2013) 14(1) *German Law Journal* 191; S Blockmans (ed), *Differentiated Integration in the EU From the Inside Looking Out* (Centre for European Policy Studies 2014); F Schimmelfennig and T Winzen, 'Instrumental and Constitutional Differentiation in the European Union' (2014) 52(2) *Journal of Common Market Studies* 354; B Leruth and C Lord, 'Differentiated integration in the European Union: a concept, a process, a system or a theory?' (2015) 22(6) *Journal of European Public Policy* 754; T Chopin and C Lequesne, 'Differentiation as a double-edged sword: member states' practices and Brexit' (2016) 92(3) *International Affairs* 531; S Weatherill, *Law and Values in the European Union* (Oxford, Oxford University Press, 2016); R Bellamy and S Kröger, 'A democratic justification of differentiated integration in a heterogeneous EU' (2017) 39 *Journal of European Integration* 625; M Demertzis et al, *One Size Does Not Fit All: European Integration by Differentiation* (Brussels, Bruegel, 2018); D Thym, 'Supranational Differentiation and Enhanced Cooperation' in R Schütze and T Tridimas, *Oxford Principles of European Union Law*, vol I (Oxford, Oxford University Press, 2018) 847; B de Witte, 'An Undivided Union? Differentiated

It is not the ambition here to engage in a thorough discussion of what is a vast subject. Rather, as part of conceptualising the Danish opt-outs, this chapter will point to the differences between the opt-outs and the other forms of differentiated integration within EU law, and more concretely to the differences emanating from the EMU and Schengen cooperation, as well as the later-introduced concepts of enhanced and permanent structured corporation. This provides the answer to the question of how the opt-outs compare to other forms of differentiated integration and whether the opt-outs fit with the concept of unity of EU law. In compliance with the scope of this book, a doctrinal and not a normative answer is sought.

An initial short presentation of differentiated integration as a concept in section II and a short account for the main treaty-based institutions of differentiated integration in section III provide a foundation for the comparison in law with the Danish opt-outs in section IV. Before conclusions are drawn in section VI, the 2017 judgment of the Danish Supreme Court in the so-called *Ajos Case* is touched upon to complete the picture (see section V).

## II. DIFFERENTIATED INTEGRATION IN GENERAL

As already established, differentiation is not a new phenomenon. Rather, it is a concept that has featured strongly in European integration from the very beginning.[4] Unlike other constitutional principles, such as the conferral of

Integration in Post-Brexit Times' (2018) 55(2/3) *Common Market Law Review* 227; M Brunazzo, 'The Evolution of EU Differentiated Integration between Crises and Dilemmas' 1 *EUIDEA Reseach Papers* (2019); B Leruth, S Ganzle and J Trondal, 'Differentiated Integration and Disintegration in the EU after Brexit: Risks versus Opportunities' (2019) 57(6) *Journal of Common Market Studies* 1383; F Schimmelfennig and T Winzen, 'Grand theories, differentiated integration' (2019) 26 *Journal of European Public Policy* 1172; M Markakis, 'Differentiated Integration and Disintegration in the EU: Brexit, the Eurozone Crisis, and Other Troubles' (2020) 23 *Journal of International Economic Law* 489; T Nguyen, 'Differentiated Integration and Accountability in the European Union. An Analytical Framework' 7 *EUIDEA Research Papers* (2020); F Schimmelfennig and T Winzen, *Ever Looser Union. Differentiated European integration* (Oxford, Oxford University Press, 2020); D Curtin, 'From a Europe of Bits and Pieces to a Union of Variegated Differentiation' in P Craig and G de Búrca (eds), *The Evolution of EU Law* (Oxford, Oxford University Press, 2021) 373; M Dawson and M Jachtenfuchs (eds), *Autonomy without Collapse in a Better European Union* (Oxford, Oxford University Press, 2022); S Kröger and T Loughran, 'The limits of support for differentiated integration in the European Union as perceived by academic experts' (2022) 4 *Political Research Exchange* 1; D Leuffen, B Rittberger and F Schimmelfennig, *Integration and Differentiation in the European Union: Theory and Policies*, 2nd edn (Cham, Palgrave Macmillan, 2022); JS Vara and RA Wessel (eds), 'New Options for Differentiated Integration in the European Union' (2022) 7(3) *European Papers* 1141; L de Blok and CE de Vries, 'A blessing and a curse? Examining public preferences for differentiated integration' (2023) 24(1) *European Union Politics* 143. See also *White Paper on the Future of Europe*, COM(2017) 2025.

[4] A Ott, 'EU Constitutional Boundaries to Differentiation: How to Reconcile Differentiation with Integration?' in Ott and Vos (eds) (n 3) 113.

power, proportionality and subsidiarity, the Treaties do not mention differentiation explicitly.[5]

The first clear suggestion regarding a differentiated integration approach is attributed to German Chancellor Willy Brandt, who, in November 1974, in light of several instances of invocation of the so-called Luxembourg Compromise,[6] called for graduated integration.[7] Since then, a multitude of designations have flourished. Variable geometry, concentric circles, a two- or multiple-speed Europe, a core group or Europe *à la carte*[8] – even 'a Europe of bits and pieces'.[9] It has been proposed to distinguish between the notions of differentiated integration and differentiated cooperation, understood as two subtypes of the more general phenomenon of differentiation, depending on whether such a phenomenon occurs in a policy area that operates along the lines of integration or cooperation respectively.[10]

Only a few of the 'fifty shades of differentiation' are mentioned above.[11] Back in 1996, the later Finnish Prime Minister and President Alexander Stubb found that the debate on differentiated integration could give even the most experienced specialist on European integration 'a severe case of semantic indigestion'.[12] Stubb identified no fewer than 30 forms of differentiated integration, which he classified as creating differences along three dimensions of time, space and policy content.[13]

The definitions and approaches to differentiated integration are indeed extensive. An array of theories has been expounded within and between multiple disciplines.[14] Stubb suggested defining differentiated integration as 'a model of integration strategies that try to reconcile heterogeneity within the European Union and allow different groupings of Member States to pursue an array of public policies with different procedural and institutional arrangements'.[15]

[5] F Schimmelfennig, 'Overcoming Crisis in the European Union. The Limits of Differentiated Integration' in Dawson and Jachtenfuchs (eds) (n 3) 48.

[6] For a more recent account of the Luxembourg Compromise, see the editorial by JH Reestman and T Beuker, 'Not dead yet. Revisiting the "Luxembourg Veto" and its Foundations' (2017) 13(1) *European Constitutional Law Review* 1.

[7] Curtin (n 3) 377.

[8] The last one attributed to R Dahrendorf, 'A Third Europe?' paper presented at the Third Jean Monnet Lecture (Florence, 26 November 1979).

[9] D Curtin, 'The Constitutional Structure of the Union: A Europe in bits and pieces' (1993) 30 *Common Market Law Review* 17. In a later contribution (Curtin (n 3) 375), Curtin concluded that 'differentiation has become not only an acceptable compromise, but even the preferred solution to potentially disaggregating forces and to the stalling of the EU integration process'.

[10] S Klose, E Perot and S Temizisler, 'Spot the Difference: Differentiated Co-operation and Differentiated Integration in the European Union' (2023) 61(1) *Journal of Common Market Studies* 259.

[11] N Koenig, 'A Differentiated View of Differentiated Integration' (23 July 2015) Jacques Delors Institut Policy Paper 140.

[12] Stubb (n 3) 283.

[13] ibid.

[14] M Kendrick, 'Brexit the Ultimate Opt-out: Learning the Lessons on Differentiated Integration' (2022) 7(3) *European Papers* 1214.

[15] Stubb (n 3) 283.

Other definitions have followed since. One such definition refers to '[t]he facilitation or accommodation of a degree of difference between Member States or regions in relation to what would otherwise be common Community or Union policies'.[16]

The different dimensions or modes of differentiated integration have been elegantly formulated by Schimmelfennig and Winzen as 'Multi-speed, Multi-tier, and Multi-menu'.[17] Thym also proposes a triple definition by dividing it into 'multiple speeds', 'federal core Europe' and 'flexibility *à la carte*'.[18] The first is essentially related to overcoming economic discrepancies and has been conceived as a transitional phenomenon.[19] The two following are more politically grounded. Thym observes that the 'core Europe' camp pursues an (often vague) vision of a *finalité fédérale*, whereas supporters of 'flexibility *à la carte*' want to orientate European integration according to the national interest.[20]

A normative debate on the issue flourishes among actors. The normative divide essentially lies between supporters who favour pragmatic reasons for differentiated integration and opponents who mostly mobilise principled reasons against it.[21] Eroding solidarity and undermining the legal unity and authority of the EU may constitute worries for some,[22] whereas others argue that differentiated integration does not produce an 'ever looser union' but facilitates and cushions an 'ever closer union'.[23] Piris is a long-standing advocate of a two-tier Europe, essentially by arguing that reluctant Member States should not hold back less reluctant ones on the European integration path, and therefore a group of member States should have the opportunity to play an avant-garde role.[24] Having occupied the position as *jurisconsulte* at the Council, Piris has first-hand experience of dealing with 'the reluctant ones', including with issues pertinent to the Danish and British/Irish opt-outs.

The foregoing is just a scratch on the surface of the extensive, colourful and at times passionate debate on the relation between European integration and differentiation from a political science point of view and from legal viewpoints. As fascinating and ever-relevant as it is, further elaboration of the debate falls outside the scope of this book. Neither is it required to extract what is of importance to this study, namely, that nowadays scholars in general find that differentiation is a key part of the EU's political and legal framework, and

[16] De Witte, Hanf and Vos (n 3) xii.

[17] Schimmelfennig and Winzen (n 3) 17.

[18] Thym, 'Supranational Differentiation and Enhanced Cooperation' (n 3).

[19] ibid 849.

[20] ibid 851.

[21] S Kröger and T Loughran, 'The Risks and Benefits of Differentiated Integration in the European Union as Perceived by Academic Experts' (2022) 60(2) *Journal of Common Market Studies* 1. See also Leruth, Ganzle and Trondal (n 3) 1384.

[22] See Kröger and Loughran (n 3) 4, with further references.

[23] Schimmelfennig and Winzen (n 3) 5.

[24] Piris (n 3).

possibly even 'a defining feature of the European Union policy, warts and all'.[25] Curtin points to a slightly shifting stance over time on the part of the CJEU as regards the uniformity of the content of the EU legal order. She mentions that whereas the concerns for coherence remain at the core of the CJEU jurisprudence, the Court leaves space for the integration of differentiation.[26] Differentiation *is* a feature of the EU's legal and institutional design.[27]

It is difficult, if at all possible, to find contemporary experts arguing that opt-outs, like the Danish ones as defined within primary EU law, challenge, as a matter of principle, the EU legal order to a degree where they should be considered legally unacceptable. It is thus safe to view them as embedded into the European legal order without their contradicting its constitutional design.

Against this background, section III produces a modest sketch of the main, treaty-based forms of differentiated integration other than the opt-outs. This provides a basis for shedding light on the characteristics of the Danish opt-outs as opposed to the other elements of differentiated integration. That is addressed in section IV.[28]

## III. MAIN TREATY-BASED INSTITUTES OF DIFFERENTIATED INTEGRATION

The Eurozone and Schengen are traditionally viewed as the most well-known instances of differentiation.[29] Incidentally, they both fall within the scope of two of the Danish opt-outs and have therefore already been studied in chapters 4 and 6, respectively in light of the provisions of the opt-outs. However, for our purposes here, the specificities each possesses as an instrument of differentiated integration in its own right are of interest.

The economic concept underlying the convergence criteria presupposed from the outset that not all EU Member States would enter the third stage of EMU (the euro) at the same time.[30] Therefore, EMU is seen as the paradigm of

[25] D Curtin, 'Brexit and the EU Area of Freedom, Security, and Justice: Bespoke Bits and Pieces' in F Fabbrini (ed), *The Law & Politics of Brexit* (Oxford, Oxford University Press, 2017) 184.

[26] Curtin (n 3) 382.

[27] R Uitz, 'The Rule of Law in the EU: Crisis, Differentiation, Conditionality' (2022) 7(2) *European Papers* 932.

[28] The many derogations traditionally gained by acceding Member States as part of the accession treaties – on a temporary basis and often with a maximum duration of five years – are left out. The same goes for flexibility pursued through intergovernmental cooperation of groups of Member States *outside* the EU legal order.

[29] S Baroncelli et al, 'Introduction to the Special Section: Differentiated Governance in a Europe in Crises' (2022) 7(2) *European Papers* 859.

[30] C Herrmann, 'Differentiated integration in the field of economic and monetary policy and the use of "(semi-)extra"' Union legal instruments – the case for "*inter se* Treaty amendments"' in B de Witte, E Vos and A Ott (eds), *Between Flexibility and Disintegration: The State of EU Law Today* (Cheltenham, Edgar Elgar Publishing, 2017) 241.

differentiated integration,[31] or, put differently, as an example of *primus inter pares* in differentiated integration.[32] Curtin finds that the Eurozone is the closest form of a 'core Europe', albeit open to all Member States who might in the future adopt the euro as their currency and join EMU.[33] The latter is important to note for the purpose of comparison with the Danish opt-out. Cooperation in EMU entails flexibility as to the pace of integration. The end goal, the euro, is legally set to apply for all Member States – except for Denmark, owing to its opt-out.[34]

When turning to Schengen as the other prominent example of differentiated integration, it is observed that in this case too, and from the outset, the (full) Schengen rules applied only to certain Member States. This has been the case ever since. Upon its integration into EU law by the Amsterdam Treaty, the dedicated Schengen Protocol specified that all future Member States were to be bound by the entire Schengen *acquis*.[35] In relation to the enlargements of the EU that followed, the issue has been further regulated by the respective accession treaties.[36] The Schengen rules on the abolition of internal border controls, cross-border hot pursuit and surveillance by police officers, the so-called Schengen Information System (SIS) and certain other elements did not apply to acceding countries until a specific Council Decision on the issue was unanimously adopted. Recently, Croatia was admitted to full Schengen membership following a positive decision by the Council pursuant to Article 4(2) of the Croatian Accession Act.[37] At the time of writing, the full Schengen *acquis* has not yet been extended to Romania and Bulgaria, as a decision of the Council to this effect is still awaited.[38] Like the euro, Schengen is a differentiation as regards the pace of integration. The legally set end-goal is full application of the Schengen rules.[39]

Whereas the euro and Schengen cooperation by their scope are confined to their respective areas, enhanced cooperation has a wider scope. Furthermore, it works 'the other way around' as a tool to overcome stalemate within the Council. Enhanced cooperation was introduced by the Treaty of Nice.[40] Essentially, it comprises a procedure by which a minimum of nine Member States, as a last

[31] S Van den Bogaert and V Borger, 'Differentiated Integration in EMU' in de Witte, Vos and Ott (eds) (n 30) 209.

[32] J-E de Neve 'The European Onion? How Differentiated Integration is Reshaping the EU' (2007) 29(4) *Journal of European Integration* 506.

[33] Curtin (n 3) 379, referring to T Beukers, 'The Eurozone crisis and the legitimacy of differentiated integration' (2013) EUI MWPWorking Paper 2013/36.

[34] See ch 4.

[35] In the current version it is Art 7 of Protocol No 19 on the Schengen Acquis integrated into the framework of the European Union [2015] OJ C326/1.

[36] Due to its specificities, Cyprus gained a special position.

[37] Council Decision (EU) 2022/2451 of 8 December 2022 on the full application of the provisions of the Schengen *acquis* in the Republic of Croatia [2022] OJ L320/41.

[38] The Commission has produced positive evaluations, yet the required unanimity in the Council to act accordingly in full is not established.

[39] The position of Denmark and the specific arrangements agreed are discussed in ch 6.

[40] Currently Art 20 TEU and Title III TFEU.

resort, may proceed to further the objectives of the Union in a particular field of cooperation, when it has become clear that the EU as a whole cannot achieve the goals of such cooperation within a reasonable period of time.

The predecessor to enhanced cooperation, the closer cooperation provisions, which had been set out in the Amsterdam Treaty, was never used in practice.[41] The use of enhanced cooperation was also met with hesitation, to such a degree that it earned the nickname 'Cinderella of differentiated integration'.[42] Not until 2010 did its first ever use come about, after a legislative proposal failed to obtain unanimous support and the Council eventually decided to proceed to authorise enhanced cooperation as regards choice of law on divorce.[43] Shortly afterwards, a decision was taken to set up unitary patent protection.[44] Interestingly, the issue on the judicial part of the matter was resolved by the Agreement on a Unified Patent Court, which was adopted under international law, thereby adding another layer of differentiation. The Member States Spain and Italy, whose position within the Council provoked the enhanced cooperation to take place, challenged the use of the instrument before the CJEU but lost their case.[45]

The crucial point to note for the purpose of this book is that a firm principle of openness underlies the entire concept.[46] The principle of openness is also embedded in the policy-specific mechanisms of enhanced cooperation within the CSDP, namely the PESCO, which was introduced by the Lisbon Treaty.[47] Provided that the defined criteria and requirements are met, any Member State may participate in the mechanism either from the outset or at a later stage. Any participating Member State may withdraw its participation by notifying its intention to do so to the Council, which then has to 'take note' that the Member State in question has ceased to participate.[48]

[41] S Peers, 'Enhanced cooperation: the Cinderella of differentiated integration' in de Witte, Vos and Ott (eds) (n 30) 78.

[42] ibid.

[43] Council Decision of 12 July 2010 authorising enhanced cooperation in the areas of the law applicable to divorce and legal separation [2010] OJ L189/12 (the 'Rome III Regulation').

[44] Council Decision of 10 March 2011 authorising enhanced cooperation in the area of the creation of unitary patent protection [2011] OJ L76/53; leading to Regulation (EU) No 1257/2012 of the European Parliament and of the Council of 17 December 2012 implementing enhanced cooperation in the area of the creation of unitary patent protection [2012] OJ L361/1. At the time of writing, enhanced cooperation has further appeared in Council Regulation (EU) 2017/1939 of 12 October 2017 implementing enhanced cooperation on the establishment of the European Public Prosecutor's Office ('the EPPO') [2017] OJ L283/1 and Proposal for a Council Directive implementing enhanced cooperation in the area of financial transaction tax, COM(2013) 71 final (currently at a standstill).

[45] Joined Cases C-274/11 *Spain v Council* and C-295/11 *Italy v Council* ECLI:EU:C:2013:240.

[46] See the reference in Art 20 TEU and provisions of Art 328 TFEU. The latter obligates the Commission and Member States participating in enhanced cooperation to promote participation by as many Member States as possible.

[47] Art 46 TEU and Protocol No 10 on permanent structured cooperation established by Article 42 of the Treaty on European Union [2008] OJ C115/275. For Denmark's position, see ch 5, including for refences to academic contributions on PESCO.

[48] Art 46(5) TEU. This provides more flexibility to Member States than what follows from the opt-in model known from Protocol (No 21) on the position of the United Kingdom and Ireland in

It may also be noted that the institute of constructive abstention, defined in Article 31(1) TEU, also represents a tool of differentiated integration. It is open to any Member State to abstain from Council decision-making in the CFSP field, with the effect that it will not be obliged to apply the decision concerned but must accept that the decision commits the Union.

## IV. THE CHARACTERISTICS OF THE DANISH OPT-OUTS AS ELEMENTS OF DIFFERENTIATED INTEGRATION

In line with the triple division of differentiated integration as formulated by Thym,[49] the Danish opt-outs no doubt belong to the third category, 'flexibility *à la carte*'. Further, Kingston generally classifies an opt-out as a 'constitutional' form of differentiation.[50] This may well be a correct classification for the Danish opt-outs, as far as the definition relates to the fact that they regulate, at treaty level, Danish exclusion from the defined areas of cooperation. However, one should be mindful of what 'constitutional' differentiation implies in the case of Denmark, to avoid surprises when Denmark, nonetheless, cooperates on the same subject matters, either because the cooperation falls outside the scope of the opt-out (EMU) or because cooperation may take place in another way as if Denmark was a third state (AFSJ). As discussed in previous chapters, notably chapters 4 and 6, unlike the situation associated with the UK, there are no spill-over effects of the Danish opt-outs. In the case of the Danish opt-outs, the 'constitutional' aspect is strictly confided to the legal definition of the opt-outs themselves.

The Maastricht Treaty, and its introduction of British and Danish opt-outs, respectively, from the third stage of EMU (the euro), has been described as forming a milestone since it paved a legal avenue for this form of differentiation.[51] In many respects that also appears to be a correct observation. However, caution is recommended when comparing what was started with the Danish and British euro opt-outs and what subsequently emerged in the form of enhanced cooperation and later PESCO.[52] The angles of approach to the opt-outs, on the one hand, and enhanced cooperation, on the other, differ. Thym has made the following reflections on the subject:

> Analytically, opt-outs and enhanced cooperation are similar as in both cases there are some member states which want more integration than others. However, we argue

respect of the Area of Freedom, Security and Justice [2012] OJ C326/295, according to which an opt-in decision is binding and cannot be revoked (see ch 6).

[49] See section II and Thym, 'Supranational Differentiation and Enhanced Cooperation' (n 3).

[50] S Kingston, 'Flexibility in EU environmental law and policy: a response to complexity, or fig leaf for expediency?' in de Witte, Ott and Vos (eds) (n 2) 337.

[51] B Rittberger, D Leuffen and F Schimmelfennig, 'Differentiated Integration of Core State Powers' in P Genschel and M Jachtenfuchs (eds), *Beyond the Regulatory Polity? The European Integration of Core State Powers* (Oxford, Oxford University Press, 2013) 192.

[52] ibid.

> that the two forms of [differentiated integration] differ with regard to their perceived purpose and nature. While opt-outs accommodate exceptions from a broad agreement on more integration, by contrast, enhanced cooperation allows some member states to do more than others. In this perspective, opt-outs are associated with resistance to more integration, while enhanced cooperation (and thus multi-speed EU) is linked to a commitment to more integration. Consequently, while the two forms are analytically similar, we expect that people perceive them as serving different purposes and, therefore, assess them differently.[53]

The most important difference in law between the Danish opt-outs and the differentiated integration within EMU and the Schengen cooperation, as well as the mechanisms for enhanced/structured cooperation, is that the position of Denmark is firmly locked,[54] whereas the door is open for Member States to join the other forms of differentiated cooperation previously mentioned. Similarly, the option in Article 36 TFEU to allow moral, public policy and human rights justification of quantitative restrictions on imports, exports or goods in transit, and in Article 52 TFEU on the public policy exception to the right of establishment, have in common that they represent options for Member States but, unlike the opt-outs, do not exclude any Member State from the otherwise prescribed effects of EU law.

The special position of Denmark is self-imposed due to a formulated political wish to prevent, in a legal form, Denmark from participating in the defined areas of EU cooperation.[55] While it is correct that Denmark has the option to abolish its position and consequently join in the cooperation, it is not a convincing argument that this equals the situation of openness that is part of other forms of differentiated cooperation. The legal approach to achieve this result in relation to the Danish opt-outs is different, as it effectively requires fundamental changes to the 'constitutional' settings at the level of primary law.[56] To achieve this, national legislation at the Danish level is required, and ultimately it all depends on the positive outcome of a Danish referendum. Despite several attempts, to date this has happened only once.

## V. PRIMACY OF THE EU LEGAL ORDER – THE *AJOS CASE*

This section will briefly address the judgment of the Danish Supreme Court in the so-called *Ajos Case* from 2017.[57] The issue of primacy, sometimes also referred

[53] Thym, 'Supranational Differentiation and Enhanced Cooperation' (n 3).

[54] Naturally, in the case of defence this is no longer so.

[55] See the discussion in ch 2. As regards the AFSJ opt-out, it should be recalled that the scope is limited to the nature of the cooperation, not the substance. See ch 6.

[56] Technically, the opt-out provisions remain but can no longer be invoked following a notification from Denmark that it will no longer avail itself of the opt-out provisions; see the situation on the defence opt-out, discussed in ch 5, section IV.

[57] Judgment of the Danish Supreme Court in Case no 15/2014, *DI, acting on behalf of Ajos A/S v Estate of A*, UfR 2017.824H.

to as the supremacy of EU law, was a prominent feature of the case,[58] and from the immediate perspective this judgment may appear out of place in this book. However, it could be argued that the outcome of the case does somehow involve an element of differentiated integration. The pertinent question then becomes whether it also involves an opt-out? Against this background, a brief account of the case is given below, with a view to then conceptualising it in light of the Danish opt-outs.

In the *Ajos Case*, the Danish Supreme Court challenged guidelines that the CJEU had set out in a preliminary ruling.[59] The case concerned a rather simple issue involving provisions of Danish labour law on severance allowances, but when that was combined with a general EU principle of prohibition of discrimination on the grounds of age, a principle established by the CJEU,[60] a collision occurred between the primacy of EU law and legal fundamentals of Danish law. By its judgment, the Supreme Court essentially dismissed the legal guidance given by the CJEU and ruled on the matter purely on the basis of Danish law. The reasoning behind the Supreme Court's judgment is rather complex, but for the purpose of this study it will suffice to summarise it as follows.[61] First, the Supreme Court found it impossible to conduct an EU-consistent interpretation of Danish law, as that would have been *contra legem*.[62] Second, weighing one general principle (prohibition of age discrimination) against another general principle (protection of legitimate expectations/legal certainty, *in casu* the certainty that the employer could derive from the explicit wording of Danish legislation) was dismissed as a way out by the preliminary ruling of the CJEU.[63] Third and decisively, the Supreme Court ruled that it lacked authority under Danish law to apply the EU principle of non-discrimination based on age with direct effect in a dispute between individuals. In this regard, the Supreme Court pointed to the Danish Act of Accession, which, according to the Supreme Court,

[58] For a short explanation of the principle of supremacy, see the official website of the EU at www.eur-lex.europa.eu/EN/legal-content/glossary/primacy-of-eu-law-precedence-supremacy.html.

[59] Case C-441/14 *Ajos* ECLI:EU:C:2016:278.

[60] Notably by Case C-144/04 *Mangold* ECLI:EU:C:2005:709.

[61] The summary is a simplification that admittedly leaves legal nuances unlit. For comprehensive and at times critical analyses, see U Neergaard and KE Sørensen, 'Activist Infighting among Courts and Breakdown of Mutual Trust? The Danish Supreme Court, the CJEU and *Ajos* Case' (2017) 36 *Yearbook of European Law* 275; R Nielsen and CD Tvarnø, 'Danish Supreme Court infringes the EU Treaties by its ruling in the Ajos case' (2017) 2 *Europarättsligt Tidsskrift* 303; M Madsen, HP Olsen and U Sadl, 'Competing Supremacies and Clashing Institutional Rationalities: The Danish Supreme Court's Decision in the Ajos Case and the National Limits of Judicial Cooperation' (2017) 85 *iCourts Working Paper Series 1*; L Hjortnæs, 'A view from the Danish Supreme Court in light of the Ajos Judgment' in W Heusel and J-P Rageade (eds), *The Authority of Eu Law – Do we Still Believe in it?* (Berlin, Springer, 2019) 73.

[62] The CJEU has ruled on the issue of *contre legem* on several occasions, eg in Joint Cases 397-403/01 *Pfeiffer* ECLI:EU:C:2004:584, para 116 and C-282/10 *Dominguez* ECLI:EU:C:2012:33, para 27. The precise scope of what constitute *contra legem* and who has jurisdiction to assess the issue is debated among scholars; see, for a narrow interpretation of the notion, R Schütze, *European Union Law*, 1st edn (Cambridge, Cambridge University Press, 2015) 400.

[63] *Ajos* (n 59) paras 38–42.

did not provide the necessary legal basis for the said application of the CJEU-established principle within the Danish jurisdiction.[64] The Supreme Court would, therefore, be acting outside of its powers as a judicial authority if it followed the preliminary ruling of the CJEU. Accordingly, on the basis solely of Danish law, the Supreme Court ruled in favour of the employer, Ajos A/S.[65]

It is not necessary to underline the significance of the Supreme Court's judgment. Besides the immediate legal implications, scholars have more generally viewed the outcome as an example of 'an imperfect judicial dialogue' between the CJEU and the Danish Supreme Court.[66] In this book, the pertinent question is how to view the *Ajos* judgment in light of the discussion of Danish EU opt-outs.

On the one hand, it seems coherent to conclude that the Supreme Court's judgment has revealed that there is a part of EU law that currently cannot be viewed as implemented in Danish law.[67] In relation to the opt-outs on the euro and the AFSJ, the supranational effects of these areas of cooperation are explicitly excluded from the Danish Act of Accession.[68] Despite this seeming similarity with the situation emerging from the *Ajos Case*, it seems less obvious to conclude, as some scholars and commentators do, that by its *Ajos* judgment the Supreme Court effectively has instituted a new Danish opt-out alongside the well-known ones from the Edinburgh Decision.[69]

The Supreme Court arguably challenged the primacy of EU law.[70] One could view the issue at stake as a conflict between the principle of supremacy and the principle of conferred powers. Rather logically, the Supreme Court concluded that the EU cannot be supreme on matters that, according to the Supreme Court, have not been conferred on it; moreover, the primacy to decide on the latter lies not with the CJEU but with the Supreme Court.[71]

In any event, the situation arising from the *Ajos Case* is different from what follows from the opt-outs, as the opt-outs do not challenge the primacy of the EU legal order; they are all unchallenged parts of it. They are also explicitly part of Danish law, regulating Denmark's EU membership. As rightly pointed out by Supreme Court Judge Hjortnæs, there is a difference between the (legal) situation established by an opt-out, as a result of the deliberate decision of the Danish Parliament not to participate in a defined area of EU cooperation, and

[64] It should be recalled that Denmark, as a general rule, applies a dualist system; see, eg, P Germer, *Indledning til Folkeretten* (Copenhagen, DJØF Publishing, 2010) 94.

[65] Neergaard and Sørensen (n 61) 23.

[66] ibid 5.

[67] ibid 27; NS Lauridsen and J Nymann-Lindegren, 'Tiltrædelsesloven dengang og nu' in U Neergaard and KE Sørensen (eds), *Danmark og EU Gennem 50 år* (Copenhagen, Djøf Forlag, 2023) 172.

[68] See ch 2, section VII.B.

[69] J Kristensen, 'Grænser for EU-rettens umiddelbare virkning i dansk ret – Om Højesterets dom i Ajos-sagen' (2017) UfR 2017B.75; M Kaae, 'Danmark har fire forbehold. Nu har Højesteret opfundet et femte' *Jyllandsposten* (Copenhagen, 12 February 2017).

[70] Neergaard and Sørensen (n 61) 37.

[71] Hjortnæs (n 61) 79.

that of the *Ajos* situation, in which Denmark, pursuant to the findings of the Supreme Court, has yet to decide whether to be part thereof at all.[72]

## VI. CONCLUDING REMARKS

Essentially, three conclusions may be drawn.

First, that the Danish opt-outs not only fit into EU law, they are part of its legal fabric. They are one of many means of differentiated integration. Although European leaders, academic scholars and others continue to discuss perceived challenges to the overall unity of EU law that differentiated integration may pose, while at the same time acknowledging that it also provides ways to ensure the persistence and further development of European integration, the legal solidity of differentiated integration, including opt-outs like the Danish ones, is not put into serious question.

Second, the opt-outs are all permanent in character, which stands in opposition to differentiation as regards the pace of integration. The latter characterises the mechanisms of differentiated integration in-built into both the EMU and Schengen areas of cooperation, as well as treaty-based flexible cooperation in the form of enhanced and permanent structured cooperation. To put it squarely: the Danish opt-outs on the euro, the AFSJ and (formerly) defence all exclude Denmark, on a permanent basis, from participating, within EU law, in the field of cooperation falling within their respective scopes. That fundamentally stands in contrast to the inclusive nature of the other forms of differentiated integration mentioned above.

Third and finally, the *lacuna* in the Danish legislation on the implementation of EU Treaty law in its national law, revealed by the judgment of the Danish Supreme Court in the *Ajos Case* , is of a different nature than the established Danish opt-outs, which are all part of EU's legal structure as well as explicitly regulated for in Danish law.

[72] ibid 84.

# 8

# *Conclusions*

## I. INTRODUCTION

THIS BOOK HAS addressed the four Danish opt-outs from operational as well as conceptual viewpoints. Their legal journey has been thoroughly recounted; from their common infancy through to their different paces to maturity and, in the case of the defence opt-out, demise.

Various legal issues that have arisen along the way are discussed and legal viewpoints offered in that connection. It has all served the purpose of identifying the legal significance that the Danish opt-outs hold within EU law, both past and present. This chapter concludes on that overall question by building on the answers to the associated questions addressed in the previous chapters.

The conclusions in chapter 2 on the original legal construction of the opt-outs highlighted the legally novel way in which it was represented, with roots in two legal orders, international law and Danish law, but not EU law even though it complemented it. A discussion of how to dissolve that construction, or more precisely of the legal framework regulating how to change the special Danish position, has taken place in chapters 4 to 6. It is a standing option for Denmark to do so. It involves different sets of regulations depending on the character of the opt-out in question and, crucially, it requires the holding of a referendum in Denmark.

Chapter 7 concluded on the conceptual issue of the opt-outs' place and character among other forms of differentiated integration within EU law, of which they form an integral part. Whereas other forms of differentiated integration in their essence are inclusive, the opposite is the case for the opt-outs due to the excluding nature they represent.

The question of how the evolution of EU law has impacted on the opt-outs, and the subsequent question on what legal effects the opt-outs have, found answers on an individual basis in chapters 3 to 6, respectively. This chapter will commence by combing those answers to provide a comprehensive overview thereof. In this respect, the findings in chapter 6 on the conceptual difference in law between the Danish opt-out on the AFSJ and the UK/Irish opt-in on the same area is recalled.

Before the overall and comprehensive conclusions are finally drawn, the issue of the terminology used to describe the special position of Denmark will be revisited with a view to concluding the discussion initiated in chapter 1.

A table setting out the legal construction of the Danish opt-outs is produced as a separate Appendix following this chapter. It provides an overview of the regulatory provisions of the opt-outs within all three legal orders: international law, EU law and national (Danish) law.

## II. CONCLUSIONS ON THE IMPACT OF THE EUROPEAN INTEGRATION PROCESS ON THE OPT-OUTS

Despite the four opt-outs' status as siblings, quadruplets in fact, all originating from the Edinburgh Decision, they have differed from one another from the outset: one was essentially not a derogation from anything (Union citizenship); another was not a derogation from anything *yet* (the AFSJ); another was an activation of a derogation option already instituted by the Treaties (euro); and one (defence) instituted a derogation from certain qualitatively defined legal measures, but only such as might materialise in the future.

Given this point of departure, it is hardly surprising that the impact of the European integration process over the years has differed from opt-out to opt-out. An account of this evolution may be summarised conclusively as follows.

The opt-out on Union citizenship became near obsolete at an early stage, as it was essentially emptied of its content by new general provisions introduced by the Amsterdam Treaty, the content of which to a large extent mirrors the wording of the Edinburgh Decision.

Given the fact that, prior to the Edinburgh Decision, a potential opt-out on the euro was already provided for in EU Treaty law by way of its own proper Protocol, combined with the relatively simple scope of this opt-out, essentially no changes to the opt-out's layout have taken place. Only technical adaptations of its wording have proved necessary in light of the European integration process.

In contrast, the AFSJ opt-out came to the fore as a consequence of the European integration process accomplished first by the Amsterdam Treaty, at which stage the opt-out took effect for roughly half of the cooperation area; and since the Lisbon Treaty the opt-out has become 'all-inclusive'. The integration process made additional legal provisions within EU law necessary to safeguard the legal scope of the AFSJ opt-out, unchanged from the definition provided by the Edinburgh Decision. Figuratively speaking, the opt-out has evolved from a bud on a branch to a tree in full bloom.

The European integration process also required the introduction of additional legal provisions to safeguard the defence opt-out following the Amsterdam Treaty. A dedicated Protocol to the EU Treaties served this purpose in relation to both the AFSJ and defence opt-outs. Yet the differences in their original character, as set out in the Edinburgh Decision, explain the drafting variations of the provisions in the otherwise common Protocol. Those regulating the AFSJ are drafted in much greater detail than is the case for those regarding defence.

The wording of the latter thus builds on the original wording from the Edinburgh Decision, whereas the wording concerning the AFSJ necessarily had to be new, as there was no precedent to build upon within the Edinburgh Decision given the particularities of the opt-out at the time of the Decision. Koutrakos has described the drafting of the defence opt-out in Article 5 of Protocol No 22 to be 'unnecessarily cumbersome', as the opt-out 'exempts Denmark from the ambit of any CFSP measure with any defence implications'.[1] The counter argument is that the drafting of Article 5 may seem cumbersome but is not necessarily unnecessary, as it served the purpose to clearly indicate that no changes were made to the scope of the opt-out as originally formulated in the Edinburgh Decision.

## III. CONCLUSIONS ON THE OPT-OUTS' LEGAL EFFECTS

The account of the legal effects of the opt-outs contains elements of individual particularities of each of the opt-outs as well as general features.

### A. Legal Effects of the Danish Opt-Outs – Individual Particularities

The *opt-out on Union citizenship* emphasises an already-established legal situation within EU law, but it does *not* represent a derogation from EU law, which is a most particular feature indeed. This also implies that it does not represent a derogation from the legal effects of Union citizenship as laid out in the Treaties and clarified over the years by the CJEU. Unlike other Member States, Denmark has never been subject to the general derogation option on certain obligations of Union citizenship provided for in Article 22 TFEU. Potentially, the Danish position on Union citizenship, as defined in the Edinburgh Decision, may evolve into a derogation per se should a future IGC aim to fundamentally change the present relationship between national citizenships and Union citizenship under EU law.

The Danish special position on access to acquire *secondary residences* in Denmark pre-dates the Maastricht Treaty and the Edinburgh Decision.[2] It does not form part of, nor does it relate to, the Danish position on Union citizenship. It constitutes an altogether separate, and fifth, derogation.

The *euro opt-out* constitutes a derogation from EU law as it, contrary to the general rules, permanently keeps Denmark outside of the third stage of EMU

[1] P Koutrakos, 'Foreign policy between opt-outs and closer cooperation' in B de Witte, A Ott and E Vos (eds), *Between Flexibility and Disintegration: The Trajectory of Differentiation in EU Law* (Cheltenham, Edward Elgar, 2017) 405, 407.

[2] Regulation at the level of primary EU law, however, only came about by way of a specific protocol introduced by the Maastricht Treaty. It had no relation to the Edinburgh Solution.

cooperation and thereby the euro currency, including the euro cooperation. It is an absolute opt-out from this particular policy area. On the other hand, there is no spill-over, either legally or politically, to other parts of the monetary cooperation in which Denmark participates actively, both within the framework of EU law and through various modes of intergovernmental cooperation taking place outside of the EU legal framework. The Danish currency is very closely pegged to the euro as part of a decades-old commitment of Denmark to a fixed exchange-rate policy. Denmark is, however, not legally bound to continue this policy.

The *defence opt-out* was a derogation from EU law as it, contrary to the general rules, kept Denmark permanently outside of a qualitatively defined part of CSDP cooperation, including on the implementation side, which in practice was a particularly complex issue to ascertain. It was an absolute opt-out from this particular policy area. On the other hand, the opt-out was only applicable within legally defined boundaries, with notably two implications: first, that cooperation within CSDP not meeting the qualification entailed in the definition of the opt-out fell outside its scope; and second, the same was the case for other forms of cooperation with a defence flavour, as long as the legal basis was within other parts of the Treaties.

Pursuant to a general right for Denmark to abolish one or all of the opt-outs at any time in accordance with its constitutional requirements, as stated both in the Edinburgh Decision and in Article 7 of Protocol No 22, Denmark did abolish the defence opt-out in 2022.[3] Following the way in which the opt-outs have been legislated for in Danish law, including a very strong political commitment in this regard to the holding of a referendum, the opt-out's abolition only came about following a positive outcome of a Danish referendum. Consequently, the opt-out on defence no longer has legal effect. Since the summer of 2022, Denmark is a party to all measures previously falling within the scope of the opt-out and which are still in force.[4] Moreover, Denmark participates fully in all new initiatives within the entire CSDP cooperation on the same conditions as all other Member States.

The *AFSJ opt-out* is a derogation from EU law as it, contrary to the general rules, keeps Denmark outside of all measures and obligations pursuant to Title VI of the TFEU. It is not, however, an absolute opt-out in the same sense as is the case is for the euro opt-out and as the case was in relation to the defence opt-out. It relates to the form (*instrumentum*) but not the substance (*negotium*). This is the only one of the opt-outs with this characteristic. It implies that Denmark may participate in AFSJ cooperation so long as it is done at an

[3] In Protocol No 16 on the special Danish position regarding the third stage of EMU, it is mentioned that steps towards Denmark's joining the thrid stage can only be taken at the request of Denmark itself.

[4] Accession to the Defence Agency as well as PESCO was not automatic but only happened later, following the completion of a specific set of procedures and requirements.

intergovernmental level. This has made it possible in certain instances, and through innovative legal solutions, to mitigate the impact of the opt-out. These mitigating solutions do not qualify as 'opt-ins', as the legal scope of the opt-out prevents AFSJ measures from becoming binding on Denmark under EU law.

A proper opt-in is set out in Protocol No 21 on the position of Ireland and (formerly) the UK. The significant feature of this model is that although the starting point is an opt-out, a political choice may be exercised by the Member State concerned on a case-by-case basis with a view to repealing the legal effects of the opt-out. In such a case, the legal position of the Member State is restored to the ordinary one.[5] This essentially explains the difference between the effects of the Danish AFSJ opt-out and the Irish AFSJ opt-in.

It is noted that a new provision in Protocol No 22 inserted by the Lisbon Treaty gives Denmark the option to convert from the current opt-out on the AFSJ to the opt-in model, which otherwise only exists in Protocol No 21. In 2015, steps were taken in this respect, but conversion was ultimately overruled in a Danish referendum, leaving the opt-out model unchanged.

## B. Legal Effects of the Danish Opt-Outs – General Aspects

The opt-outs are all legally defined and subject to legal interpretation. They relate to legally adopted measures and obligations. Other types of documents, like conclusions, strategies, etc, that do not have this explicit legal character are not covered.[6] There are no political spill-over effects from any of the opt-outs, a fact that essentially stems from the 1992 Memorandum 'Denmark in Europe', drafted by the political parties in Denmark.

Whereas the legal scope of the Treaties has been subject to immense development since the Maastricht Treaty as part of the ongoing European integration process, the legal scope of the opt-outs, as originally defined in the Edinburgh Decision, has not changed over the years. Adaptions of the opt-outs in light of the European integration process have occurred, notably in relation to the ones on defence and the AFSJ. This has been done with a specific view to ensuring the unfettered scope of the opt-outs. Following the Lisbon Treaty, scholars described the Danish opt-out on the AFSJ as having been expanded to cover cooperation on police and criminal matters.[7] While that is true, it does not imply that the Danish position changed; on the contrary. With the changes made by the Lisbon

[5] Certain specific modifications apply. See discussion in ch 6.

[6] All documents from the Euro Group do fall within the scope of the euro opt-out as Denmark does not participate in the euro cooperation at all.

[7] See, eg, C Matera, 'Much Ado About the Opt-outs? The Impact of Variable Geometry in the AFSJ on the EU as a Global Security Actor' in S Blockmans (ed), *Differentiated Integration in the EU From the Inside Looking Out* (Brussels, Centre for European Policy Studies, 2014) 75, 78; D Thym, 'Supranational Differentiation and Enhanced Cooperation' in R Schütze and T Tridimas, *Oxford Principles of European Union Law*, vol I (Oxford, Oxford University Press, 2018) 847, 860.

Treaty to the said cooperation, transferring it to the ordinary, supranational cooperation of the TFEU, the effects of the pre-defined opt-out followed suit. Had they not, the Edinburgh Decision would have been breached.

This goes to show that the choice to opt out, also from the euro and on defence, was taken once and for all by Danish politicians, confirmed by the Danish electorate and accepted by Denmark's partners in 1992–93. The Danish position has since been legally locked. From the outset, the key to unlocking this position has rested in the hands of the Danish electorate. This constrains the room for manoeuvre of any Danish government of the day.[8] It took 30 years before a change was made following the positive outcome of the 2022 referendum on the defence opt-out.

The opt-outs regulate the position of the Member State of Denmark in relation to the defined legal measures and obligations. Denmark, as a Member State, is represented as such in the European Council and the Council.[9] In relation to EU rule-making, the implication of the opt-outs notably consists of the exclusion of Denmark from taking part in the Council's adoption of legal acts. The Danish seat in the Council, including its Working Groups and Coreper (Committee of Permanent Representatives), is, however, not vacated and Denmark is not barred from taking the floor on matters falling within the scope of the opt-outs.[10]

The opt-outs have no legal effects on the Member of the Commission appointed by the Danish Government. It should be recalled that the role of the Commission is to promote the general interest of the Union and that the Commissioners are 'completely independent' in their role.[11] It would thus constitute a misconception to assume that a Danish national cannot be appointed to the position of President of the Commission as an effect of the opt-outs. At least there are no legal obstacles in this respect. Neither are there any restrictions on which portfolio a Danish national may hold within the Commission. In practical and political terms, however, it may be assumed that other actors, including the European Parliament, may not find it helpful to have a Danish national heading a specific policy area from which the country known best to the individual has opted out. In any case, that has not happened.

Regarding the CJEU, the independence of the judges appointed by the Danish Government is not affected by the opt-outs, and neither is the free hand the Court and its Presidents have to organise its work internally. It is also clear that Denmark fully enjoys the general right under the Treaties for any Member State to intervene or submit observations before the Court in cases involving matters falling within the scope of the opt-outs.

[8] No Danish government has entered an IGC on treaty change with the formulated aim of challenging the Edinburgh Decision.

[9] Art 10(2) TEU.

[10] The political weight with which Denmark potentially speaks is another story that falls outside the scope of this study. See on that issue notably the contributions of Adler-Nissen cited in ch 1. Prior to the Lisbon Treaty, the defence opt-out prevented Denmark from assuming the Council Chair (but not the Danish Chair) on defence matters.

[11] Art 17 TEU.

No effects of the opt-outs are replicated within the European Parliament either.[12] Members of the European Parliament (MEPs) are not elected representatives of their home countries. They are representatives of the Union's citizens, and as such are European voices and European co-rule makers in an independent European Parliament. Formally, the MEPs do not divide themselves according to nationalities but according to general political observations.[13] This explains why the opt-outs do not constrain the scope of the mandate of the Danish MEPs. A normative discussion on the matter flourishes among scholars who challenge the current legal situation, with some finding the unaffected voting rights of MEPs elected by citizens from a Member State with an opt-out to be undemocratic given that a legislative measure under debate would not apply in that Member State.[14] How the concerns raised could be reconciled with ideas among certain MEPs to create transnational lists/constituencies seemingly remains to be addressed.

Returning to the legal-doctrinal situation, it should be noted that the opt-outs are not directed to the private sector. Danish businesses are thus fully entitled to bid on the same terms as all other eligible parties on tenders, etc, even when the subject matter falls within the scope of an opt-out.[15]

## IV. CONCLUSIONS ON THE ISSUE OF TERMINOLOGY TO DESCRIBE THE DANISH POSITION

In chapter 1, there was discussion of the terminology used to describe the special Danish position, with the preliminary conclusion that 'opt-outs' is used throughout this book.

Recalling the definition of the term 'opt-out' as meaning 'choosing not to participate', the conclusion to be drawn on the basis of the discussions in the previous chapters is that the term 'opt-out' is a suitable description for the Danish legal position on the euro and the AFSJ, and formerly on defence. It should be recalled that the choice not to participate is made only once, at the outset, and that it defines, in a legally binding manner, the position of Denmark within the defined areas of cooperation without any spill-over effects.

[12] It is recalled that in the case of the AFSJ, the European Parliament is co-legislator.

[13] See Art 14 TEU.

[14] D Thym, '"United in Diversity" – The Integration of Enhanced Cooperation into the European Constitutional Order' (2010) 6/11 *German Law Journal* 1731. See also R Corbett, 'Two-Tier Europe – Really?' in S Blockmans (ed), *Differentiated Integration in the EU From the Inside Looking Out* (Brussels, Centre for European Policy Studies, 2014) 8; D Curtin and C Fasone, 'Differentiated Representation: Is a Flexible European Parliament Desirable?' in de Witte, Ott and Vos (eds) (n 1) 118; M Herrmann and D Leuffen, 'No Representation without Integration! Why Differentiated Integration Challenges the Composition of the European Parliament' (2020) 58(4) *Journal of Common Market Studies* 1016.

[15] This was perhaps mostly relevant in practice during the time of the defence opt-out.

Denmark does not have any 'opt-ins'. Denmark holds an option to convert its AFSJ position into an opt-in model, but at the time of writing this has not been successfully exercised. Various legally defined and legally-binding mitigation solutions have been established, though none qualify in law as proper opt-ins.

The Danish position on Union citizenship is neither special nor a derogation. Consequently, it is not an opt-out.[16] That should be kept in mind even though reference to the 'four Danish opt-outs' from the Edinburgh Decision nonetheless is widely used – also in this book.

Finally, as has been recalled, Denmark also enjoys a special position on the acquisition of secondary residences in Denmark. That position pre-dates the Maastricht Treaty and the Edinburgh Decision, although it became formalised at the level of primary law by the Maastricht Treaty. It regulates for a derogation from what otherwise follows from EU law. Contrary to the opt-outs from the Edinburgh Decision, its scope and legal effect are narrow. Nonetheless, it does constitute a legally binding Danish choice, accepted by all other Treaty parties, not to be part of those specific elements of EU law, which otherwise would allow for a broader access to acquire secondary residences in Denmark. On that basis, it is concluded that it may be correctly labelled as 'a fifth Danish opt-out'. This stands in contrast to the legal situation following the judgment in the *Ajos Case*, which does not represent any active choice on the side of Denmark not to participate in the corner of EU law addressed in that ruling and therefore should not be labelled as 'an opt-out'.

## V. FINAL AND OVERALL CONCLUSIONS ON THE COMPREHENSIVE ANALYSIS OF THE DANISH OPT-OUTS

The previous sub-conclusions distil into an answer to the main question asked in this book. This concluding answer is that the Danish opt-outs hold legal significance in EU law in several ways. That is so both in the past and in the present. Indeed, the present is to a large degree governed by the past. That and the other dimensions of significance are summarised in the remaining part of this chapter, to serve as the comprehensive, final conclusions.

### A. The Opt-Outs Hold Significance as a Result of their Unique Legal Journey

In chapter 2 we have seen how the Edinburgh Solution came about by way of a comprehensive set of documents, at the centre of which is the Edinburgh

[16] It does hold the potential to be turned into an opt-out, should European integration collide with its definition of the legal relationship between Union citizenship and national citizenship.

Decision, an instrument binding the parties, the EU Member States, under international law but not forming part of EU law, although it clearly complemented the Maastricht Treaty – a novelty in the evolution of EU law indeed.

The Edinburgh Decision has been described as a 'concession' (rendered to Denmark)[17] and as representing 'a felicitous interpretation of certain parts of the TEU'.[18] Others find that the concession was made on the part of Denmark, which gave up its 'veto', and that it therefore could hardly be classified as a Danish victory.[19] Indeed, beauty is in the eye of the beholder. The essential argument put forward in this book is that the Edinburgh Decision was a legal possibility due to the characteristics of the opt-outs, which at the time were all pointing towards potential, future developments of European integration. Denmark would not become part thereof, but at the same time Denmark would not prevent such further integration from happening. The crucial feature of the Edinburgh Decision is that it did not aim to change the Maastricht Treaty; neither did it breach any of the obligations arising from it and it did not aim to roll back on the already established *acquis* – a significant and rather unique feature of the opt-outs' past.

Chapters 3 to 6 have explored how the opt-outs have adapted to a continuous European integration process, which has led to all of the opt-outs becoming part of the EU Treaty framework.

At the same time, the Danish position on the Union citizenship was no opt-out at all, nor was it a derogation from anything else. It catered for provisions of general applicability that were inserted into the Treaties by the Amsterdam Treaty. In this way, it has, rather significantly, served as an unprecedented piece of the *travaux préparatoires* for specific EU treaty provisions with general applicability that emerged later.

From the outset, the euro opt-out already had its legal roots within EU primary law by way of a Protocol that was part of the Maastricht Treaty. The two remaining opt-outs, on defence and the AFSJ, respectively, were given their own common Protocol by the Amsterdam Treaty. Later, the Protocol was updated in light of changes introduced by the Lisbon Treaty, this all with a view to preserving Denmark's legal position within EU law, which, rather significantly, had already been defined in a legal instrument outside its scope, namely, the Edinburgh Decision.

Also significant is the fact that throughout their history, the *scope* of the opt-outs has stayed unchanged. The *effects* of the respective opt-outs, with the exception of the one on Union citizenship, have, however, widened as a consequence of the European integration process.

[17] R Schütze, *European Union Law*, 2nd edn (Cambridge, Cambridge University Press, 2018) 22.

[18] CWA Timmermans, 'The Genesis and Historical Development of the European Communities and the European Union' in PJ Kuijper et al (eds), *The Law of the European Union*, 5th edn (The Hauge, Wolters Kluwer, 2018) 1, 26.

[19] D Howarth, 'The compromise on Denmark and the Treaty on European Union: A legal and political analysis' (1994) 31 *Common Market Law Review* 765, 801.

## B. The Opt-Outs Hold Significance Due to their Endurance

In chapter 2 it is concluded that the opt-outs in the Edinburgh Decision did indeed introduce 'something new'. It is also concluded that the Edinburgh Decision came to define the position of Denmark within the specific areas of EU cooperation for the next 30 years. That was not necessarily what was envisaged at the time.

Some scholars have argued that the euro opt-outs, for both Denmark and the UK, were presented as temporary, although no timeline was laid down for those countries to join EMU.[20] Others find that the individual opt-outs within EMU negotiated by the UK and Denmark, respectively, were permanent in nature.[21] There can hardly be much doubt, on the face of the opt-outs themselves, that the latter, at least formally, is correct. As discussed in chapter 2, this corresponds with the directives issued by the Danish political parties that the sought-after agreement on the Danish opt-outs not only should be legally binding but also should be concluded for an unlimited period. The question to pose is rather: For how long was 'permanence' envisaged to endure? Before answering that, let us turn to the AFSJ opt-out.

In relation to the AFSJ opt-out, scholars have argued that an underlying purpose behind this opt-out should perhaps mainly be understood as a signal to the rest of the Union that Denmark wished to maintain intergovernmentalism in cooperation on Justice and Home Affairs.[22] Signal or not, the fact of course is that Denmark secured for itself a legal position whereby Denmark, for its part, and as the only Member State,[23] henceforward cooperated only on an intergovernmental basis. This study has argued that the signal arguably was a different one and that it was made through the Declaration of Denmark on the AFSJ, which forms part of the Edinburgh Solution. Denmark points to the constitutional requirements to be observed with a view to Denmark's participating on a supranational level in the AFJS cooperation. By doing so, Denmark may well have signalled that the legal position of Denmark, whereby Denmark only participates on an intergovernmental basis, was not necessarily meant to be as long-lasting as it turned out.

It may well have been a belief also in relation to the euro opt-out that 'permanence' had its limits. This view is supported by De Witte, who claims that 'sooner or later, it was thought, the opting-out countries would join the rest'.[24]

[20] B de Witte, 'EMU As Constitutional Law' in F Amtenbrink and C Herrmann (eds), *The EU Law of Economic and Monetary Union* (Oxford, Oxford University Press, 2020) 278.

[21] D Curtin, 'From a Europe of Bits and Pieces to a Union of Variegated Differentiation' in P Craig and G de Búrca (eds), *The Evolution of EU Law*, 3rd edn (Oxford, Oxford University Press, 2021) 385.

[22] R Adler-Nissen and T Gammeltoft-Hansen, 'Straitjacket or Sovereignty Shield? The Danish Opt-Out on Justice and Home Affairs and Prospects after the Treaty of Lisbon' (2010) *Danish Foreign Policy Yearbook* 137, 140.

[23] It is recalled that Protocol No 21 on the British/Irish position allows for opting into a supranational cooperation.

[24] B de Witte, 'The Law as Tool and Constraint of Differentiated Integration' in M Dawson and M Jachtenfuchs (eds), *Autonomy without Collapse in a Better European Union* (Oxford, Oxford

Alas, it took 30 years before one opt-out, on defence, was abolished. A slight irony is that this particular opt-out, at the time of the Edinburgh Decision, was viewed as the one likely to be most permanent, given the then close relation of the yet to be established CSDP to the defence alliance WEU, which was on a Danish 'no-go' list.

Nonetheless, for those 30 years, and still going strong as far as the euro and AFSJ opt-outs are concerned, it is a significant feature just how locked the Danish position has remained to the legal definition insisted upon by Denmark and granted by the Edinburgh Decision.[25]

## C. The Opt-Outs Hold Significance Because of their Scope

It has been argued by some that the list is almost endless regarding the various possibilities for differentiated integration within the current framework of the Treaties.[26] That may well be true, but the immense difference in character and the legal effects of the different forms of differentiating measures and institutes should be kept in mind; the same applies to their scope.

This study has recalled that the Danish position on Union citizenship, as defined in the Edinburgh Decision, has at no time constituted a derogation from EU law. However, the Danish position on the euro and the AFSJ, and formerly on defence, are constitutional opt-outs in the sense that they are legally based at the level of primary law, and they cover entire areas of central elements of EU cooperation, not only one single aspect. Furthermore, they are all permanent.[27] Their vast scope is in itself as significant as it is unique.

At the same time, Denmark remains a full Member State and no institutional separation of Denmark takes place. In the European Commission, the European Parliament and Court of Justice, there is no differentiated voting.

## D. The Opt-Outs Hold Significance Due to their Complexity

The euro opt-out is essentially not complex. A perceived complexity may derive from the no spill-over effect, which at times has led scholars to express surprise

University Press, 2022) 63, 65. See also the interview with retired ambassador and former Permanent Representative of Denmark to the EU, Poul Skytte Christoffersen, 'Danmarks grå EU-eminence: "Vi var på mange måder et besværligt medlemsland fra starten"' *Altinget* (12 January 2023) at www.altinget.dk (accessed 26 May 2023).

[25] Ch 5 on the defence opt-out has clarified that an adjusted interpretation of the definition given by the Edinburgh Decision took place to cater for the slow demise of the WEU as part of the European integration process.

[26] S Blockmans, 'Introduction' in S Blockmans (ed), *Differentiated Integration in the EU from the Inside Looking Out* (Centre for European Policy Studies, 2014) 5.

[27] They do not compare to, say, the Swedish 'mini opt-out' from the secondary legislation ban on *snus* (loose tobacco), see the accession treaty on Sweden and others, Annex XV – List provided for in Article 151 of the Act of Accession – X. Miscellaneous, point (a).

at Danish participation in numerous fields of EMU cooperation, including the very tight pegging of the Danish currency to the euro as part of a long-enduring Danish fixed exchange-rate policy.

On the other hand, the opt-out on defence was, and the one on the AFSJ is, complex as a consequence of its legal definitions and, not least in relation to defence, the complexity of the subject matter itself.

The defence opt-out implied not only that Denmark did not participate in the elaboration and adoption of concrete CSDP measures with defence implications, but also that it did not contribute to their implementation either. The legal meaning of both 'defence implications' and the borderlines of the implementation aspect had to be determined in light of life as it unfolded in practice, complex as it is. Given the nature of the defence opt-out, the holes that it left in the fabric of CSDP cooperation were lasting and could not be patched up.

The drafting of the combined set of provisions governing the position of Denmark – and Ireland and formerly the UK – on the AFSJ following the Lisbon Treaty, including the transitional provisions as a consequence of the dismantling of the third pillar, in itself adds a substantial layer of complexity.[28] Moreover, the nature of the AFSJ opt-out, different as it is from the defence and euro opt-outs, holds a particular element of complexity.

The AFSJ opt-out is an unconditional opt-out, although related solely to the form and not the substance of cooperation. The various legal mitigating measures, in different configurations as established over the years, essentially treat Denmark as if it were a third country, yet it is not.

The so-called Schengen Technicality within the Danish opt-out Protocol No 22 uniquely institutes a legal basis at the level of EU primary law that provides for Denmark's participation, including in the EU agency of FRONTEX, on an intergovernmental basis. On aspects of external relations within the AFSJ, Denmark necessarily has to act vis-à-vis third countries in a separate capacity, often in parallel with the EU.

By borrowing terminology from the medical profession, the diagnosis of the position of Denmark on AFSJ admittedly contains an element of legal schizophrenia.[29]

## E. The Opt-Outs Hold Significance as Trendsetters, Yet at the Same Time Remain Unique Contributions to the Concept of Differentiated Integration

In chapter 7 it is established that not only do the Danish opt-outs not contradict the EU law but also they form part of its very fabric. Even though they

[28] Dashwood points out that the sheer complexity of the provisions governing the AFSJ perhaps is testament to the dangers of excessive flexibility within the Union legal order. Dashwood adds that it is 'militating against sheer comprehension, let alone effective scrutiny, by the interested public and affected stakeholders', see A Dashwood et al, *Wyatt and Dashwood's European Union* Law, 6th edn (Oxford, Hart Publishing, 2011) 127.

[29] A further yet minor element of complexity is the fact that visa issues are exempted from the scope of the opt-out.

were tailormade and held particularities from a legal point of view, they may have had significance more generally as catalysts for differentiated integration as developed further in its many forms since then. At least that is what some scholars argue.[30]

However, what this study has shown is the importance of perceiving the Edinburgh Decision, first and foremost, as a tool of its time to overcome political constraints on the European integration process. The opt-outs have subsequently formed an organic part of that process.

This background explains why the opt-outs do not necessarily serve as templates that can be copy-pasted.

Schimmelfennig has come to these general conclusions:

> In sum, the supply conditions of differentiated integration are most favourable in a context of no or shallow prior integration of regulatory or distributive policies, in which a large group of states agree on further integration and externalities between them and the outsiders are low. By contrast, demand for differentiation is most difficult to realize when constitutional and redistributive issues are at stake in deeply and uniformly integrated policies and differentiation threatens to shrink the size of the insider group and create significant externalities between them and the outsiders.[31]

The Edinburgh Decision that granted Denmark its opt-outs came about in a context that corresponds to the first part of Schimmelfennig's observations. It seems increasingly difficult to envisage materialisation of a similar situation again, given the current stage of the European integration process.

An attempt to use the model of an intergovernmental decision was made in 2016 to cater for the then British concerns.[32] Yet although it aimed to increase the level of flexibility for the UK in a number of areas, including on free movement of persons, it could not, and therefore did not, repatriate powers to the national level. Ultimately, that remained the British request and the rest is history, albeit another story than the one told in this book.[33]

## F. The Opt-Outs Hold Significance for the Future – Or Do They?

As concluded in section V.E, the Danish opt-outs do not necessarily serve as templates for solutions to future requests for further differentiated integration.

[30] See the debate unfolding in the references to literature given in ch 7.

[31] F Schimmelfennig, 'Overcoming Crisis in the European Union. The Limits of Differentiated Integration' in Dawson and Jachtenfuchs (eds) (n 24) 43, 49.

[32] 'Decision of the Heads of State and Government, meeting within the European Council, concerning a New Settlement for the United Kingdom within the European Union', Annex 1 to the Conclusions of the European Council of 18 and 19 February 2016, 'A New Settlement for the United Kingdom within the European Union' [2016] OJ C691/1.

[33] On the failed UK deal, see Paul Craig, 'The United Kingdom, the European Union, and Sovereignty' in Richard Rawlings, Peter Leyland and Alison L Young (eds), *Sovereignty and the Law, Domestic, European and International Perspectives* (Oxford, Oxford University Press, 2013);

At least, not templates that are likely to undertake a similar journey, from being solely a legal solution put in place outside yet parallel to EU law, later to become part of primary EU law, while at the same time the original solution remains in force as a legal anchor.

The euro and the AFSJ opt-outs are in force at the time of writing and, as such, their legal effects within EU law continue to apply. Departing from the legal-doctrinal scope of this book at this conclusion stage, the pertinent question would be: Will these opt-outs likely endure for yet 30 more years to come?

The late Danish writer, actor, painter and much more, Robert Storm Petersen ('Storm P') allegedly once said 'It is difficult to predict, especially the future.'[34]

In light of this indisputable wisdom, this author will limit himself to concluding that the abolition of the defence opt-out in the Summer of 2022 represents a milestone for the Danish opt-outs.[35]

After 30 years, the lock on the Edinburgh Decision has been turned.

Stefani Weiss and Steven Blockmans, 'The EU deal to avoid Brexit: take it or leave' (2016) 131 *CEPS Special Report*.

[34] (Author's own translation.) The original version in Danish reads: 'Det er svært at spå, især om fremtiden'.

[35] C Thorning, 'De Danske Forbehold' in U Neergaard and KE Sørensen (eds), *Danmark og EU gennem 50 år – en milepæl* (Copenhagen, Djøf Forlag, 2023) 186.

# *Appendix: The Legal Construction of the Opt-Outs*

This Appendix provides an overview of the main regulatory framework of the opt-outs within all relevant legal orders: international law, EU law and national (Danish) law. The 'fifth' opt-out, concerning the acquisition of secondary residences in Denmark, is also included.

| **Opt-out** | **International law** | **EU law** | **Danish law** |
|---|---|---|---|
| Union citizenship | Edinburgh Decision, Section A | Article 9 TEU and Article 20(1) TFEU | Act on Denmark's accession to the Edinburgh Decision and the Maastricht Treaty, Article 1, read in conjunction with a referenda commitment given in the explanatory notes.<br>Act of Accession to the EU, Article 4, no 11[1] |
| Euro (3rd stage of EMU) | Edinburgh Decision, Section B | Protocol No 16 to the TEU and TFEU on certain provisions relating to Denmark | Act on Denmark's accession to the Edinburgh Decision and the Maastricht Treaty, Article 1, read in conjunction with a referenda commitment given in the explanatory notes<br>Act of Accession to the EU, Article 4, no 11 and no 14, litra b[2] |
| *Defence* | *Edinburgh Decision, Section C* | *Protocol No 22 to the TEU and TFEU on the Position of Denmark, Part II*[3] | *Act on Denmark's accession to the Edinburgh Decision and the Maastricht Treaty, Article 1, read in conjunction with a referenda commitment given in the explanatory notes*<br>*Act of Accession to the EU, Article 4, no 11* |

*(continued)*

[1] Inclusion of the Edinburgh Decision on the list of 'treaties, etc' forming basis of the Danish EU Membership.

[2] Exclusion of the Treaty provisions on the euro (supranational effects).

[3] In 2022, Denmark made use of the general provision entailed in Part IV of Protocol No 22 to abolish the opt-out. Consequently, its legal effects have ceased to exist.

*(Continued)*

| Opt-out | International law | EU law | Danish law |
| --- | --- | --- | --- |
| AFSJ | Edinburgh Decision, Section D | Protocol No 22 to the TEU and TFEU on the Position of Denmark, Parts I and III. | Act on Denmark's accession to the Edinburgh Decision and the Maastricht Treaty, Article 1, read in conjunction with a referenda commitment given in the explanatory notes<br>Act of Accession to the EU, Article 4, no 11 and no 14, litra a[4] |
| Summerhouses (secondary residences) | | Protocol No 32 on the Acquisition of Property in Denmark[5] | |

[4] Exclusion of the AFSJ Treaty provisions (supranational effects).

[5] The opt-out is not mentioned in the political document 'Denmark in Europe' and it is not part of the subsequent Edinburgh Solution. Although Danish law on acquisition of summerhouses entails provisions that legislate on the effect of the opt-out, no particular provisions regulate the status of the opt-out as such. Unlike the opt-outs originating in the Edinburgh Decision, there are thus no specific requirements on the holding of a referendum as a precondition for a potential abolition of this opt-out.

# *Bibliography*


Adler-Nissen, R, 'The Diplomacy of Opting Out: A Bourdieudian Approach to National Integration Strategies' (2008) 46(3) *Journal of Common Market Studies* 663

——, 'Behind the scenes of differentiated integration: circumventing national opt-outs in Justice and Home Affairs' (2009) 16(1) *Journal of European Public Policy* 62

——, 'Opting Out of an Ever Closer Union: The Integration *Doxa* and the Management of Sovereignty' (2011) 34(5) *West European Politics* 1092

——, R, *Opting out of the European Union* (Cambridge, Cambridge University Press, 2014)

——, 'The Vocal Euro-outsider: The UK in a Two-speed Europe' (2016) 87(2) *The Political Quarterly* 238

Adler-Nissen, R and Gammeltoft-Hansen, T, 'Straitjacket or Sovereignty Shield? The Danish Opt-Out on Justice and Home Affairs and Prospects after the Treaty of Lisbon' (2010) *Danish Foreign Policy Yearbook* 137

Allemand, F, 'The Impact of the EU Enlargement on Economic and Monetary Union: What Lessons Can Be Learnt From the Differentiated Integration Mechanisms in an Enlarged Europe?' (2005) 11(5) *European Law Journal* 586

Amtenbrink, F and Herrmann, C (eds), *EU Law of Economic & Monetary Union* (Oxford, Oxford University Press, 2020)

Amtenbrink, F, Geelhoed, LA and Kingston, A, 'Economic, Monetary and Social Policy' in PJG Kapteyn et al (eds), *Kapteyn & VerLoren van Themaat – The Law of the European Union and the European Communities* (The Hague, Kluwer Law International, 2008) 881

Avbelj, M, 'Differentiated Integration – Farewell to the EU-27?' (2013) 14(1) *German Law Journal* 191

Baroncelli, S, 'Differentiated Governance in European Economic and Monetary Union: From Maastricht to Next Generation EU' (2022) 7(2) *European Papers* 867

Baroncelli, S et al, 'Introduction to the Special Section: Differentiated Governance in a Europe in Crises' (2022) 7(2) *European Papers* 857

Bellamy, R and Kröger, S, 'A democratic justification of differentiated integration in a heterogeneous EU' (2017) 39 *Journal of European Integration* 625

Beukers, T, 'The Eurozone Crisis and the Legitimacy of Differentiated Integration' (2013) EUI MWP Working Paper 2013/36

Beukers, T and Van der Sluis, M, 'Differentiated Integration from the Perspective of Non-Euro Area Member States' in T Beukers, B de Witte and C Kilpatrick (eds), *Constituitonal Change Through Euro-Crisis Law* (Cambridge, Cambridge University Press, 2017) 143

Blockmans, S (ed), *Differentiated Integration in the EU from the Inside Looking Out* (Brussels, Centre for European Policy Studies, 2014)

Blockmans, S and Crosson, DM, 'Differentiated integration within PESCO – clusters and convergence in EU defence' (2019) CEPS Research Report 2019/04

Blumann, C and Dubouis, L, *Droit institutionnel de l'Union européenne*, 2nd edn (LexisNexis Litec, 2005)

Bribosia, H, 'Les nouvelles formes de flexibilité en matière de défense' in G Amato, H Bribosia and B de Witte (eds), *Genesis and Destiny of the European Constitution* (Brussels, Bruylant, 2007) 835

Brunazzo, M, 'The Evolution of EU Differentiated Integration between Crises and Dilemmas' 1 *EUIDEA Reseach Papers* (2019)

Butler, G, 'The European Defense Union and Denmark's Defense opt-out: A Legal Appraisal' (2020) 25 *European Foreign Affairs Review* 117

Cardwell, PJ, 'The End of Exceptionalism and a Strengthening of Coherence? Law and Legal Integration in the EU Post-Brexit' (2019) 57(6) *Journal of Common Market Studies* 1407

Chalmers, D, Davis, G and Monti, G, *European Union Law*, 4th edn (Cambridge, Cambridge University Press, 2019)

Chamon, M, 'Op-Ed: AG Hogan's Opinion in Avis 1/19 regarding the Istanbul Convention' *EU Law Live* (2021)

Chopin, T and Lequesne, C, 'Differentiation as a double-edged sword: member states' practices and Brexit' (2016) 92(3) *International Affairs* 531

Closa, C, 'The Concept of Citizenship in the Treaty on European Union' (1992) 29 *Common Market Law Review* 1137

——, 'Citizenship of the Union and Nationality of Member State' (1995) 32 *Common Market Law Review* 487

Christensen, JP, Jensen, JA, Jensen, MH, *Grundloven med kommentarer* (Copenhagen, Jurist- og Økonomforbundets Forlag, 2015)

Corbett, R, 'Two-Tier Europe – Really?' in S Blockmans (ed), *Differentiated Integration in the EU From the Inside Looking Out* (Brussels, Centre for European Policy Studies, 2014) 8

Craig, P, 'The United Kingdom, the European Union, and Sovereignty' in R Rawlings, P Leyland and AL Young (eds), *Sovereignty and the Law, Domestic, European and International Perspectives* (Oxford, Oxford University Press, 2013) 165

Craig, P and Búrca, G, *EU Law – text, cases, and materials*, 7th edn (Oxford, Oxford University Press, 2020)

Cremona, M, 'Enhanced cooperation and the common foreign and security and defence policy' (2009) EUI Working Papers LAW 2009/21

Curtin, D, 'The Constitutional Structure of the Union: A Europe in bits and pieces' (1993) 30 *Common Market Law Review* 17

——, 'Brexit and the EU Area of Freedom, Security, and Justice: Bespoke Bits and Pieces' in Federico Fabbrini (ed), *The Law & Politics of Brexit* (Oxford, Oxford University Press, 2017) 183

——, 'From a Europe of Bits and Pieces to a Union of Variegated Differentiation' in P Craig and G de Búrca (eds), *The Evolution of EU Law*, 3rd edn (Oxford, Oxford University Press 2021) 373

Curtin, D and Fasone, C, 'Differentiated Representation: Is a Flexible European Parliament Desirable?' in B de Witte, A Ott and E Vos (eds), *Between Flexibility and Disintegration. The Trajectory of Differentiation in EU Law* (Cheltenham, Edward Edgar Publishing, 2017) 118

Curtin, D and Van Ooik, R, 'Denmark and the Edinburgh Summit: Maastricht without tears: A Legal Analysis' in D O'Keeffe and PM Twomey (eds), *Legal Issues of the Maastricht Treaty* (Chichester, Wiley Chancery, 1994) 349

Dahrendorf, R, 'A Third Europe?' paper presented at the Third Jean Monnet Lecture (Florence, 26 November 1979)

Danielsen, JH, 'Delegation of Sovereignty – Article 20 of the Danish Constitution: The story of a successful operation but a dead patient?' in H Koch et al (eds), *Europe, The New Legal Realism* (Copenhagen, DJØF's Forlag, 2010) 135

Danielsen, JH et al (eds), *EU-Karnov*, vol 1 (Copenhagen, Karnov Group Denmark, 2015)

Dashwood, A, 'Guest Editorial. Living with the Eurozone' (2016) 53(1) *Common Market Law Review* 3

Dashwood et al, *Wyatt and Dashwood's European Union* Law, 6th edn (Oxford, Hart Publishing, 2011)

Dawson, M and Jachtenfuchs, M (eds), *Autonomy without Collapse in a Better European Union* (Oxford, Oxford University Press, 2022)

De Blok, L and De Vries, CE, 'A blessing and a curse? Examining public preferences for differentiated integration' (2023) 24(1) *European Union Politics* 143

Demertzis, M et al, *One Size Does Not Fit All: European Integration by Differentiation* (Brussels, Bruegel, 2018)

De Neve, J-E, 'The European Onion? How Differentiated Integration is Reshaping the EU' (2007) 29 *Journal of European Integration* 503

De Witte, B, 'Euro Crisis Responses and the EU Legal Order: Increased Institutional Variation or Constitutional Mutation?' (2015) 11 *European Constitutional Law Review* 434

——, 'An Undivided Union? Differentiated Integration in Post-Brexit Times' (2018) 55 (2/3) *Common Market Law Review* 227

——, 'EMU As Constitutional Law' in F Amtenbrink and C Herrmann (eds), *The EU Law of Economic and Monetary Union* (Oxford, Oxford University Press, 2020) 278

——, 'The Law as Tool and Constraint of Differentiated Integration' in M Dawson and M Jachtenfuchs (eds), *Autonomy without Collapse in a Better European Union* (Oxford, Oxford University Press, 2022) 63

De Witte, B, Hanf, D and Vos, E (eds), *The Many Faces of Differentiation in EU Law* (Antwerp, Intersentia, 2001)

De Witte, B, Ott, A and Vos, E (eds), *Between Flexibility and Disintegration: The Trajectory of Differentiation in EU Law* (Cheltenham, Edward Edgar Publishing, 2017)

Dinan, D, 'The Arc of Institutional Reform in Post-Maastricht Treaty Change' (2012) 34(7) *European Integration* 843

Duttle, T et al, 'Opting out from European Union legislation: the differentiation of secondary law' (2017) 24(3) *Journal of European Public Policy* 406

Elholm, T, 'Det retlige forbehold og strafferetten' in BE Olsen and KE Sørensen (eds), *EU-Retten i Danmark* (Copenhagen, DJØF's Forlag, 2018) 87

Engel, A, 'Opting in or opting out? The EU's variable geometry in the area of freedom, security and justice' in R Pereira, A Engel and S Miettinen (eds), *The Governance of Criminal Justice in the European Union* (Cheltenham, Edward Elgar Publishing, 2020) 39

——, 'Op-Ed: The New EAW Regime Upheld by the Court of Justice – An Olive Branch Extended to the UK?' *EU Law Live* (2021)

Fabbrini, S, 'Emerging from the Euro Crisis: The Institutional Dilemmas of a Political Union' in M Dawson et al (eds), *Beyond the Crisis: The Governance of Europe's Economic, Political and Legal Transformation* (Oxford, Oxford University Press 2015) 94

Ferran, E, 'European Banking Union and the EU single financial market: more differentiated integration, or disintegration?' (2014) University of Cambridge Faculty of Law Research Paper 29/2014

Folsom, RH, *European Union Law including BREXIT in a nutshell*, 9th edn (Saint Paul, MN, West Academic Publishing, 2017)

Gade, I et al, *Det Politimæssige og Strafferetlige Samarbejde i Den Europæiske Union* (Copenhagen, Jurist- og Økonomforbundets Forlag, 2005)

Germer, P, *Indledning til Folkeretten* (Copenhagen, DJØF Publishing, 2010)

Hartley, TC, 'Constitutional and international aspects of the Maastricht Treaty Agreement' (1993) 42(2) *International and Comparative Law Quarterly*

Haslach, R, 'The Western European Union: a defence organisation in search of a new role' (1991) *Europe* 17

Heber, C, *Enhanced Cooperation and European Tax Law* (Oxford, Oxford University Press, 2021)

Herlin-Karnell, E, 'Between flexibility and disintegration in EU criminal law' in B de Witte, A Ott and E Vos (eds), *Between Flexibility and Disintegration: The State of EU Law Today* (Cheltenham, Edward Elgar Publishing, 2017) 384

Herrmann, C, 'Differentiated integration in the field of economic and monetary policy and the use of "(semi)extra" Union legal instruments – the case for "*inter se* Treaty amendments"' in B de Witte, E Vos and A Ott (eds), *Between Flexibility and Disintegration: The Trajectory of Differentiation in EU Law* (Cheltenham, Edgar Elgar Publishing, 2017) 237

Herrmann, M and Leuffen, D, 'No Representation without Integration! Why Differentiated Integration Challenges the Composition of the European Parliament' (2020) 58(4) *Journal of Common Market Studies* 1016

Hillion, C and Wessel, RA, 'The Good, the Bad and the Ugly: Three Levels of Judicial Control over the CFSP' in S Blockmans and P Koutrakos (eds), *Research Handbook on EU Common Foreign and Security Policy* (Cheltenham, Edward Elgar Publishing 2018) 65

Hjortnæs, L, 'A view from the Danish Supreme Court in light of the Ajos Judgment' in W Heusel and J-P Rageade (eds), *The Authority of EU Law – Do we Still Believe in it?* (Berlin, Springer, 2019) 73

Howarth, D, 'The Compromise on Denmark and the Treaty on European Union: A Legal and Political Analysis' (1994) 31 *Common Market Law Review* 765

Inglish, K, 'The Union's Fifth Accession Treaty: New Means to make enlargement possible' (2004) 41 *Common Market Law Review* 937

Jensen, CB and Slapin, JB, 'Institutional hokey-pokey: the politics of multispeed integration in the European Union' (2012) 17 *Journal of European Public Policy* 779

Jensen, MD and Nedergaard, P, 'Danish European Union Policies: Sailing Between Economic Benefits and Political Sovereignty' in PM Christiansen, J Elklit and P Nedergaard (eds), *The Oxford Handbook of Danish Politics* (Oxford, Oxford University Press, 2020) 487

Kaae, M, 'Danmark har fire forbehold. Nu har Højesteret opfundet et femte' *Jyllandsposten* (Copenhagen, 12 February 2017)

Kendrick, M, 'Brexit the Ultimate Opt-out: Learning the Lessons on Differentiated Integration' (2022) 7(3) *European Papers* 1211

Kingston, S, 'Flexibility in EU environmental law and policy: a response to complexity, or fig leaf for expediency?' in B de Witte, A Ott and E Vos (eds), *Between Flexibility and Disintegration. The Trajectory of Differentiation in EU Law* (Cheltenham, Edward Edgar Publishing, 2017) 336

Klose, S, Perot, E and Temizisler, S, 'Spot the Difference: Differentiated Co-operation and Differentiated Integration in the European Union' (2023) 61(1) *Journal of Common Market Studies* 259

Koch, H, 'Grundlovsstridige EU-folkeafstemninger' in H Koch et al, *Politik og jura. Festskrift til Ole Espersen* (Copenhagen, Forlaget Thomson, 2004) 497

Kochenov, D (ed), *EU Citizenship and Federalism* (Cambridge, Cambridge University Press, 2017)

Koenig, N, 'A Differentiated View of Differentiated Integration' (23 July 2015) Jacques Delors Institut Policy Paper 140

Kölliker, A, 'Bringing together or driving apart the union? Towards a theory of differentiated integration' (2001) 24(4) *West European Politics*

Kostakopoulou, T, 'The Area of Freedom, Security and Justice and the European Union's Constitutional Dialogue' in C Barnard (ed), *The Fundamentals of EU Law Revisited: Assembling the Impact of the Constitutional Debate* (Oxford, Oxford University Press, 2007) 152

Kostakopoulou, T, 'European Union Citizenship: The Journey Goes On' in A Ott and E Vos, *Fifty Years of European Integration: Foundations and Perspectives* (The Hague, TMC Asser Press, 2009) 271

Koutrakos, P, 'Foreign policy between opt-outs and closer cooperation' in B de Witte, A Ott and E Vos (eds), *Between Flexibility and Disintegration: The Trajectory of Differentiation in EU Law* (Cheltenham, Edward Edgar Publishing, 2017) 405

Kristensen, J, 'Grænser for EU-rettens umiddelbare virkning i dansk ret – Om Højesterets dom i Ajos-sagen' (2017) *Ugeskrift for Retsvæsen* 2017B.75

Kröger, S and Loughran, T, 'The limits of support for differentiated integration in the European Union as perceived by academic experts' (2022) 4 *Political Research Exchange* 1

Kröger, S and Loughran, T, 'The Risks and Benefits of Differentiated Integration in the European Union as Perceived by Academic Experts' (2022) 60(2) *Journal of Common Market Studies* 702

Krunke, H, 'Peoples' Vengeances. From Maastricht to Edinburgh: The Danish Solution' (2005) 1 *European Constitutional Law Review* 339

Kuijper, PJ et al (eds), *The Law of the European Union*, 5th edn (The Hague, Wolters Kluwer, 2018)

Ladenburger, C, 'Police and Criminal Law in the Treaty of Lisbon. A New Dimension for the Community Method' (2008) 4(1) *European Constitutional Law Review* 20

Laffan, B, 'Sovereignty: Driving British Divergence' in F Fabbrini (ed), *The Law & Politics of Brexit* (Oxford, Oxford University Press, 2021) 240

Larik, J and Wessel, RA, 'The EU–UK Post-Brexit Trade Agreement: Forging Partnership or Managing Rivalry?' in A Cygan and A Łazowski (eds), *Research Handbook on Legal Aspects of Brexit* (Cheltenham, Edward Elgar Publishing, 2022) 122

Lastra, R, *International Financial and Monetary Law*, 2nd edn (Oxford, Oxford University Press, 2015)

Lauridsen, NS and Nymann-Lindegren, J, 'Tiltrædelsesloven dengang og nu' in U Neergaard and KE Sørensen (eds), *Danmark og EU Gennem 50 år – en milepæl* (Copenhagen, Djøf Forlag, 2023) 155

Łazowski, A, *Inside but out? The United Kingdom and the European Union* (Oxford, Oxford University Press, 2017)

Leruth, B, Ganzle, S and Trondal, J, 'Differentiated Integration and Disintegration in the EU after Brexit: Risks versus Opportunities' (2019) 57(6) *Journal of Common Market Studies* 1383

Leruth, B and Lord, C, 'Differentiated integration in the European Union: a concept, a process, a system or a theory?' (2015) 22(6) *Journal of European Public Policy* 754

Lenaerts, K and Van Nuffel, P, *Europees Recht*, 6th edn (Antwerp, Intersentia, 2017)

Leuffen, D, Rittberger, B and Schimmelfennig, F, *Integration and Differentiation in the European Union. Theory and Policies*, 2nd edn (Cham, Palgrave Macmillan, 2022)

Madsen, M, Olsen, HP and Sadl, U, 'Competing Supremacies and Clashing Institutional Rationalities: The Danish Supreme Court's Decision in the Ajos Case and the National Limits of Judicial Cooperation' (2017) 85 *iCourts Working Paper Series* 1

Markakis, M, 'Differentiated Integration and Disintegration in the EU: Brexit, the Eurozone Crisis, and Other Troubles' (2020) 23 *Journal of International Economic Law* 489

Matera, C, 'Much Ado About the Opt-Outs? The Impact of Variable Geometry in the AFSJ on the EU as a Global Security Actor' in S Blockmans (ed), *Differentiated Integration in the EU From the Inside Looking Out* (Brussels, Centre for European Policy Studies, 2014) 75

Miles, L and Wivel, A (eds), *Denmark and the European Union* (Abingdon, Routledge, 2014)

Møller, JØ, 'Brexit: Lessons from Denmark' *OMFIF* (11 October 2016) at www.omfif.org/2016/brexit-lessons-from-denmark

Møller, PS, 'Dansk Udenrigspolitik og EU-medlemskabet' in U Neergaard and KE Sørensen (eds), *Danmark og EU Gennem 50 år – en milepæl* (Copenhagen, Djøf Forlag, 2023) 75

Naurin, D and Lindahl, R, 'Out in the cold? Flexible integration and the political status of Euro opt-outs' (2010) 11(4) *European Union Politics* 485

Neergaard, U, 'Euro Forbeholdet' in BE Olsen and KE Sørensen (eds), *EU-retten i Danmark* (Copenhagen, Jurist- og Økonomforbundets Forlag, 2018) 133

——, '"A More United Union" and the Danish Conundrum' in AB Engelbrekt and X Groussot (eds), *The Future of Europe: Political and Legal Interaction Beyond Brexit* (Oxford, Hart Publishing, 2019) 249

——, U, 'ERM II' in F Amtenbrink and C Herrmann (eds), *The EU Law Of Economic and Monetary Union* (Oxford, Oxford University Press, 2020) 736

Neergaard, U and Butler, G, 'Denmark's Defence opt-out, the Forthcoming Referendum, and the Changing Face of EU Defence and Security Arrangements' (2022) 95 *EU Law Live* 2

Neergaard, U and Sørensen, KE, 'Activist Infighting among Courts and Breakdown of Mutual Trust? The Danish Supreme Court, the CJEU and *Ajos* Case' (2017) 36 *Yearbook of European Law* 275

Nguyen, T, 'Differentiated Integration and Accountability in the European Union. An Analytical Framework' 7 *EU Idea Research Papers* (2020)

Nielsen, PA, 'Det retlige forbehold og civilretten' in BE Olsen and KE Sørensen (eds), *EU-Retten i Danmark* (Copenhagen, DJØF's Forlag, 2018) 69

Nielsen, R and Tvarnø, CD, 'Danish Supreme Court infringes the EU Treaties by its ruling in the Ajos case' (2017) 2 *Europarätsligt Tidsskrift* 303

Olesen, TB, 'Denmark in Europe 1973–2015: Processes of Europeanization and "Denmarkization"' (2015) 11(4) *Journal of Contemporary European Research* 312

——, *Den svære dans. Danmark og det europæiske samarbejde* (Copenhagen, Gads Forlag, 2022)

——, 'Danmark i Europa – de lange linjer 1945–2022' in U Neergaard and KE Sørensen (eds), *Danmark og EU gennem 50 år – en milepæl* (Copenhagen, Djøf Forlag, 2023) 29

Olsen, GR, 'How Strong is Europeanisation, Really? The Danish Defence Administration and the Opt-Out from the European Security and Defence Policy' (2011) 12(1) *Perspectives on European Politics and Society* 13

Olsen, BE and Sørensen, KE (eds), *EU-retten i Danmark* (Copenhagen, Jurist- og Økonomforbundets Forlag, 2018)

Ott A, 'EU Constitutional Boundaries to Differentiation: How to Reconcile Differentiation with Integration?' in A Ott and EVos (eds), *Fifty Years of European Integration: Foundations and Perspectives* (The Hague, TMC Asser Press, 2009) 113

Ott A and Vos E (eds), *Fifty Years of European Integration: Foundations and Perspectives* (The Hague, TMC Asser Press, 2009)

Papagianni, G, *Institutional and Policy Dynamics of EU Migration Law* (Leiden, Martinus Nijhoff Publisher, 2006)

Peers, S, 'In a World of Their Own – Justice and Home Affairs Opt-Outs and the Treaty of Lisbon' (2008) 10 *Cambridge Yearbook of European Legal Studies* 383

——, 'Legislative Update: EU Immigration and Asylum Competence and Decision-Making in the Treaty of Lisbon' (2008) 10 *European Journal of Migration and Law* 219

——, *EU Justice and Home Affairs Law*, vols I and II (4th edn, Oxford, Oxford University Press, 2016)

——, 'Enhanced cooperation: the Cinderella of differentiated integration' in B de Witte, E Vos and A Ott (eds), *Between Flexibility and Disintegration: The State of EU Law Today* (Cheltenham, Edgar Elgar Publishing, 2017) 76

——, 'Differentiated integration and the Brexit process in EU Justice and Home Affairs' in AR Servent and F Trauner (eds), *The Routledge Handbook of Justice and Home Affaires Research* (Abingdon, Routledge, 2017) 253

Petersen, N, 'Denmark and the European Union 1985–96. A Two-level Analysis' (1996) 31(2) *Cooperation and Conflict* 185

Piris, J-C, *The Lisbon Treaty: A Legal and Political Analysis* (Cambridge, Cambridge University Press, 2010)

Piris, J-P, *The Future of Europe. Towards a Two-Speed EU?* (Cambridge, Cambridge University Press, 2011)

Rasmussen, H, *EU-ret i kontekst* (Copenhagen, Gad Jura, 1995)

Reestman, JH and Beuker, T, 'Not dead yet. Revisiting the "Luxembourg Veto" and its Foundations' (2017) 13(1) *European Constitutional Law Review* 1

Rittberger, B, Leuffen, D and Schimmelfennig, F, 'Differentiated Integration of Core State Powers' in P Genschel and M Jachtenfuchs (eds), *Beyond the Regulatory Polity? The European Integration of Core State Powers* (Oxford, Oxford University Press, 2013) 188

Rohan, S, *The Western European Union, International Politics Between Alliance and Integration* (Abingdon, Routledge, 2014)

Rosas, A and Armati, L, *EU Constitutional Law. An Introduction*, 3rd edn (Oxford, Hart Publishing, 2018)

Schimmelfennig, F, 'Overcoming Crisis in the European Union. The Limits of Differentiated Integration' in M Dawson and M Jachtenfuchs (eds), *Autonomy without Collapse in a Better European Union* (Oxford, Oxford University Press, 2022) 43

Schimmelfennig, F and Winzen, T, 'Instrumental and Constitutional Differentiation in the European Union' (2014) 52(2) *Journal of Common Market Studies* 354

Schimmelfennig, F and Winzen, T, 'Grand theories, differentiated integration' (2019) 26 *Journal of European Public Policy* 1172

Schimmelfennig, F and Winzen, T, *Ever Looser Union. Differentiated European Integration* (Oxford, Oxford University Press, 2020)

Schmidt, P, 'The Western European Union in the 1990s: searching for a role' (Washington, DC, 6 May 1993) *Strategic Outreach Roundtable Paper and Conference Report*

Schmitt, MN (ed), *Tallinn Manual on the International Law Applicable to Cyber Warfare* (Cambridge, Cambridge University Press, 2013)

Schraff, D and Schimmelfennig, F, 'Does differentiated integration strengthen the democratic legitimacy of the EU? Evidence from the 2015 Danish opt-out referendum' (2020) 21(4) *European Union Politics* 590

Schütze, R, *European Union Law*, 1st edn (Cambridge, Cambridge University Press, 2015)
——, *European Union Law*, 2nd edn (Cambridge, Cambridge University Press, 2018)
Servent, AR and Trauner, F (eds), *The Routledge Handbook of Justice and Home Affairs Research* (Abingdon, Routledge, 2017)
Shaw, J, 'The Treaty of Amsterdam: Challenges of Flexibility and Legitimacy' (1998) 4(1) *European Law Journal* 63
Stubb, A, 'A Categorization of Differentiated Integration' (1996) 34(2) *Journal of Common Market Studies* 283
Svensson, P, 'The Danish Yes to Maastricht and Edinburgh. The EU Referendum of May 1993' (1994) 17(1) *Scandinavian Political Studies* 69
Sørensen, KE, 'Notat om sommerhusprotokollen og mulighederne for at skærpe kontrollen og sagsbehandlingen', Europaudvalget 2022–23 (2. samling) EUU Alm.del – Bilag 434
Sørensen, M, 'Udtalelse til Folketingets Markedsudvalg af januar 1971' (1971) *Juristen* 431
Timmermans, CWA, 'The Genesis and Historical Development of the European Communities and the European Union' in PJ Kuijper et al (eds), *The Law of the European Union*, 5th edn (The Hague, Wolters Kluwer, 2018) 1
Thorning, C, 'EU's institutioner' in JH Danielsen et al (eds), *EU-Karnov 2015*, vol 1 (Copenhagen, Karnov Groupe Denmark, 2015) 106
——, 'Forsvarsforbeholdet' in BE Olsen and KE Sørensen (eds), *EU-retten i Danmark* (Copenhagen, Jurist- og Økonomforbundets Forlag, 2018) 155
——, 'The ERTA Doctrine Post-Lisbon: Opinion 1/13 (Convention of the Civil Aspects of International Child Abduction)' in RA Wessel and G Butler (eds), *EU External Relation Law: The Cases in Context* (Oxford, Hart Publishing, 2022) 745
——, 'De Danske Forbehold' in U Neergaard and KE Sørensen (eds), *Danmark og EU gennem 50 år – en milepæl* (Copenhagen, Djøf Forlag, 2023) 175
Thym, D, '"United in Diversity" – The Integration of Enhanced Cooperation into the European Constitutional Order' (2010) 6/11 *German Law Journal* 1731
—— (ed), *Questioning EU Citizenship* (Oxford, Hart Publishing, 2017)
——, 'Supranational Differentiation and Enhanced Cooperation' in R Schütze and T Tridimas (eds), *Oxford Principles of European Union Law*, vol I (Oxford, Oxford University Press, 2018) 847
Trauner, F, 'Increased Differentiation as an Engine for Integration? Studying Justice and Home Affaires' in G Falkner (ed), *The EU's Decision Traps: Comparing Policies* (Oxford, Oxford University Press, 2011) 145
Uitz, R, 'The Rule of Law in the EU: Crisis, Differentiation, Conditionality' (2022) 7(2) *European Papers* 929
Usher, J, 'The Evolution of Economic and Monetary Union – Some Legal Issues' in A Arnull, P Eeckhout and T Tridimas (eds), *Continuity and Change in EU Law: Essays in Honour of Sir Francis Jacobs* (Oxford, Oxford University Press, 2008) 297
Van den Bogaert, S and Borger, V, 'Differentiated Integration in EMU' in B de Witte, E Vos and A Ott (eds), *Between Flexibility and Disintegration: The State of EU Law Today* (Cheltenham, Edgar Elgar Publishing, 2017) 209
Van Eekelen, W, 'The WEU is a crossroads institution' (1990) 23(3) *International Defense Review*
Vara, JS and Fahey, E, 'Transatlantic relations and the operation of AFSJ flexibility' in S Blockmans (ed), *Differentiated Integration in the EU From the Inside Looking Out* (Brussels, Centre for European Policy Studies, 2014) 103
Vara, JS and Wessel, RA (eds), 'New Options for Differentiated Integration in the European Union' (2022) 7(3) *European Papers*
Vedsted-Hansen, J, 'Det retlige forbehold og personers mobilitet' in BE Olsen and KE Sørensen (eds), *EU-retten i Danmark* (Copenhagen, Jurist- og Økonomforbundets Forlag, 2018) 105
Wagner, E, 'Integration of Schengen into the Framework of the European Union' (1998) 25 *Legal Issues of European Integration* 1
Walker, N, 'Sovereignty and Differentiated Integration in the European Union' (1998) 4 *European Law Journal* 355

Ware, R and Millar; V, 'The Maastricht Debate: Clarifications, "Opt-Outs" and Amendments' (1993) House of Commons Research Paper 93(3).
Weatherill, S, *Law and Values in the European Union* (Oxford, Oxford University Press, 2016)
Weiss, S and Blockmans, S, 'The EU deal to avoid Brexit: take it or leave' (2016) 131 *CEPS Special Report* 1
Werts, J, *The European Council* (The Hague, TMC Asser Instituut, 1992)
Wessel, RA, *The European Union's Foreign and Security Policy: A Legal Institutional Perspective* (The Hague, Kluwer Law International, 1999)
——, 'The EU as Black Widow: Devouring the WEU to Give Birth to a European Security and Defense Policy' in V Kronenberger (ed), *The European Union and the International Legal Order – Discord or Harmony?* (The Hague, TMC Asser Press, 2001) 405
——, 'Integration and Constitutionalisation in EU Foreign and Security Policy' in R Schütze (ed), *Globalisation and Governance. International Problems, European Solutions* (Cambridge, Cambridge University Press, 2018) 339
——, 'Legality in EU Common Foreign and Security Policy: The Choice of the Appropriate Legal Basis' in C Kilpatrick and J Scott (eds), *Contemporary Challenges to EU Legality* (Oxford, Oxford University Press, 2021) 71
Wessel, RA and Szép, V, *The implementation of Article 31 of the treaty on European Union and the use of Qualified Majority Voting: Towards a more effective Common Foreign and Security Policy?* (Strasbourg, European Parliament, 2022)
Wind, M and Adamo, S, 'Is Green Better than Blue? The Danish JHA opt-out and the Unilateral Attempt to Attract Highly Skilled Labour' (2015) 17 *European Journal of Migration and Law* 329
Wivel, A, 'As Awkward as They Need to Be: Denmark's Pragmatic Activist Approach to Europe' in M Stegmann McCallion and A Brianson (eds), *Nordic States and European Integration: Awkward Partners in the North* (Cham, Palgrave Macmillan, 2018) 13

# Index

NB – page number in **bold** denote information in tables

www.ingramcontent.com/pod-product-compliance
Ingram Content Group UK Ltd.
Pitfield, Milton Keynes, MK11 3LW, UK
UKHW020844290926
15470UKWH00004B/1534

9 781509 980949